BEST PRACTICES IN INFORMATION TECHNOLOGY: HOW CORPORATIONS GET THE MOST VALUE FROM EXPLOITING THEIR DIGITAL INVESTMENTS

by
James W. Cortada

Other Books by James W. Cortada

Best Practices in Information Technology: How Corporations Get the Most Value from Exploiting Their Digital Investments

by
James W. Cortada

To join a Prentice Hall PTR Internet mailing list,
point to: **http://www.prenhall.com/mail_lists/**

Prentice Hall PTR
Upper Saddle River, NJ 07458

Library of Congress Cataloging-in-Publication Data

Cortada, James W.
  Best practices in information technology : how corporations get
the most value from exploiting their digital investments / by Jim
Cortada.
     p.   cm.
  Includes index.
  ISBN 0-13-756446-5
  1. Information technology--Management. 2. Management information
systems.   I. Title.
HD30.2.C669 1997
658.4'038--dc21   97-26392
                                                CIP

Editorial/production supervision: *Eileen Clark*
Cover design director: *Jerry Votta*
Cover design: *Design Source*
Manufacturing manager: *Alexis R. Heydt*
Acquisitions editor: *Paul Becker*
Editorial Assistant: *Maureen Diana*
Marketing Manager: *Dan Rush*

Published by Prentice Hall PTR
Prentice-Hall, Inc.
A Simon & Schuster Company
Upper Saddle River, New Jersey 07458

Prentice Hall books are widely used by corporations and government agencies for training, marketing, and resale. The publisher offers discounts on this book when ordered in bulk quantities. For more information, contact:

        Corporate Sales Department
        Phone: 800-382-3419
        Fax: 201-236-7141
        E-mail: corpsales@prenhall.com
Or write: Prentice Hall PTR
        Corp. Sales Dept.
        One Lake Street
        Upper Saddle River, NJ 07458

Printed in the United States of America
10   9   8   7   6   5   4

ISBN 0-13-756446-5

Prentice-Hall International (UK) Limited, *London*
Prentice-Hall of Australia Pty. Limited, *Sydney*
Prentice-Hall Canada Inc., *Toronto*
Prentice-Hall Hispanoamericana, S.A., *Mexico*
Prentice-Hall of India Private Limited, *New Delhi*
Prentice-Hall of Japan, Inc., *Tokyo*
Simon & Schuster Asia Pte. Ltd., *Singapore*
Editora Prentice-Hall do Brasil, Ltda., *Rio de Janeiro*

to
my parents who were the first to
teach me to do things
well

TABLE OF CONTENTS

FOREWORD

The one thing we can take to the bank is that the competitive frenzy which was started by the pundits who suggested that Japan was far ahead of the United States in productivity, that we were slipping into oblivion as a nation, will continue forever. Competitive pressures will not subside; they will only intensify as companies understand what it takes to compete in a global economy. As the survivors continually improve their operations by concentrating and truly managing their critical competencies, the price of staying in business will continue to go up. The need to stay lean and mean will also not go away. In addition, as Europe moves out of the doldrums and gets back into fighting shape, we will see increased competitive pressure. We must realize that all of us are in survival mode for the duration.

To survive, and to thrive, companies will have to be focused on their customers. They will need to stay focused on their competition and on the organizations interested in coming into their industry, often to skim the cream, to capture the most profitable segments. Constant vigilance of the marketplace and its forces will be necessary to focus intensely on the competencies of the organization which provide it with a competitive advantage. This advantage can be gone tomorrow unless we continually make the necessary investments in those competencies, stay tuned to their relevancy in the market, and adjust as conditions change. We are finding that the most successful managers remain focused on the value they provide to their customers and never forget who and what makes them successful.

The tool, the technological marvel that will make it possible for us to stay ahead of our competition is Information Technology (I/T). This tool has matured and is demonstrating over and over again that it can and will allow companies to compete successfully in a very volatile, intensely competitive marketplace. It allows us to leverage our global capabilities by providing a forum for collaboration. We are now able to create products and services using the best and most creative minds in our organizations, no matter where in the world they are located, and do it in a cost-effective manner using this technology. Companies which have mastered the management of that tool have realized handsome returns on their technology investments. More importantly, we now have a body of knowledge which allows us to suggest to companies how best to manage information technology.

With this book, Jim Cortada provides management with a very practical tool. He identifies the areas that require management attention to successfully manage information technology. Once the areas of concern have been identified, he discusses the management practices which make it possible for management to apply I/T and which will allow organizations to build a capability which creates competitive advantage in the marketplace. This is done by demonstrating how companies are using "best practices" to leverage this tool and also by showing how companies have mismanaged this area, spending millions of dollars without any return, because they failed to pay attention to the basics. Cortada argues that the management of I/T is not any different from managing any other major competency within the organization. The reason for not generating the necessary returns is senior management's lack of attention to this area and in believing that it takes very special processes to manage I/T. This myth is exploded by Cortada's candid and straightforward review of how companies have successfully managed this technology. It is all explained in language that senior management understands. While some I/T professionals might argue that Cortada is stating the obvious, we all know that the obvious deserves, no, must be stated in clear and practical language, particularly since many executives outside of I/T are today making decisions concerning I/T.

The most important point senior management must take away from this book is that I/T is a tool used to solve business problems. It is not something I/T professionals should engage in to satisfy their own curiosity and need, but rather, it is something they need to practice to help the business achieve its objectives. Unless we can demonstrate that the application of this technology assists in the creation of business value to the company and its customers, we should not waste our resources "playing" with it just because it is fashionable to do so. This book will help management align its business and I/T strategy. It will then discuss how to do this as well as how not to do it. From there the book shifts to help management with the realization of an adequate return on the investment in this technology. Again we see examples of how and how not to do this.

A most helpful chapter deals with how companies can apply this technology to have a major impact on the business. It shows how companies have applied I/T to successfully reduce costs, improve overall efficiencies, and how this technology has been used to leverage the intellectual capital of companies to create new products and services. It is the usage of best practices which assists companies to take effective advantage of I/T.

Another important contribution of this book deals with the management of current assets within a company's I/T portfolio. While we may complain about our business applications and the lack of their flexibility, the point is that unless these applications are managed as assets and are contributing to the success of the organization, we waste resources. Cortada helps us understand how we need to manage these assets and how they need to be leveraged in the future. The I/T infrastructure of the future must be defined so that the role of these old assets can be understood and used in the new context. This book shows how organizations create new operating visions for the business, how I/T can help create this new environment, and how the old assets need to be managed to provide a strong return on the company's investment.

Cortada leverages his knowledge of Total Quality Management (TQM) to the management of I/T. He discusses the need to stay focused on the customer, external as well as internal, and the need to develop a set of measurements to understand how the organization is doing. The application of quality management techniques is a best practices technique that is paying handsome dividends to many organizations. The development of performance measurements has already demonstrated to many companies how to improve dramatically return on our I/T investments. But, as Cortada demonstrates, we must make sure that these measurements of performance are developed by the business and not just by the I/T organization. Only when we truly understand the business requirements, and I/T's potential impact on the operations of the business, can we produce a meaningful set of performance measures. The author leads us through the development of a set of performance measures, allowing the organization to manage I/T successfully.

This book provides you with one additional pearl, a discussion on the need to understand and to manage the cultural alignment of the business and the I/T professionals. Many I/T professionals do march to a different drummer than the business community. This must be understood by the functional areas of the business to provide the right guidance in the management of a company's business needs. Understanding what makes an I/T professional tick can help an organization create the right environment where I/T professionals are challenged and rewarded for the creation of value to the business. These are valuable people who can have a dramatic impact on the financial success of a business; we need to understand how best to apply their skills in a way that aligns I/T with the objectives of the business as a whole.

The bottom line: This book is long overdue. It is a very practical guide for management in that it outlines succinctly the areas that managers must pay attention to within the I/T domain to get appropriate return on their technology investments. It goes further to outline how to scan the external environment to see what other companies are doing to manage this vital area successfully, supplying detailed suggestions on how these techniques can be implemented within one's own organization. Once the first set of fixes are in place, Cortada shows how to use quality management practices to maintain an edge in the marketplace by managing I/T to support your business objectives.

> — *Michael Albrecht, Jr.*
> *General Manager*
> *Consulting Services North America*
> *IBM Corporation*

PREFACE

There are two things we can all agree on when it comes to computers: We spend a lot of money on them and they are too hard to use. Many people would add a third: "I am not sure I am getting real value for my information technology investment." The third point is keeping today's Chief Information Officers (CIOs) and Chief Executive Officers (CEOs) awake at night. But let's begin with several facts.

First, worldwide, over $400 billion has been spent on hardware and software and another $600–700 billion using them during the mid-1990s. Most medium to large organizations in the industrialized world today spend between 1.5 and 5 percent of their total budgets on Information Technology (I/T). PCs alone sell by the tens of millions each year; in fact, in some countries like the United States, sales are approaching or exceeding the number of television sets purchased. This is big business.

Second, the toughest barrier to break through for the maximum exploitation of computers to their ultimate advantage is their relative poor usability. They are still, after 50 years, difficult to install, maintain, and, most important, to use. I doubt you can find a single executive or PC user who doesn't have a complaint about the lack of ease of use of these technologies. And yet they have become so important to our businesses—that we cannot afford to let cost or usability get in the way of our exploiting their power. So we go to extraordinary lengths to overcome problems. Companies support expensive Help Desk functions, 800 hot lines, and assign armies of computer experts to departments to help people connect and use their PCs. Many PC users buy their own books in attempts to use business assets more effectively. Every major PC manual—and there are thousands of them—sell in the millions and in dozens of languages. The bottom line is we really want to use computers effectively.

Third, I, along with thousands of other "computer experts," spend a great deal of time explaining to senior business management how best to use this technology. Indeed, enormous sums are spent each year by corporations such as IBM and Microsoft, major universities, such as Harvard, MIT, and Cal Tech, and by effective computer users like GE, Westinghouse, and Ford Motors to figure out how to use this expensive technology properly. Whole bodies of knowledge have emerged to help in the search for easier and more effective ways to use computers. The strategists have taught us the importance of aligning technologies with business plans; the technologists have figured out how to give us computers for centralized, decentralized, distributed, and network-centric computing. The quality experts have taught us the value of process management and the value of sensible measures applied in practical ways. In other words, we can align our strategies, technologies, and processes to just about any size, flavor, cost, or shape that we want. Whole countries are betting big chunks of their economic futures on getting it right: India with programmers and East Asia with its hardware manufacturing, the United States with software and basic R&D.

This is all well and good, but for those of us who have to run businesses, solve problems, get basic information to make decisions, and exploit technology before our competitors do, there is no time to become an expert in the one area we spend so much money on and yet feel so insecure about. For both this community and the business-focused managers who are increasingly coming to dominate information technology operations, a new strategy is emerging, born out of the quality management movement and the popular application of benchmarking techniques. Simply put, the new strategy is the application of "best practices." It has become quite fashionable to copy what someone else has figured out, modifying it to fit one's own operations. It turns out that across many organizations, functions, topics, and issues, finding out what others are doing well and attempting to replicate their features—best practices—are emerging as a practical strategy for improving overall organizational performance in the immediate future.

This book is about best practices in I/T. It will not give you *the* answer, but I will show you how to arrive at it because the answer will keep changing and I would like to have you not lose sleep at night because of that fact. Constantly applying best practices makes it possible for you to discover and then achieve the ways to get the most value out of your investment in computing. That is the long and the short of why I wrote this book.

This book follows in a long string of volumes I have written over the past two decades on how to improve productivity and effectiveness of computing. But more specifically, it is a companion to a book I published in 1995: *TQM for Information Systems Management: Quality Practices for Continuous Improvement.* In that book I documented many wonderful management practices that were seeping into the world of computers and specifically into the information technology organizations of large corporations. My original intent was to say, "look, the quality management folks have clearly demonstrated important ways to improve the value delivered by I/T organizations." I accomplished that objective to the extent that the reader could walk away from the book knowing what to change and with a sense of what other people were doing. I did not want to write another treatise on how to do process reengineering or change corporate culture through seminars, posters, and empowered teams. It was enough to say that those things were going on, why, and what benefits people were enjoying.

But what became obvious to me after completing that book was the fact that the quality management practitioners were leading with a powerful strategy—best practices. They would benchmark what others were doing, conduct literature surveys, interview people, bring home their findings, and look for ways to duplicate them. By the way, this was also going in sales, marketing, manufacturing, finance, personnel management, and in accounting. The various activities have been merging into a best practices strategy and it is now rearing its head in computing. The TQM book had the usual collection of war stories about who was cleverly doing what in computing. What was needed next, however, was a more explicit statement of what are the best practice strategies in I/T, a better sense of what are best practices in key areas of concern to management, and then finally, how to apply those strategies on an ongoing basis since the examples in the chapters that follow will, in time, be yesterday's news. So what is needed is an explanation of best practices, and also insight into patterns of best practices to look for in I/T. Providing some easy-to-use nontechnical methodologies and tools to apply best practices in I/T also appeared of imminent importance.

Let's discuss what a best practices strategy is not. It is not a one-time event in which you go out and find how someone is doing something very well, drop it into your organization, and then declare victory. It is not a substitute for doing the hard thinking about where your business is going and why (visioning). It is not a substitute for continuous improvement. What it is, however, is a strategy for finding and applying the best thinking and experience independent of your own and that of your company. Well executed, best practices in I/T and in every other functional area cause you to continuously keep up with what others are doing well, learning from their mistakes, and giving you confidence and a path to your own practices which are better than anyone else's. Those who implement best practices the worst way are those who use it merely to look through the rear view mirror on what to do. Those who use it best look over the bow of their ship to what is ahead. I cannot emphasize this point enough because too many people fail to realize that the effective use of best practices lies in getting you to a novel future.

The foundation for this book is built on three sources of information. First, there is my own personal work as manager, consultant, and user of computing for a quarter of a century. During that period of time, I have studied, implemented, used, and written about the management of computing, learning a few tricks along the way. Second, colleagues at IBM have constantly studied problems associated with the management of information technology for over a half century; their reservoir of studies and insights on what works well is profound and still a highly underutilized body of knowledge by the industrialized world. I have tapped into those pools of best practices to buttress the book, particularly in support of comments I make about general trends. Be assured that those comments are based solidly on surveys of many I/T organizations and practices. Third, secondary research on such topics as strategic alignment, operational practices, and measurements has been made possible by the fact that there has been an enormous growth in the volume of solid research and experimentation in the management of computing over the past decade.

Like all my other books, this one will be light on war stories and heavily focused on management practices. It succeeds or fails to the extent that it makes sense and is actionable. I have written it for management in general, not targeting it at a technical audience. It is a companion to my *TQM for Information Systems Management* but also can stand on its own. I have purposefully kept the book short—a difficult thing to do since it is far easier to write a 400- to 600-page volume that explains everything in full detail. I kept it short so you would focus only on the most important issues—a key element of a best practices strategy—and not be caught up in the vast quantity of narrowly focused discussions about specific machines, software, application development strategies, and service delivery approaches. The literature on each is vast and has been growing steadily over the past five decades. Yes, the computer has been around for over a half century; it is about time to find out what really works well!

Different audiences can read the book in several ways. While I wrote the book so any business person could read it cover to cover, you have options. The first four chapters are intended for all audiences, particularly management in functional areas trying to figure out what information technology can do, and for I/T management trying to learn what they should do. The same applies to Chapter 10 and marginally for Chapter 9. Chapters 4 through 8 are clearly targeted at the tactical issues related to the management of information technology. At a minimum they should be read by I/T professionals; however, I have material in each chapter for all managers and professionals. For example, Chapter 5, on legacy systems, teaches senior management what value older systems have but teaches the I/T professional what to do with them. The same chapter discusses I/T architectures but points out for senior management why the discussion is not arcane but rather crucial to any strategy they might have to sign up for and spend millions of dollars on. Throughout the book, there are various discussions about the value of I/T, which should always serve as the underlying basis for all important conversations about the role and management of computers, regardless of where one sits in the organization. Each chapter has boxed inserts that tell stories of specific company experiences. I also end each chapter with a box entitled "Implementing Best Practices Now" in which I list several steps you can take right now to get started implementing the ideas found in the chapter. The steps are those normally taken by well-managed companies.

I could not have written this book without the help of so many experts on the wise use of computer technology. Colleagues within IBM and also across the information processing industry have taught me a great deal and so many contributed advice and information for this book. However, I would like to call out the help of several individuals in particular. Mary T. Curnane of the IBM Consulting Group is one of those individuals who I am convinced can create successful I/T strategies in her sleep. She went through this manuscript with a fine-tooth comb making many suggestions for improvement. Tom Jenks, also of the IBM Consulting Group, taught me a great deal about measurements and management systems, critical elements in this book. Mike Albrecht, general manager of consulting services for IBM in North America, went through the manuscript line by line, making many suggestions for improvements based both on his experience in consulting and as an I/T executive. I also want to thank him publicly for contributing the foreword to this book. John W. Dunn, group vice president and chief technology officer at Northern Indiana Public Service Company (NIPSCO), demonstrated how to build massive systems that contributed directly to the bottom line while the I/T organization at Delmarva Power could write a book on how to make computing end-user focused!

This project renews a business relationship with the first editor to publish one of my management books—Paul Becker—at Prentice Hall. I thought he was excellent 15 years ago, but now he is even better. It was wonderful working with him again. I also want to thank Eileen Clark for shepherding the project from manuscript to book and Martha Williams for copyediting my original manuscript. Gene Barone, an I/T support specialist at IBM, prepared all the art work, taking my hand-drawn squiggles and turning them into important messages. Finally, I want to thank my family for making it possible for me to find the time to write this book.

This book has benefited from the help of my many friends across the world of I/T, and from colleagues within IBM. However, it is the product of my thinking and is not a statement of how IBM or my colleagues and friends necessarily feel about computing. If you like the book, thank you; if you find errors of facts, judgment, or effectiveness, that is my fault, but let me know so I can improve my practices. Write to me c/o of my publisher, Prentice-Hall, Inc., 1 Lake Street, Upper Saddle River, NJ 07458, to share your best practices experiences because we are only just starting to understand the power of this strategy. I will find ways to share your good stories with other readers.

—James W. Cortada

Why Best Practices: The Shortcut to Productivity and Results

Imitation is the sincerest form of flattery.

—**Charles Caleb Colton, 1820**

*T*his chapter introduces the concept of best practices and describes its importance as a strategy in the management of Information Technology (I/T). The reader is also introduced to "bad practices" and told how to avoid these common problems. I provide an explanation of how best practices are part of any business transformation strategy. How the rest of the book supports the concept of best practices as a body of practices is also explained.

If you spend 2 to 5 percent of your organization's budget on computers, you probably want to know the best way to use them. If you spend less, you will probably want to know if that is a good or bad indicator of your effective investment in I/T. We have a history of suspecting that we don't use them efficiently and experiencing the frustration of not always getting out of them what we want. As in so many other parts of our working lives, we are frequently looking for the "silver bullet," the "shortcut," or the "quick fix." While these terms suggest that doing it the "easy way" is somehow wrong, in fact finding very quick ways to improve productivity does

1

make good business sense. Best practices helps support that strategy—but using best practices has to be done properly.

What Is a Best Practice?

What are "best practices"? The most widely held definition is that best practices are processes which are recognized as being the best by function or within an industry. For example, perhaps the best billing system in the world belongs to American Express. This company rarely bills you inaccurately; it also gives you more information than probably any other firm on what you charged on your card. In addition to that, it collects and analyzes those data as efficiently and effectively as any other company, thereby driving down administrative costs, finding new marketing opportunities, and linking card users with vendors who supply the services they most frequently charge. If I wanted to set up a credit card business or improve my billing process to customers, my first phone call would be to American Express. I would want to know how they bill, what it costs, how they manage the process, what they do with the data, and what are the economic benefits of the enormous investment they have made in the process. I would also like to know how they manage to be one step ahead of so many other billing operations in providing new services to its customers, merchants, and itself.

If I wanted to learn how to move things from one town to another and wanted to talk to the very best, I would turn to Federal Express, which is acknowledged as having the best practices in logistics. If I wanted to implement an employee suggestion process, I would turn to Milliken. If I wanted to change my corporate culture in the direction of teams, I might turn to Delmarva Power, 3M, or to Xerox, or to one of the Japanese companies such as Toyota. Teams at 3M, for instance, made it possible for the company to maximize its use of R&D dollars by reusing ideas spread across many people.

The criteria for a best practice can range widely. Good public press for an organization's activities can excite your curiosity. Awards of excellence, such as the ones made by *Beyond Computing,* also help. But today, the greatest majority of criteria emerge out of benchmarking studies, about which I will have more to say throughout this book.

Best practices should not be confused with best product, however, since there is a difference. Federal Express does not produce a product; it does perform a service; the same with American Express. Toyota knows a great deal about teaming, but I am not always sure they have the best automobile. The U.S. Army may know more about inventory control and logistics than most corporations and clearly has one of the great military organizations of the late twentieth century, but we do not think of them as producing a world-class product—no war is. Yet we all saw how the U.S. armed services worked as a team to deliver vast quantities of supplies fast to the Middle East as part of the Persian Gulf War—certainly the greatest logistical victory of the second half of this century! You can have a great product and not have a best practice. A good indicator might be a great product that is way overpriced, this suggests the manufacturer or service provider has not figured out how to drive down costs. Many outstanding hotels are like this—great service, too many employees running around, and your bill almost has to be presented to you on a flatbed truck. Best practices are collections of activities within an organization that are done very, very well and ultimately, are recognized as such by others.

Another concept to keep in mind is that a best practice is a case study suggesting better ways to do things. Such a case study—take American Express' billing—can then serve as a base for benchmarking performance. Benchmarking helps you answer a variety of questions:

- What value do end users place on this process or a proposed improvement?
- How effective does it have to be in order to make me competitive?
- How much opportunity exists for improvements in efficiency and effectiveness?

Best practices can suggest opportunities for improvement in very precise ways. The more specific a suggestion is, the more actionable it becomes. To say that we should improve our backroom operations in the credit card business is useless; everyone knows they should improve. But to then go and learn how Sears manages its credit card databases for millions of cardholders gets you something that can be done.

Best practices are rapidly becoming a way of improving cycle time. Industry in the past decade has come to recognize the full power of reducing the amount of time it takes to do things. Costs come down, customers are willing to pay for something done or delivered quicker, competition is strained, and improvements come earlier. But how do you achieve these benefits? There are a variety of proven techniques. One of them is to go find out how somebody else is doing something and then figure out how to transplant the best of the best practices in your organization in a way that makes sense within your environment. This strategy applies to all departments in all organizations and across all industries.

In summary, best practices give you access to five sources of ideas for improving your operations:

- Inspiration—because somebody else has already done it and it works.
- Benchmarking—because it provides a way to measure and analyze your effectiveness.
- References—because these can become potential benchmarking partners and people to learn from.
- Skills transfer—because you do not have time to reinvent the wheel.
- Continuous improvement—because there is always opportunity to squeeze more productivity out of the work you do.

Types of "Bad Practices"

Are there such things as "bad practices"? It turns out that the answer is yes and that most people are guilty of practicing these until they learn better. It is very important to understand this because bad practices block your ability to get to best practices and frequently hide the fact that you are not doing things well. They hide things because on the surface they look terrific. The problem lies in their implementation. The five "bad practices" listed below are statements about bad implementation challenges, not necessarily about best practices that are really not the best. Remember the value comes from how you implement a best practice. This is even more important than finding one in the first place.

Bad Practice 1: Copy "as is." This is the act of literally reproducing in your organization how a process is done by somebody else. The problem with this "quick fix" strategy is that the reason the other person has made it into a best practice is because the practice was tailored to their specific needs, not yours. No two organizations have the exact same operating conditions; thus to utilize a "best practice," it has to be tuned to your particular circumstances. A common example is the wide adoption of employee suggestion or customer survey processes. If Company A, for instance, has a culture in which suggestions have rarely been taken seriously, you cannot just drop in Milliken's process. Milliken has a culture in which individual leadership on coming up with new ideas for improving efficiencies is celebrated and encouraged. So in Company A you probably would still have to pay for suggestions while at Milliken, it is recognized as part of everyday work.

Bad Practice 2: No validation. You hear that some company has the best practice in a particular process and you rush over to see it, become enamored with it, and try to emulate it in your organization without checking to see if it is, *in fact,* a best practice. You may, *in fact,* have a better practice to begin with. It is important, therefore, to have a set of criteria by which to determine what a best practice is so you know one when you see it and can measure it against your current practices. That means you have to understand in detail how well your current practice functions and what the opportunities are to improve it. To do that requires that you measure performance quantitatively and methodically. But more on that later in this book.

Bad Practice 3: Not current. Not everybody's best practice continues to remain best. To do that requires a process of continuous improvement and innovation and not everyone does that. Quite frequently some manager or executive will invest in a particular process for reasons unique to them at a particular time, but successor managers may not have the same interest or necessity to sustain the best practice. Meanwhile, people will have written articles and made presentations at conferences on their best practice, often presenting information that is one or more years old. To avoid this very common trap, you have to determine if the process you are looking at is the most current. Otherwise you may be attempting to model your own process against one that is not as efficient or effective as an already existing one. The owner of a well-run process will typically be a good source of information on how current his or her process is, usually because they are continuously benchmarking against other companies. Benchmarking results, therefore, are outstanding sets of evidence of currency.

Bad Practice 4: Relevance not established. This is another way of saying that the business value of implementing a best practice has not been established. We see this phenomenon with processes that are not linked to what the business is attempting to accomplish. It is a problem because implementing a best practice can consume substantial resources and time, so you might as well go through the effort for processes that can significantly enhance your organization's operations. Quality management experts frequently want to reengineer all processes. No. You do not have enough resources to do that so pick the ones that are most critical to your operations. Understand why they are critical to your success and how that success must be demonstrated through operational results. Then go forward and explore best practices, continuous improvement, or reengineering.

Bad Practice 5: Done for fashion. Corporations and government agencies are as susceptible to fashion in management practices as teenagers are to fads in music and clothes. Let's face it; every several years there is a new management paradigm: management by objectives, just-in-time manufacturing, total quality management, agile manufacturing, business transformation, and so on. Each has merit, but only if applied in ways that improve your organization. Common examples are everywhere: outsourcing of I/T without having a good business case, advertising on the Internet without understanding what the Internet can do for you, PCs for executives when so many still can't even type. You still have to ask yourself a very basic question: How will a refurbished process that is now a best practice help my organization achieve its objectives? If you cannot properly answer that question and you still feel the impulse to go forward with the work, you may be guilty of succumbing to fashion.

Closely linked to the problem of fashion is politics. If yours is a culture in which careers are made by rapidly moving through jobs, then employees will feel a need to demonstrate the launching of an initiative during their watch. That calls for dramatic gestures that are seen as demonstrating action and results within the context of currently accepted (fashionable) management practices. There are two problems with this pattern of behavior: First, the person who started it may not have made the correct decision about what the organization really needed and, second, will probably not be around to do the real hard work of getting the process working and continuously improved. Yet it is that latter phase of implementing a best practice where you get the real benefits and these activities are not glamorous or dramatically visible.

So we come to the issues of motivation and business case. Implementing best practices is hard work and expensive, but worth it. So you have to have a good reason for being interested in a best practice and building one yourself.

Role of Benchmarking

Whether for I/T or some other function in an enterprise, the strategy most frequently deployed for identifying and learning from best practices is the use of benchmarking. Two types are very evident in the best run I/T organizations: measurement based and process based.

Traditionally, information processing organizations have relied on measurement-based benchmarking to understand vendor performance, and to conduct data-center audits, product testing, and cost measurements. I/T organizations know how to do these things. As Figure 1.1 illustrates, there are 11 characteristics that define measurement-based benchmarking. Some are very obvious: The focus is on efficiency (i.e., cost), impact is narrow and tactical (i.e., uptime of the computer, cost of data on a particular type of information storage medium), and approach is comparative (i.e., one type of device versus another, purchase versus lease, my department versus your department). These types of benchmarks are quite inexpensive (less than U.S. $50,000 in the 1990s). They are valuable for less than a year because technology and circumstances change. Most are conducted by technical management within the I/T organization. These studies are not necessarily of limited value and, when well done, are useful for years.

Process-based benchmarking is used to understand how to exploit I/T to improve the value of a process. You are using best practices to improve the value of a process. Here benchmarking becomes more complex, expensive, and the answers can be quite subtle. Yet this kind of benchmarking gets to

FIGURE 1.1

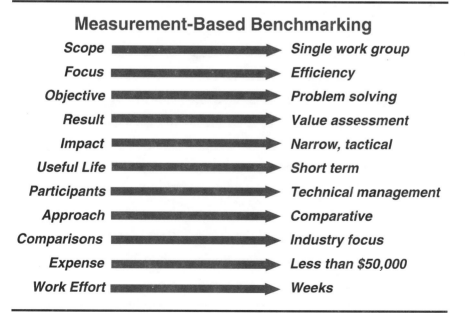

Measurement-Based Benchmarking

Scope	*Single work group*
Focus	*Efficiency*
Objective	*Problem solving*
Result	*Value assessment*
Impact	*Narrow, tactical*
Useful Life	*Short term*
Participants	*Technical management*
Approach	*Comparative*
Comparisons	*Industry focus*
Expense	*Less than $50,000*
Work Effort	*Weeks*

the heart of best practices. It involves multiple departments and invariably makes it possible to fall into one of the "bad practices" traps if you are not careful. Figure 1.2 catalogs 11 characteristics evident in I/T organizations that conduct process benchmarking. As in Figure 1.1, the characteristics on the left are the same, but they play out differently on the right.

As with measurement-based benchmarking, well-run shops tend to demonstrate similar patterns of effective behavior. For example, process benchmarking is typically linked to broader business objectives, answering the question, How can we support the corporate objective through an improved process? However, note that well-run organizations use benchmarking routinely to understand major issues: They ask broad and strategic questions, hunt for the best in their industries, and are prepared to spend a great deal of money on these. If you can build a best practice, you can make a fortune. Federal Express demonstrated that with its logistics processes, American Express with its billing services.

A couple of other features of this approach are important to understand. They are insight based, which means management is looking less at how one does a task mechanically within a process—although that is important too—and more at the effects of the process on such issues as

FIGURE 1.2

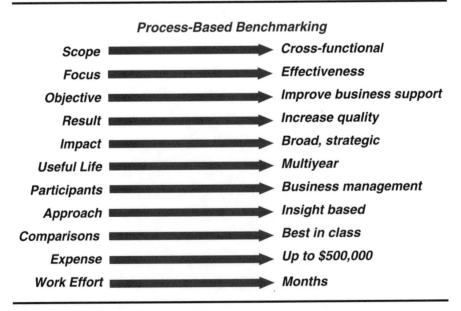

Process-Based Benchmarking

Scope	Cross-functional
Focus	Effectiveness
Objective	Improve business support
Result	Increase quality
Impact	Broad, strategic
Useful Life	Multiyear
Participants	Business management
Approach	Insight based
Comparisons	Best in class
Expense	Up to $500,000
Work Effort	Months

corporate culture, customer perceptions, productivity, ability to grow the business, improve quality, flexibility, and reduce wasted effort. To do this also requires that benchmarking be ongoing, for years in many cases, not a one-time event.

Best in Class versus World Class: Which Is Best?

Since your ability to be competitive and always to arrive at a market early with an outstanding product or service is dependent on your organization's speed and capability of performing, minimum standards of performance and results have to be set. Just as there are best practices, there are sets of standards which emerge within one industry or across many industries. Let's make sure we are clear on what they are.

If you are trying to be best at something within your industry, we speak of that as attempting to be "best in class." This is particularly important in an industry where there are unique things going on, unique in that they do not necessarily appear in other industries. For example, transporting gas is almost entirely done exclusively within the utility industry. Being able to perform this work the cheapest and provide it the most reliably would be a form of "best in class."

If you are trying to be very good, or best, at something that crosses industries, then we think of this as attempting to be "world class." For example, you and I know that customers judge service personnel based on experiences across all service industries. Thus, if we are used to not waiting in long lines to pay for goods at a small clothing store, we expect our supermarkets to do the same. If Hertz gets you into your rental car with no waiting, then waiting in line at a hotel to register becomes unacceptable. The hotel would have to become as good as Hertz—a member of a different industry—because we customers have developed an expectation for judging quality service.

Well-run companies that have best practices are very clear about which arena their practice must operate in. These people can tell you quickly whom they benchmark against—their industry or cross-industry—and why. The assumption is that world class is a higher standard than best in class and that the former is more expensive to reach than the latter. There is insufficient evidence to suggest if that is true. Companies care because one costs more; companies choose where to benchmark based on expected results. The point is, don't confuse the two.

Using ABC Accounting to Measure Productivity: Charles Schwab, Of Course

This leading stockbroker, long a pioneer in the effective use of I/T, quietly built a comprehensive Activity-Based Cost (ABC) accounting system that gives it relevant detail on the cost of its processes. Called Model for Understanding Schwab Economics (MUSE), it has enabled employees to increase their insights on how to improve productivity, changing marketing strategies, devising what new products and services to add, while figuring out where best to cut costs. MUSE is moving to a client/server platform to speed up the process for gathering and analyzing data. MUSE could not exist without I/T focused on how to capture and make user-friendly data needed to run the business real time.

For more information, see Peter Fabris, "CIO 100—Best Practices: Inspired Accounting," *CIO* 8, no. 19 (August 1995): 110–112.

What about I/T? Don't we have to compare ourselves cross-industry since everyone has computers? Maybe. It all depends on what you are trying to do. Being world class for many people is like going to church or brushing your teeth every day. Your mother taught you to do these things as a child in the belief that they were good for you. But as an adult, that is not enough. To really want to go to church and get the maximum benefit out of that experience requires that you have certain religious convictions. To brush your teeth everyday, you must appreciate the medical and social consequences of not brushing them, particularly as you get older and your teeth start getting looser! The same applies to I/T. Like brushing your teeth, doing things that make your operations world class, for example, can be done today in expectation of benefits tomorrow, such as still having your teeth five years from now.

If your I/T organization needs to move from highly centralized to a decentralized model as part of a critical business strategy for the corporation, you would probably want to find the best practices for such a transformation regardless of industry, but always looking at what happened in your industry just to be on the safe side. On the other hand, if your I/T organization needs to provide you with a customer service support application that is unique to an industry (e.g., taking orders for stocks and bonds), you would probably limit your concerns to what other brokerage firms are doing. Yet even here, unique features can be very attractive. For example, Levi's customer service processing system collects measurements on the size of individual customers so the company can make a pair of pants to order. It won't be long before its competitors will have to do the same thing, changing Levi's "world-class" process to a "given" in the industry. In short, the target keeps changing.

Best Practices as Part of Business Transformation

In the rest of this book, we will discuss many issues related to how I/T becomes more effective when it is a closely integrated part of the rest of the enterprise. Every major survey and published benchmark study done in the past several years has demonstrated that the best run I/T organizations do not operate in relative isolation from the rest of the corporation or government agency. Hard to believe, but there has been a concerted and often highly successful effort to link computers and their support staff more closely to mainstream business operations. Nothing has caused this situation to occur in a more compelling fashion than the growth in the size of I/T budgets, which in turn are driving the value issue. Process reengineering across corporations has also contributed to the discussion of value from I/T. Although in the mid-1990s we have broadened the view of process work to take into account such other issues as corporate cultural and organizational considerations—hence terms like business transformation and learning organizations, among many, are currently overtaking the phrase reengineering—it is nonetheless relevant for our immediate discussion.

One of the "best practices" that companies have increasingly strived for is effective redesign of critical operational processes. Process redesign has been going on for decades but in the late 1980s and early 1990s "process reengineering" was essentially rediscovered, made fashionable, and the thing to do. This was closely followed by press reports that 70 percent or more of reengineering projects were failing, which resulted in vast quantities of speculation pro and con. Brushing aside all that debate, what about the 30 percent or whatever the number is that were successful? While the answer to that question would easily take up a chapter on its own and is beyond the scope of our concerns, one of the facts to keep in mind is that successful reengineering projects have very high I/T content. In other words, just simplifying a process, reducing levels of authorization, and empowering front-line workers with authority to make decisions, or setting wild expectations born out of hype and sloppy thinking are not enough. The best redesigns exploit I/T to the fullest to capture and present information, analyze data, perform work previously done less cost-effectively, and share operational responsibilities for the performance of processes across organizational boundaries both inside and outside your enterprise.

As a result, the I/T community in well-run organizations is very actively involved in staffing and guiding major process reengineering projects with very strong business executive sponsorship. For example, NIPSCO, a leading gas and electric utility company in the midwestern section of the United States, assigned responsibility for developing a whole new approach to servicing customer inquiries and billing to a senior executive who also happened to be a technologist. The answer I saw him come up with involved designing and implementing a major customer service software application. Through his actions, John W. Dunn, and his president Gary Neale, who is also steeped in I/T, fundamentally changed many things at NIPSCO: How and for what I/T is used, skills and responsibilities of customer-contact employees, what NIPSCO's value proposition is in the market, and the culture of the company. The same story could be told about many other firms across multiple industries. But in each successful case, I/T personnel were intimately involved in the redesign and implementation of a new process. There is no published record of a best practice that does not have a heavy dose of I/T. Consequently, if you want to increase the odds of success in transforming your processes or your organization, the I/T community must be able to provide leadership and personnel to implement best practices. That is why it is so essential to implement the ideas discussed in this book.

Conclusions

Three points should be kept in mind about best practices. First, it is a strategy and a mindset for how to improve the efficiency and effectiveness of any organization. It crosses such bodies of management disciplines as accounting, quality management, virtual organizations, reengineering, and so forth, bringing order and clarity to our thinking about what to do. Closely tied to this point is the fact that best practices include customer focus while considering issues of efficiency and effectiveness. Second, it is a strategy that companies, consultants, and practitioners are beginning to talk about publicly, making it possible to collect insights on what best practices are. Third, it is almost, if not always, impossible to implement best practices today if your I/T organization does not participate. I/T organizations also need to be able to break out their own costs to know what current expenses are, although not necessarily to benchmark these against those of other companies.

In most large companies, best practices are being applied in various departments with or without conscious recognition by senior management. The quality management movement alone forced that change of behavior. What is not so clearly evident is that I/T organizations are doing the same. Yet there is growing interest on the part of I/T managers to find out what the best practices are within their discipline. What they are now turning to, however, is the question: "What are best practices in I/T?" The how has been demonstrated by those who do process reengineering and understand the nuts and bolts of changing corporate cultures. The I/T community needs to understand what has to change in order to ensure that their performance is the most effective. We started that discussion with my previous book, *TQM for Information Systems Management*, but now we must take the issue one step further to define what is being done very well.

Exploiting I/T for Best Customer Service: The Case of Northern Indiana Public Service Company

The U.S. utility industry of the 1990s began to be deregulated with competition encouraged by state and federal authorities. Recognizing that customer service had to be outstanding—and very cost-effective—in order to be a winner in the new utility industry, the senior management team at Northern Indiana Public Service (NIPSCO) decided that they would be the best at working with customers. To do that effectively one of their first actions was to develop a world-class system that would handle a variety of tasks from collecting information from customers, to logging in meter readings, to generating accurate bills, while collecting data of use to marketing.

John W. Dunn, chief technology officer at NIPSCO, partnered with IBM to leverage the knowledge of what a utility needed in order to provide outstanding customer service with IBM's knowledge of how to build large systems. Together they created a client/server-based system linked to NIPSCO's mainframe. They worked with their employees as well to define what information they needed in order to respond to customer inquiries, redesigned many processes, codified policies, redesigned invoices, and surveyed customers to stay "tuned in" to what was important. The result is that NIPSCO today has a world-class customer service system, is much closer to their customers, and is even selling copies of their software system to other firms.

For further information, see James W. Cortada, Donald P. Hammer, and Alana J. Meeker, "Down in the Trenches! Role of Procedures in Standardizing Processes," *Quality Engineering* 8, no. 3 (1996): 455–464.

For that, there is a growing body of material, both published and unpublished, of case studies, benchmarks, and academic research which, when rolled up together, gives us good composite targets to look at. The chapters of this book reflect what well-run organizations are focusing on in the 1990s. Armed with that information, you will be able to prioritize what best practices I/T has to major in and, just as important, what benefits to expect.

These practices can then be applied to fix immediate problems and improve operations right now, while guiding your transformation for the long term. The best at applying best practices do both. They know this year's operations need to improve and that they must be profitable. Best practices helps clearly in this arena. For more substantive changes that require multiple years or are true reengineering transformations, they give you a solid basis of what has worked, where things are going, and design points to encourage boldness and innovation in your thinking. But before we can get down to the nuts and bolts of this effective strategy, we need to be clear about what the value of I/T is to the enterprise as a whole, the subject of our next chapter, because otherwise the effort is not worth it. Properly done, you can build whole new industries, dominate yours, and contribute substantial gross profits to the balance sheet. The key is doing it right and that begins by knowing what value you need.

Implementing Best Practices Now	
Action	**Why**
Understand your company's business strategy.	Will make it possible for you to start making I/T decisions in support of it.
Understand any existing I/T strategies.	Begin to align I/T with the rest of the business.
Find one to two major I/T activities critical to your business to benchmark.	Find out how bad or good they are and how to improve them quickly.
Create or reenergize a very senior level I/T steering committee.	Forces end users to begin taking ownership of I/T while making the "techies" focus more on business issues.
Become a student of best practices; it is not a fad.	Allows you to start applying what works elsewhere now.

References

1. Braithwaite, Timothy. *The Power of Maximizing Your Technology Investments.* Milwaukee, WI: ASQC Quality Press, 1996.
2. Cortada, James W.; Donald P. Hammer, and Alana J. Meeker. "Down in the Trenches! Role of Procedures in Standardizing Processes," *Quality Engineering* 8, No. 3 (1996): 455–464.
3. Cortada, James W. *TQM for Information Systems Management: Quality Practices for Continuous Improvement.* New York: McGraw-Hill, 1995.
4. Davenport, Thomas H. *Process Innovation.* Boston: Harvard Business School Press, 1993.
5. Donovan, John J. *Business Re-engineering with Information Technology.* Englewood Cliffs, NJ: Prentice Hall, 1994.
6. Harmon, Roy L. *Reinventing the Business: Preparing Today's Enterprise for Tomorrow's Technology.* New York: Free Press, 1996.
7. Lorin, Harold. *Doing IT Right: Technology, Business and Risk of Computing.* Greenwich, CT: Manning Publications Co., 1996.
8. Tapscott, Don and Art Caston. *Paradigm Shift: The New Promise of Information Technology.* New York: McGraw-Hill, 1993.
9. Walton, Richard E. *Up and Running: Integrating Technology and the Organization.* Boston: Harvard Business Review, 1989.

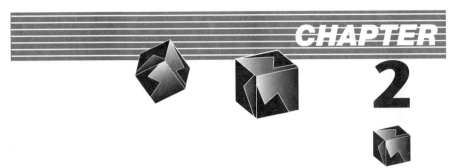

CHAPTER 2

THE VALUE OF ALIGNING I/T WITH BUSINESS STRATEGIES

The greatest thing in this world is not so much where we are, but in what direction we are moving.

—Oliver Wendell Holmes, 1870s

his chapter's main theme is that well-run enterprises align their business and I/T strategies and then develop processes to ensure that both work together for results. How that is done as a process is the subject of this chapter. Two types of alignment are also defined.

The loudest message to come from consultants, successful I/T executives, and the academic community over the past decade has been the need to link very closely what the I/T community does to the goals of the corporation at large. Taking that one step alone increases the odds of I/T's being applied in ways that deliver far more value to the corporation or agency as a whole. Such a linkage sets the agenda for what best practices any I/T organization has to worry about. They should improve the organization's high-value processes. For those reasons, the very first step in any serious effort to exploit the benefits of best practices must involve a deep understanding of how they link to the fundamental purposes and realities of the organization of which I/T is a part. It appears that the question of whether to align or not is over. A survey of I/T organizations conducted by *Informa-*

tionWeek in 1996 (published September 30) reported that more than two-thirds of I/T executives said that today their organizations were more aligned with the goals of business units than they were several years earlier. This alignment, and the resultant relationships it fostered with end-user communities, had also become highly collaborative. Almost all recent management studies about the application of I/T for competitive advantage have also been reporting a greater emphasis on alignment in the late 1980s and 1990s than had been the case earlier.

Some Fundamental Business Realities

Everything begins with a clear understanding of the fundamental business realities influencing the success or failure of your corporation. You ignore these at your peril. Some Malcolm Baldrige National Award winners have almost gone out of business; the story of what nearly happened to the U.S. automotive industry in the 1970s and 1980s is well understood. Computer chip manufacturers declined similarly and turned their situation around by facing the economic realities staring them in the face. The point is, organizations filled with smart people sometimes avoid business realities which suggests that the great French politician and veteran of George Washington's army, the Marquis de Lafayette was right: The obvious is worth stating.

Well-run companies begin with a basic assumption: Strategies in any industry must be targeted to respond to the forces at work within their industries. To be successful a company must implement efficient market-driven supply and distribution strategies that also deliver quality. Today this requires an I/T-intensive set of processes. Successful corporations have to go to market with a combination of strategies that on the surface and, to some experts, may seem contradictory, and make them all work. The obvious ones include

- Establishing leadership as the low-cost or high-value provider
- Forming relationships and alliances with partners and suppliers to arrive at the market suited up for selling and service
- Complying with often expensive social costs, such as environmental regulations
- Segmenting customers, often to the individual, for special mass-customized offerings

- Shifting value propositions to customer delighters in an age when customers are increasingly demanding better quality products and services, and on lowering costs
- Thriving in a global market where your next competitor can suddenly come from a country you never heard of.

If these sound obvious, so be it. But they all have one thing in common: Today the best at handling these issues use a great deal of I/T, acknowledge and deal with frequently and constantly changing circumstances, and have found ways to do so.

The corollary comment for just about any industry is that the forces of change bearing down on old, new, and newly emerging industries are more dynamic than at any time in the past. Governments interfere with world markets through taxes, regulations, and monetary policies. New entrants come in from all over, many times from other industries which have different ways of doing things and, of course, varying types of best practices. The bargaining power of customers grows each day due to three conditions: rising standards of living, expanded educational levels, and the application of technology in communications, finance, and transportation. Today you and I can buy whatever we want anywhere in the world 24 hours a day. Traditional rivals implement best practices, giving us all a run for our money. Substitute products and services seem to be everywhere. While one characteristic over another may be more strongly or moderately felt this year versus last year, the reality is fundamentally the same: Pressure on the business comes from many sources, requiring exploitation of advantages and protection against the siege, all done quickly and effectively.

Curiously, so many small- to medium-sized companies do not have robust I/T strategies. IBM's own surveys over the years on the topic suggest that smaller companies tend not to have I/T strategies while the very largest do. In an unpublished survey done in 1995, for example, IBM researchers noted that 95 percent of all large companies had a plan. Increasingly over the past few years, however, companies have developed and implemented I/T strategies. These plans have evolved from architecture- and technology-based plans, laced with budget targets, to statements and tactical "to dos" related to business strategy. While plan development remains primarily the responsibility of the chief information officer, senior management has increasingly become involved in the planning process as I/T has become more important to the strategic success of the firm.

Early Adoption of I/T as a Corporate Strategy: The Case of 3M

We know 3M as the Scotch tape company and the makers of Post-It Notes and Scotchgard Fabric Protector. With continuous growth in 3M's revenues, profits, and value of stock in the 1990s, you have to ask, What is the secret? Part of the answer lies in the fact that 3M tends to sucessfully use new technology earlier than many other corporations. So where is 3M aiming its technology investments? 3M considers I/T critical in running its supply chain, in supporting corporate financial and human resource processes, and in providing the channel for internal communications. The entire work force uses I/T, 80 percent via PCs. The heavy use of graphics, versus text-only, for example, is driving up the use of data by about 10 percent each year in cost, 30 to 40 percent in raw volume.

3M is also experimenting with the Internet, with the emphasis on experimenting. When you tend to use new technologies early, you have to experiment to learn how best to do things; this is an important feature of 3M's I/T view of technology. 3M has all the usual home pages, and so forth, but its employees currently use "the Net" to do research.

What lies in the future for this leading-edge user of technology? Its I/T executives reported recently to the Economic Intelligence Unit that helping the company move, with a product-oriented culture, from host-based systems to a worldwide network is their primary objective.

For further information, see Economic Intelligence Unit, *Global Telecommunications to the Year 2000* (New York: Economist Intelligence Unit, 1996): 74–77.

If I had to summarize briefly how corporations have been responding to the pressures of the marketplace and to the availability of I/T as technical tools and weapons, it would be the list in Figure 2.1. For each industry you can develop a similar chart; the same applies for your company. This one happens to depict what is happening in the utility industry. I chose it because that is an industry undergoing profound and rapid change today as it moves from a highly regulated to a deregulated global market. I think its problems are yours, only stated more graphically. Look at I/T. It moves from backroom processing of accounting to competitive weapon. While business pundits have been saying that for a very long time, the fact remains many, many corporations still do not know how to make I/T a strategic enabler of the company's objectives. Implementing best practices is one way to get to the right-hand side of the chart although to succeed fully, you cannot ignore taking action across the other eight dimensions. If you want a best practices for business transformation, this is a good blueprint of the answer!

FIGURE 2.1

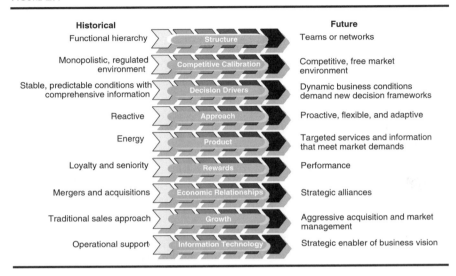

Historical		Future
Functional hierarchy	Structure	Teams or networks
Monopolistic, regulated environment	Competitive Calibration	Competitive, free market environment
Stable, predictable conditions with comprehensive information	Decision Drivers	Dynamic business conditions demand new decision frameworks
Reactive	Approach	Proactive, flexible, and adaptive
Energy	Product	Targeted services and information that meet market demands
Loyalty and seniority	Rewards	Performance
Mergers and acquisitions	Economic Relationships	Strategic alliances
Traditional sales approach	Growth	Aggressive acquisition and market management
Operational support	Information Technology	Strategic enabler of business vision

Companies that display best practices in I/T will tell you to focus on a broader set of critical technology- and business-sensitive issues than might have been done in the past. While Figure 2.2 is quite simple in concept, it nonetheless captures the essence of what so many are doing today that yields significant value. Michael Albrecht, with the IBM Consulting Group, originally developed this model to keep management focused on all the components they had to balance. It represents an important challenge once you get past the simple words. For example, cost leadership can be both low or high price, depending on the value and competitive forces at work. All the processes required to deliver value and thus make a corporate cost strategy work are dependent on I/T. Much of that dependence requires that I/T be effective in managing the rapid development and delivery of new applications, making information of the right kind available across the entire enterprise, and keeping costs in line with peer I/T organizations.

In its 1996 annual survey on how I/T is being used and managed, *Beyond Computing* (April issue) reported that those companies that use computers well find benefits. Nearly 66 percent said that leveraging technology could deliver value; the bad news is, almost 34 percent still questioned it. Regardless of the effectiveness of I/T, nearly 90 percent of all respondents wanted I/T to deliver value in improving customer service, speeding employee access to information, streamlining operations, and lowering costs. These topics will be the subject of Chapter 4.

FIGURE 2.2

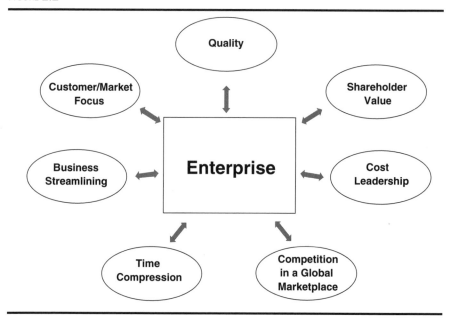

Changing Realities in the World of I/T

What makes all of this terribly complicated is the fact that the world in which I/T was created to operate and support is no longer the environment it finds itself competing in. This applies to almost every industry because large, stable, long-lasting systems increasingly no longer deliver the same value to the corporation which now finds itself in more fluid environments. Moving from slow to quicker depreciation of equipment, for example, changes all the economics of the cost of hardware with the real-world chaos that it imposes on both the I/T executive and his or her chief financial officer. For that reason many I/T executives do not get along with key line managers and executives but the reason is usually simple: The process for acquiring technology is changing. In a best practices model, that acquisition process becomes the subject of reengineering, about which we will have more to say.

Changes continue, for example, in reporting structure. *Information-Week* reported in September 1996 that senior I/T executives were increasingly being moved from reporting directly to CEOs (the fashionable thing to do in the 1980s) to chief operating officers, that is to say, to the senior executive responsible for daily operations. The long-evident trend of decentralizing

I/T is continuing, but nearly 16 percent of those surveyed are centralizing. Simultaneously, changing technologies and cost performance continue to ensure churn in platforms, tools, and deployment of I/T professionals.

Across many industries very elegant and complex processes were developed to build comprehensive and massive systems designed to last over a decade. These expensive systems are now under siege. We live in an environment where those methods for developing systems have to give way to new ones where applications can be developed in parts, rapidly, and then thrown away in a few years, where object technology, for instance, has come into its own. The use of near-throw-away tools (unless they are objects designed to be reused) have included such things as PC-based query packages. That is a massive change in the way I/T organizations have operated. Debates about large mainframes versus client/server or object-oriented systems pale in significance to the culture and operational processes that I/T shops have lived with when you start talking about how systems have to be built. Many of the best-run I/T organizations throughout the world are now deploying best practices strategies in the development of application creation processes. Figure 2.3 captures the essential changes that this kind of environment is imposing on I/T communities.

Using I/T as a Central Part of the Business: Banking at NatWest Group

This is a major British bank holding corporation with 3,500 offices around the world, of which over 2,300 are in the United Kingdom. I/T provides products and delivery capabilities for the bank, linking together legacy systems, various companies, and customers so the bank can use its information about finance and customers as a strategic tool. I/T supports six different distribution channels, accounts management, cash management, and even interactive video. The I/T organization provides 20 fundamental services, all of which are partially outsourced. In this company telecommunications is viewed as more strategic than simply I/T because it supports call centers and telesales—two growing areas of banking in the 1990s. Here I/T is used to get close to the company's customers, making it easier to communicate back and forth.

This is a best practices company when it comes to electronic banking, expanding its service lines and its customer base around the world. To a large extent, this was made possible through the strategic use of I/T.

For further information, see Economist Intelligence Unit, *Global Telecommunications to the Year 2000* (New York: Economist Intelligence Unit, 1996): 54–58.

FIGURE 2.3

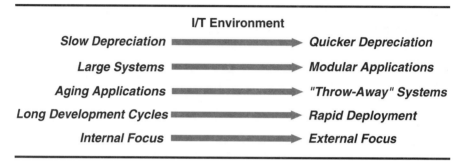

I/T Environment

Slow Depreciation	*Quicker Depreciation*
Large Systems	*Modular Applications*
Aging Applications	*"Throw-Away" Systems*
Long Development Cycles	*Rapid Deployment*
Internal Focus	*External Focus*

To a large extent we are talking about the technologies and skills needed by information processing professionals changing rapidly. Every major study or survey that I have seen over the past decade focuses on the same issues. For convenience, I have listed them in Figure 2.4. They are a combination of fundamental changes in technology platforms, technical tools, and programming strategies. We need not spend a great deal of time going through these; suffice it to say, the transitions from the left-hand side of the figure to the world depicted on the right are as massive as the I/T community has seen since the invention of the computer forced them from punch cards and tabulators to computers and software in the 1950s. For many shops many old skills are under siege while few understand what skills they really have to port over to their changing world.

FIGURE 2.4

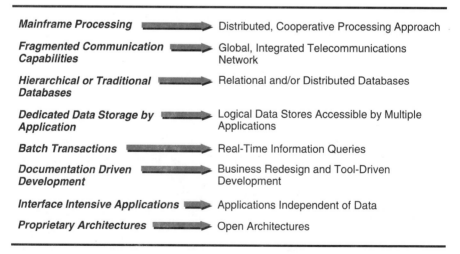

Mainframe Processing	Distributed, Cooperative Processing Approach
Fragmented Communication Capabilities	Global, Integrated Telecommunications Network
Hierarchical or Traditional Databases	Relational and/or Distributed Databases
Dedicated Data Storage by Application	Logical Data Stores Accessible by Multiple Applications
Batch Transactions	Real-Time Information Queries
Documentation Driven Development	Business Redesign and Tool-Driven Development
Interface Intensive Applications	Applications Independent of Data
Proprietary Architectures	Open Architectures

Regardless of quality of performance, overall management is frustrated with I/T. In *Beyond Computing*'s September 1996 survey on the subject, only 1 percent of the respondents said I/T had met all their goals; another 52 percent said most were met—many were best practices organizations—while another third reported only some objectives were met. In short, there is a lot of work yet to be done to exploit technology.

The motivation that most frequently drives I/T organizations to apply best practices strategies is the need to cope with change to get things done that add value. All the issues touched on above converge around the search for the best I/T transformation management and process practices. Thus we have on the one hand the need for a strategy on how the best have changed their I/T worlds and, on the other, lower on the food chain, the nuts and bolts of better processes common to most, if not all, I/T organizations.

Normally the questions management pursues regarding I/T value continue along the three lines that have always concerned technical managers: people, technology, and process. Strategies for developing best practices invariably wind up under one of these three umbrellas.

Under the issue of people, two fundamental concerns exist; one related to human resources, the other to company culture. The first is how do companies manage human resources to achieve business objectives? The second is how does rapid change affect the ability of companies to transform? While the answers to these questions cover the entire enterprise and come from many sources—usually not I/T shops—they are, nonetheless, the initial triggers for the hunt for best practices. Increasingly, businesses are learning that these "soft" issues are the hard ones because if you cannot answer these two questions effectively, the transformation is slowed. Processes are being redesigned faster than people can change. The challenge is to recognize that fact and then deal with it, hence the great interest today in change management strategies, most of which depend on organized collections of experience (i.e., best practices) drawn from previous change initiatives across many industries.

Within the sphere of strategic technology issues, concerns hover around technology architectures and what to do with existing software (known as legacy systems). The fundamental question on architecture, about which we will have more to say, is how information technology is designed and assimilated. Concerning legacy systems, we want to ask the question: How do companies manage their application portfolio to maximize return on investment?

How to Create Value: Becton Dickinson & Co.

This medical device manufacturer created a supply chain process that drove down costs and increased service and productivity. Through extensive use of I/T and process management methods, it built its state-of-the-art Combuilt, an electronic data interchange network. The key lesson to making this work was clear: Build a corporate culture that rewards use of partnerships and alignment with business strategy. In this case, the partnership involved working with IBM and Premenos Corporation and multiple departments within the company to create a unified, cohesive supply chain unit.

For more information, see E.B. Baatz, "CIO—Best Practices: Unlimited Partnerships," *CIO* 8, no. 19 (August 1995): 56–58.

The third facet—value—has been the most difficult to deal with. To begin with, it has a terrible reputation dating back to the late 1950s and early 1960s. While the history of that problem need not concern us here, what does is the perception that I/T frequently does not pull its own weight. The lack of an effective process for demonstrating the validity of that perception, be it true or false, has complicated the debate, bringing much passion into it. However, more rational, well-run companies are trying to address the problem in a practical way. The good news is they are making headway; their results are reported throughout this book. Specifically, companies are beginning to focus on three sets of issues: alignment, governance, and delivery of value. While I will devote a whole chapter to the topic of value, the questions being asked are clear. Alignment concerns the issue of how to get information processing lined up with what the company needs to get done, working off the corporate agenda and not their own. So the basic question is how can business and I/T plans, funding, and communication best be coordinated? The management of I/T—the fashionable term used today is governance—addresses the issue of how internal and external options should be leveraged. Notice that well-run companies no longer ask the older question: How should Information Systems (IS) be run? There is a recognition today that I/T comes from many places, both inside and outside the legally constituted enterprise. Finally, on the issue of value delivery, what techniques are most effective for selecting, justifying, and monitoring initiatives to ensure value?

In all three facets, companies are applying benchmarking methodologies, signing up for studies across many industries. We are entering a golden age for benchmarks because the recent ones done by IBM, various industry associations, and privately by I/T shops are generating useful and actionable data on how well-run organizations are dealing with these three sets of issues. While only a small portion of the results have been made public so far, what is seeping out is significant. The reason the data are frequently not getting out the way early reengineering results did is that these data are perceived to represent competitively valuable data. As you increase your reliance on computing to be competitive, it stands to reason that you would be very reluctant to tell people outside the firm what you are doing well. This is particularly the case with applications that concern customers and marketing and results of major I/T reengineering projects. What most are willing to share are such technical debates as how to write software faster and cheaper (e.g., using object-oriented technologies and client/server systems).

Operational and Strategic Alignments

The key message delivered by well-run I/T organizations over the past decade has been that value is fundamentally delivered when the technical community aligns its activities with those of the enterprise as a whole. The evidence in support of this position is overwhelmingly compelling. Historically too, when information processing organizations delivered systems and services that were tightly linked to the corporation, serendipity occurred. Over the past decade there has been a resurgence of research findings reinforcing what must appear to many readers as terribly obvious. But, I/T organizations have also been accused, quite rightly in many cases, of marching to their own drum beat, building their own culture and being profoundly swayed by the nature of the hardware and software technologies they use.

The real challenge, of course, is not in persuading anybody to align I/T with the overall objectives of the enterprise; it is, instead, how to do it. Benchmarks and surveys all suggest that the best-run I/T organizations see issues of alignment as their number one problem to resolve. Two sets of alignment issues on the minds of senior executives have emerged: operational and strategic. Key issues and practices are emerging along three lines: planning, funding, and communications.

The key planning questions being asked are

- Do I/T activities fit business unit plans?
- Do we have the right balance between long- and short-term plans?

**Using Information to Get Competitive:
Hunting for Knowledge and Flexibility**

Increasingly executives in international companies that are successful are arguing that faster, less expensive and smarter movement of information through networks is making them more competitive. Although tough to document, they nonetheless say that they are asking their I/T organizations to not only cut costs but, increasingly more important, also increase knowledge and facilitate the corporation's being more flexible. The ability to measure I/T's success is coming through benchmarking. They are insisting that this activity become an integral part of I/T routine operations.

For more information, see Nilly Landau, "The Hard Job of Measuring I/T's Soft Parts," *International Business* 7, no. 9 (September 1994): 28–30.

How I/T organizations arrive at these answers is perhaps the most compelling insight from well-run I/T departments. The best practices in evidence all boil down to continuous I/T and business planning going on to ensure ongoing alignment. The best organizations do not have a planning exercise once a year; they do it continuously with constant, monthly reviews of how they are doing against plans. I/T plans emerge as a piece of business plans. I/T strategy is the umbrella under which technical projects and activities are kept linked to the overall business strategy of the corporation. The second pattern of behavior is that time lags are built into the planning process which make it possible for I/T and business units to adjust before linking plans. Everyone wants breathing room to go try things and execute plans; these are simply structured into the planning cycle.

The second facet—funding—invariably generates three questions regardless of the size and scope of the I/T organization:

- Are we investing the right amount on computing?
- Are we making the right investment decisions?
- Are we investing adequately in infrastructure?

The answers are derived from the ongoing review of progress against plans, and the degree to which I/T activities are in alignment with, or to put it another way, support what the business is trying to accomplish. The most effective companies are putting their money where their mouths are. They allocate operating and capital budget funds to strategic projects and to infrastructure investments as a way of ensuring that day-to-day decisions support the strategy. For example, if the company needs to have distributed processing, it invests in object-oriented skills development, establishes a robust client/server competency center, and buys software that exploits these technologies.

Communications is the third facet. By this I do not mean telecommunications or networks, but rather good-old fashioned "tell people what you are doing and why" type of communications. Senior I/T executives will tell you that they struggle with two questions:

- Does I/T communicate its strategic value to its constituency?
- Does I/T coordinate appropriately with its customers or significant stakeholders?

Communications as a process is probably the most poorly executed one in any company regardless of department. The same applies to the I/T community; in fact, one might argue it is historically worse there because for decades I/T organizations have done little or no communicating with their end users about what they are doing. However, well-run I/T operations have done a great deal. Besides all the usual newsletters and performance reports, effective technology managers go out and participate in planning sessions, and physically station their people across the organization and don't allow them to huddle behind the barriers of the data center. They are out there in various departments participating in staff meetings where they explain their activities. In other words, they treat communications as a series of critical activities and assign people and their own time to it. Communications evolves from being ad hoc activities into a well-organized process that includes shared goals and objectives. These are reviewed, modified, and improved, just like any other properly managed process.

Figure 2.5 summarizes the issues and the best practices currently evident. The important concept to keep in mind is that regardless of whether you are focusing on operational or strategic issues, the three areas of concern and action apply. Now let's discuss how the planning process appears in well-run organizations.

FIGURE 2.5

Key Issues	"Best Practices"

Planning
- Do I/T activities fit business unit plans?
- Do we have the right balance between long and short term?

- Continuous I/T and business planning ensures ongoing alignment.
- Time is allocated to allow I/T and business units to link plans.

Funding
- Are we investing the right amount on I/T?
- Are we making the right investment decisions?
- Are we investing adequately in infrastructure?

- Earmarking funds to strategic projects and/c infrastructure guarantees that day-to-day decisions support the strategy.

Communications
- Does I/T communicate its strategic value to its constituency?
- Does I/T coordinate appropriately with its customers?

- Treating communications as a series of critical activities and assigning dedicated personnel, rather than an ad hoc activity, establishes shared goals and objectives.

Operational versus Strategic Planning

Organizations always have the option of using computer technology to enable business plans or to provide business differentiation. This breakdown to a cost versus competitive advantage view has been an age-old debate among technologists, senior executives, and the "experts." The professors and consultants tend to argue in favor of using computers to differentiate a business from its competitors. We all know the story of how American Airlines built a reservation system that led to three decades of great successes and, more recently, how Federal Express tracks packages so closely that it can offer dramatic improvements in its guarantees for next day delivery services. Yet many I/T executives have argued an equally compelling case that they should provide services that make business plans function. Thus, if someone wants to respond to customer inquiries effectively, they build telephone/software systems that allow banks of operators to talk to customers while looking at their records on-line. There is no right or wrong on the issue, well-run companies usually have both.

Figure 2.6 suggests how one versus the other influences strategic decisions in I/T.

Figure 2.6

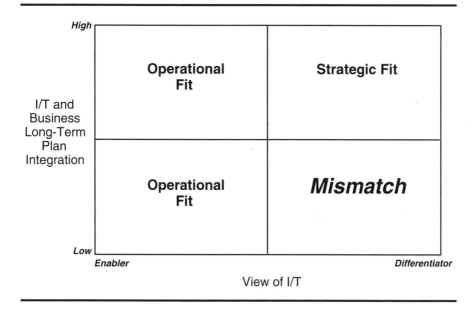

Operational fit focuses on executing business strategy by improving productivity (cost reductions). An enormous amount of work has been done to define how this should be done, and this process is already evident in many well-run organizations. Using the model developed by John C. Henderson and N. Venkatraman, now widely used by many corporations, alignment is across a variety of points of contact. Figure 2.7 illustrates how you begin by understanding the business strategy across scope, competencies, and governance. Then you look at organizational infrastructure and processes to define how they will support the business objectives. Then the I/T organization steps in and aligns itself against those business operational intents. What that does is generate a set of functional requirements, a portfolio of applications, and a capacity plan to meet those business requirements. Figure 2.8 lists the types of questions which must be answered to manage the I/T delivery system. Robust operational plans always comment on each of these themes.

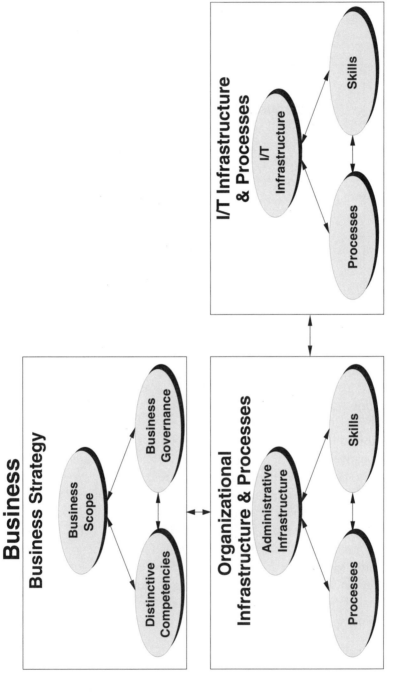

Business

Business Strategy

- Business Scope
- Business Governance
- Distinctive Competencies

Organizational Infrastructure & Processes

- Administrative Infrastructure
- Skills
- Processes

I/T Infrastructure & Processes

- I/T Infrastructure
- Skills
- Processes

FIGURE 2.7

Figure 2.8

• **Hardware and Network Systems**
  – Scope
  – Benefits
  – Costs (initial & ongoing)
  – Resources/skill requirements
  – Migration path
	• **Budget**
	  – What
	  – Where
	  – When
	  – How much

• **Application and Network Systems**
  – User
  – Purpose/scope
  – Risks
  – Costs
  – Benefits
  – Implementation resources
	• **I/S Management Plan**
	  – Organization
	  – Hiring/training
	  – Standards
	  – Methodology
	  – Policies/procedures

Organizations that have best practices in planning clearly execute adaptive planning and funding. This is especially the case in I/T organizations that have an operational fit with the enterprise they support. What are evident patterns of behavior?

Planning: Four features are almost always in evidence.

- I/T plans are responsive to business unit requirements for technology even though invariably there is limited turnaround time to deliver hardware, software, and systems. They somehow find a way. That "somehow" is structured in the way I/T is responsive to end users as a company would be to its customers.
- Priorities for I/T activities and investments are made by the business units, not by some lone I/T executive in their department.
- I/T plans are kept flexible and are reviewed frequently by the business community (usually quarterly). Priorities are adjusted in response to such changes as business volumes and market realities. In this situation, I/T plans are very tactical and end-user focused.
- Approvals for major I/T initiatives are made in a timely fashion (in other words, quickly) and are linked to funding. Decisions to go ahead on a project are accompanied by budget allocations to get them going.

Funding: Three patterns of behavior are in evidence.

- Invariably you notice that business units are playing a pivotal role in obtaining funding for I/T initiatives. Today, we can even say that the phrase "I/T initiatives" is becoming outdated, being replaced with "business initiatives" which have an I/T content. Historically, it has usually been the I/T organization that defined an initiative and sought funding. In these best practices organizations, it is the other way around. Often it is the business unit that funds I/T initiatives by either giving up budget for that or aligning with I/T to convince senior executives to offer up capital and operational funding. This is a very significant departure from business as usual.
- Budgets are more fluid, changing during the course of the year. The key is flexibility. This stands in sharp contrast to the normal pattern where an I/T executive gets his or her budget for the year and is told to make it and not come back for another 12 months. In best practices organizations, as requirements for change ebb and flow, so too do the capital and operational budgets keep in lock step with decisions. This too is a sharp departure from business as usual. This pattern is more in evidence in the private sector than in government agencies.
- Investments in infrastructure are deliberately made with clearly understood intents. Since many executives, particularly in the United States, are measured on short-term quarterly profit targets, they thus frequently have the incentive to put off capital investments for the future. In best practices companies, however, their measurements, incentives, and bonus payment plans have been aligned with the recognition that investments must be made this quarter, this year for the future. That pattern is a radical departure from business as usual but is emerging as a clearly evident feature of well-run companies.

Communications: So far two attributes are in evidence.

- End users—invariably business units and not individuals—keep I/T organizations well-informed about their plans, almost always including technologists in their development and execution. This ensures a timely dialogue and facilitates buyin from everyone who has responsibility for implementing business plans.

- In a clear demonstration of the practice of organizations learning, teaming, and applying core competencies to business issues, instant teaming of subject experts takes place in response to business problems or market opportunities. Thus, one can frequently see, for example, marketing experts working with data mining technicians to figure out what information can be extracted out of the computer files that will help identify new markets or new products. In fact, this last best practice is *the* model for planning. Such planning is done up front in a team form.

These are the patterns evident in companies that have I/T organizations that have elected to focus on aligning by operational fits. Invariably the initiative for developing this pattern of behavior begins with I/T, but it only works in companies that practice similar decision making and planning across the enterprise.

Those I/T organizations and their companies that want to apply strategic fit follow a different, yet not radically different, tact. Strategic fit results when you align I/T strategic plans to the business strategy. This is the main theme, for example, to emerge from the research done by Henderson and Venkatraman. Using their chart to demonstrate what is happening—see Figure 2.9—well-run organizations have aligned business and I/T strategies almost on a one-to-one basis. For example, once the business scope has been settled on, the technology required to support it must be resolved. Developments in technology, in turn, also influence business scope; that is how you find companies linking opportunities created by technological innovations.

The same applies to the competencies of a company and its systems, with how a business will govern (manage) itself, and with how I/T will manage its operations. This holds true for organization, infrastructures, and processes on both sides. And as with strategy, one influences the other. These two researchers also discovered that well-run organizations also have infrastructures and processes influencing strategy. In short, it is a holistic process, one which is consciously understood to be operating. Management intentionally encourages a holistic response to strategy and deployment of resources.

In this scenario what has become a pattern is that a business plan with a strong I/T component results in a strategic fit. That fit also falls along three lines of activities: planning, funding, and communications. As with operational fit, we can identify behaviors at work.

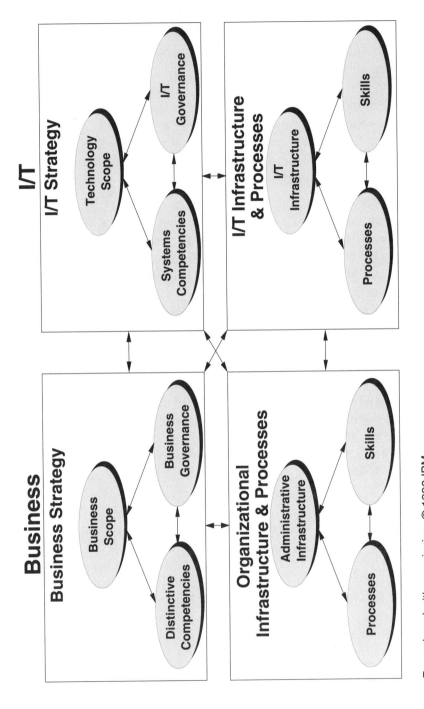

Reproduced with permission. © 1993 IBM

FIGURE 2.9

Planning: Two features are evident.

- The planning effort includes involvement by all the key stakeholders who are touched by these plans: business units, I/T, and partners.
- The planning process invariably leads to a single well-integrated business plan that includes a clearly stated I/T component. The plan is executed as a whole, with I/T and business units operating in tandem.

Funding: Four activities are very much in evidence.

- Since these plans are strategic, they are invariably multiyear; thus funding is provided for key I/T initiatives across more than one fiscal year; two to three years is not uncommon and the funding plan is adhered to.
- Because these are usually major plans, senior business and I/T executives remain actively engaged in the allocation of cross-firm resources.
- Since conflicts are inevitable, management creates forums for resolving cross-business unit disagreements or other problems.
- Funding of I/T infrastructures is made in the strong belief that these are crucial to the future competitiveness of the company, so much so that they are pursued aggressively by both I/T and the affected business units.

Communications: Two central features are normally evident.

- As with operational planning processes, collaboration exists between business units and I/T organizations to ensure alignment. Thus, for example, a business unit discussing a problem might call upon an I/T expert to participate in its discussion. The relationship evolves into a collaborative one, leading to mutual understanding and respect on the one hand and, to joint execution of tasks on the other.
- A byproduct of this approach is that I/T executives invariably wind up within the "inner circle" of senior managers making the key strategic decisions. This is a logical and yet important pattern of behavior because, historically, I/T executives have frequently complained that they were left out of the key decisions, often serving as second-class executives. As I/T executives add value and are critical to the implementation of a plan, particularly those who have high I/T content, it becomes essential that they be part of that inner circle.

Regardless of which approach you take—for operational or strategic fit—those who do it well strive for synergy among planning, funding, and communications. That three-part process creates focus and mission. The net result is improved implementation, an effective bias for action (Figure 2.10). Mechanically, action emerges from an integrated and comprehensive road map for the future and managers do not avoid the discipline of good paperwork (Figure 2.11).

FIGURE 2.10

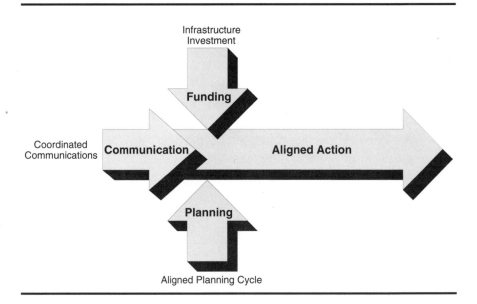

Infrastructure
Investment

Funding

Coordinated
Communications   **Communication**   **Aligned Action**

Planning

Aligned Planning Cycle

Conclusions

What these organizations have obviously done is to find straightforward but powerful ways to link planning intentions with daily actions. While this may sound simple, and clearly the descriptions provided in this chapter are, the resulting benefits are powerful.

- This process of folding I/T and business plans together does, in practice, lead to continuous alignment of plans and actions.
- This process generates a strong vision of I/T's role, fostering collaboration which, in turn, leads to increased value coming from information technology.

- This process places great emphasis on shared accountability for the governance of I/T, encouraging improved allocation of I/T resources from the perspective of the business units.

The inevitable results of this process are business centric: sales, reduced operating expenses, growth in market share, higher customer satisfaction, more productive employees, and so forth. It takes the bumper sticker message—enabling you to exploit your strategic advantages—and makes it actionable!

Armed with a clearer understanding of what is valuable from I/T, the inevitable next question has to be; "Well, how do I get the technologists to give me what I want?" It is a very good question and the subject of the next chapter. The question is not only outstanding from an obvious and practical perspective; it is also important because many firms do not know how to get their I/T organizations in line with what the corporation as a whole wants to get done! Once we get the buyin from I/T, then the rest of this book becomes very possible.

I began this book by stating that best practices strategies are being widely implemented and that they are generating results. Is everyone doing this today? No. Complaints about the lack of I/T value remain very high,

FIGURE 2.11

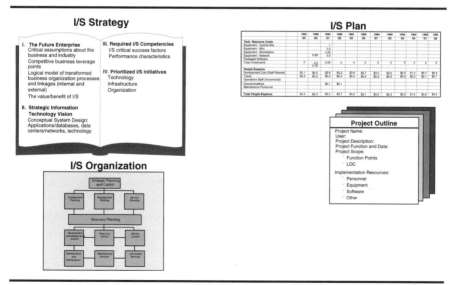

but so too do the number of organizations not yet doing anything serious about it. In *Beyond Computing*'s September 1996 survey, respondents were asked what plans they had for improving I/T. The evidence suggests that only a third are in the hunt for quality by using best practices. Of those who were not even claiming to leverage I/T for specific values, 43.5 percent even admitted not having any plans while another 20 percent said they would get around to it in the next two to five years! Bottom line: There is plenty of room for improvement in the use of I/T. The rest of the book deals with the nuts and bolts of how that is being done today.

Implementing Best Practices Now	
Action	**Why**
Focus on the value of I/T the next time an I/T project comes up for consideration.	Begins to get everyone focused on the business results expected.
Force every new I/T project to be aligned with end users with the latter defining the value needed.	Ensures I/T is focusing on business results while obtaining buyin from line management in functional areas.
Begin formal I/T planning with end users if you are not doing so already.	So you pick the right I/T things to do.
Ask other senior executives in other companies how they hunt for value in I/T.	They might know something you can use right away.

References

1. Allen, Thomas J., and M.S. Scott Morton (Eds.). *Information Technology and the Corporation of the 1990s.* New York: Oxford University Press, 1994.
2. Cash, J.J., and B. Konsynski. "I/S Redraws Competitive Boundaries," *Harvard Business Review* 63, no. 2 (1985): 134–142.
3. Editors, Harvard Business Review. *Revolution in Real Time: Managing Information Technology in the 1990s.* Boston: Harvard Business Review Books, 1990.
4. Harmon, Roy L. *Reinventing the Business: Preparing Today's Enterprise for*

Tomorrow's Technology. New York: Free Press, 1996.

5. Hax, A.C., and N.S. Majluf. *Strategic Management: An Integrative Perspective.* Englewood Cliffs, NJ: Prentice Hall, 1984.

6. Henderson, John C., and N. Venkatraman. "Understanding Strategic Alignment," *Business Quarterly* (Winter 1991): 72–78 and their other article "Strategic Alignment: Leveraging Information Technology for Transforming Organizations," *IBM Systems Journal* 32, no. 1 (1993): 4–16.

7. "IS Gears Up For The Next Millennium," *InformationWeek* (September 30, 1996): 65.

8. Kleinschrod, Walter A. "Leveraging Technology," *Beyond Computing* (April 1996): 20–22.

9. Pollalis, Yannis A. "A Systemic Approach to Change Management: Integrating IS Planning, BPR, and TQM," *Information Systems Management* 13, no. 2 (Spring 1996): 19–25.

10. Walton, Richard E. *Up and Running: Integrating Technology and the Organization.* Boston: Harvard Business School Press, 1989.

11. Weizer, Norman, et al. *The Arthur D. Little Forecast on Information Technology and Productivity: Making the Integrated Enterprise Work.* New York: John Wiley & Sons, 1991.

RECEIVING VALUE FROM COMPUTERS AND THE HIGH PRIESTS OF TECHNOLOGY

Value—A fair return in money, goods, or services, for something exchanged.

—Webster's Dictionary

*T*his chapter describes how world-class companies make decisions to acquire new I/T services and define what value they want from these. Their strategies for identifying and ensuring they receive value are also reviewed.

But what is a fair return? The quality gurus would argue that fair return is in the eye of the beholder: "I know it when I see it!" More rationally, however, value is closer to what *Webster's Dictionary* calls it; a fair return on investment. Yet the hard part is always defining what is fair, particularly in an age when in many industries the correct adjective has to be *compelling* because of customer expectations. For decades management has had a difficult time defining what value from information technology is. In the 1950s and early 1960s it was almost easy since companies were automating functions that were already being performed by people. So you could take their salaries and costs and divide that total by what it would be if done by a computer and make a decision about value very quickly. When new applications came on-line, particularly through the use of databases and terminals, life got complicated. Since then there has been a raging debate about the value provided by computers.

The body of literature on the topic is massive. Almost every survey of senior management done on the issue since the late 1960s has indicated that they have not been convinced for years that I/T was pulling its weight. At best, it was usually a necessary expense, although on occasion some data processing manager would be respected for his or her business acumen. But why dredge up all this history? It is to state that executives have stopped tolerating the unknown about I/T benefits because these expenses, and their potential return to their corporations, are too great to ignore the issue. Once again, if we turn to companies and agencies that have addressed the problem in a practical manner, we find new processes being developed to identify, measure, and exploit value.

A Strategy for Reaping Value

The value which I/T is perceived as delivering to an enterprise is increasingly being linked to a process for the selection of initiatives, their justification, and monitoring what is end-user and customer focused. The heart of the process has two halves:

- Selecting the I/T initiative
- Monitoring the initiative

These are then coupled with a measure of the value anticipated. Well-run organizations usually do this by linking measures to customer focus, a set of balanced criteria across service lines or functions, and continuous improvement. These three parameters are of equal value. Figure 3.1 describes the flow of the value process. Now let's see what each component of the process looks like.

FIGURE 3.1

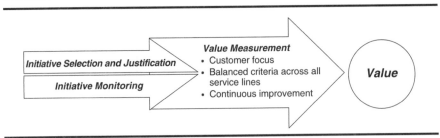

**Using Technology to Lead in a Market:
Nintendo and the World of Games**

This company has won approximately 40 percent of the $15 billion electronic game market by combining sound strategies and tactics with information technology. In 1985 it launched its first home video game and in 1989, Game Boy, the first portable, handheld game system that also included interchangeable games. The company applied its knowledge to produce games that had active characters—like Mario, Link, Yoshi, and Kirby. Next it built a customer support structure of people, telephone hot lines, and systems to help customers and to gather market data. Results: By 1995 the company had received over 40 million telephone calls from customers, giving the company millions of ideas about how to improve games. To provide software, the firm also formed alliances with software firms around the world, constantly adding new and better games, largely in response to what the callers and other market gathering channels suggest.

For further information, see W.W. Williams, "Games for Growth: Nintendo Co., Ltd.," *Hemispheres* (April 1996): 29–30, 32.

In the case of selecting an initiative and its cost justification, we are speaking about the process by which a company decides its I/T investment priorities. While you would be hard put to find any I/T executive who has a crisp statement as to what their justification process is, increasingly the best practice in this area boils down to eight steps which are executed with end-user organizations. Briefly put they are

1. Maintain a customer focus, using a balanced set of criteria laced with a strategy for continuous improvement. Value, in other words, is couched in the language of customers, growth, and profits.

2. Maintain good communications and strong working relationships with end users as that will improve their judgment of I/T staffers. We will discuss how to make sure senior management is involved.

3. Pick the right projects to take on—projects that are linked to business strategies and selected jointly with stakeholders.

4. Develop cost tracking, coupled with an initial benefits analysis that includes verification of business results. Add in some evaluation of customer satisfaction.

5. Link measurements to delivery of business value. Define service quality indicators in customer terms to ensure customer/market focus.

6. Don't just install applications. Reengineer processes. Use I/T as the centerpiece of new ways of doing business.

7. Provide users with tools that can enable them to measure and prevent waste. Help users do it right the first time and teach them how they can simplify their own processes.

8. Let your users cost-justify the value of new I/T projects rather than take full responsibility. Make sure they also share accountability for the results of your joint work. I/T owns accountability for cost and functionality of I/T components.

Sounds great; put the monkey on the end-user's back! Not quite; best practice enterprises, we saw in Chapter 2, collaborate across departments to figure out what makes sense to take on.

On selecting initiatives and developing justification, the key is to develop a process by which the company decides its I/T investment priorities. There are many paths that can be taken, but they all involve formal statements of economic and strategic benefits and who is responsible for delivering them. Decisions are made by all those involved in making these come alive. Some companies use teams, others, senior I/T councils or strategic investment task forces, but the good ones never leave it to the CIO or CEO to do alone. That approach simply ensures confusion, lack of buyin, and limited accountability, and possibly the wrong decision.

Monitoring the I/T initiative as it moves from proposal to implementation and results achieved requires looking at how to evaluate the performance of I/T projects relative to their original plans. The literature on how to do this is vast; we do not need to spend time on it here. What differentiates best practices companies from others is that they actually do implement rigorous project control techniques. Your company has these kinds of skills typically in three places: the I/T department which is used to managing complex projects; quality process reengineering teams if your company has taken on process redesign work; and finally, consultants who are always expected to complete projects on time and within budget. Tap any of those sources for the basics of project management because that is what is called for here.

Measuring value is a great deal more complicated. Essentially what well-run companies do is begin by developing indicators of I/T contributions to business results through performance measures which

- Define expected results in customer and stockholder terms.
- Include measures covering the totality of I/T objectives across all service lines.
- Provide actionable data for incremental progress.

While the subject of measurements of I/T is complicated (I covered it in a chapter in *TQM for Information Systems Management*), the Gospel is: Don't just measure financial return on investment. Develop a set of balanced measures that speak to such issues as how pleased users and victims of a project are with I/T's performance, economic data that address issues such as sales, growth, and cost of waste, and process performance characteristics such as speed, flexibility, simplicity, and accuracy, and finally, about how well the organization is learning from the experience (e.g., employee skills development, project reviews of on time and on budget performance and why).

All these actions take us to value. Companies that understand how to define value have overwhelmingly concluded that value is the perception of I/Ts contribution to business results. Effective measurements enable fact-based discussion by management about the performance of an I/T initiative relative to their expectations. But in the end, it is the conclusions of all those affected by an I/T initiative that determines value.

Delivering Value with I/T: USAA Focuses on Customers

United Services Automobile Association (USAA) is considered by most executives and business consultants as one of the best-run corporations in the world. USAA focuses on providing unparalleled customer service, using I/T to get the job done. One major area of emphasis is the application of computers in keeping the voice of USAA's customer loud and clear. From the CEO down to the data center floor, the customer comes first. Revenues flow as a result. I/T management had contributed applications that made it possible for USAA to have best practices in relationship management process, complaint handling, satisfaction measurements, and market and customer needs assessments. Instead of cutting I/T budgets, management is investing more in computing than the national average.

For more information, see Carol Hildebrand, "CIO 100—Best Practices: Satisfaction Guaranteed," *CIO* 8, no. 19 (August 1995): 98–100.

What about value of the I/T organization as a whole? Assessments in well-run organizations tend to come from two sources: analysis of ongoing projects, as we have just reviewed, and surveys of overall performance done by I/T organizations targeting customers, end users, partners, vendors, and senior management. They report these data back to all their constituencies, thank them for the compliments, and then focus on how to address deficiencies. Increasingly the Baldrige criteria, or a variation, is the tool being used. One best practices I/T organization, Appleton Paper Company, for example, uses the Baldrige criteria across the entire company. Citizens Utilities also does this. In short, it is not industry specific; cases appear in many industries. So when the senior I/T executive at Appleton Paper, John L. Tucker, has to review the performance of his department, he does it in language familiar to all his stakeholders. Because they participate in so many of his decisions, the assessments are as much of their performance as they are of his. Now that is team-based value assessment!

Let's summarize. Across all industries I/T is under pressure to demonstrate and defend its contribution to business performance. A byproduct of that pressure is the debate among executives and their staffs concerning selection and justification of initiatives, monitoring them and measuring value. The debate always seems to boil down to three questions that best practices companies take seriously and go through great pains to answer:

- On the selection and justification of initiatives: Are we selecting and funding the right I/T projects?
- On monitoring initiatives: Are we getting our money's worth?
- On measuring value: Do our measurements tell us how well we are achieving our goals?

Well-run companies do not ask just one or even two of these questions, they ask all three. For the life of a project or for the assessment of an I/T department, these are good questions to ask, even greater when you have believable answers.

If you think that this preceding discussion was too elementary, you may want to think again. *InformationWeek* reported in October 1996 that less than 20 percent of all corporations even have a process in place to cost-justify I/T. In a survey done by consultants working for Grant Thornton, a similar finding demonstrated how few do the obvious. The best practice is not so much finding Return-On-Investment (ROI) in I/T as it is in identifying payback on a process that happens to include I/T. The shift to a process-centric analysis of ROI differentiates the best I/T management teams from the rest when it comes to articulating the value of their services. To a large extent, when IBM consultants help clients articulate the value of their I/T, they focus on the results of I/T within the context of applications and processes as seen by end users and customers, not just by I/T professionals.

How the Best Select I/T Initiatives

The selection of major I/T initiatives has always been a complicated process. The decision is fraught with risk: risk of spending too much money, risk of technical failure, risk of delay in the delivery of benefits, risk of not getting the benefits anticipated, risk of the economic environment changing, risk that someone won't follow through to completed implementation, risk of an industry shift. Then there are options: Do nothing, incrementally improve what you have, or radically change what you have. If you change what you have, there are options here too: options based on what technological platforms are available to you, what business strategies you are attempting to execute, and where you will place responsibility for the I/T initiative within the organization. In short, the selection and justification of an initiative is both a complicated and sloppy process in most organizations. Monitoring, which one would think would be easier than selection, is equally complicated.

So what do companies do to minimize risk and increase the odds that they got it right? The most common answers are to have good communications and strong working relationships among all involved, and the right knowledge and skills. In some cases yet another ingredient is needed: the ability to be creative, particularly in industries experiencing great change. The issue of creativity in such a case does not mean simply borrowing great ideas from a different industry; it means really coming up with something new that had not been done before, as Citicorp did nearly two decades ago when it became an early user of ATM systems. Today we are seeing such creativity at work, for example, in Internet-based and network-based applications, particularly at the borders of disaggregating industries reaching customers electronically. In case after case where management believed an initiative proved successful, these two strategies were at work.

Regarding communications, seven best practices attributes are evident:

- Two-way
- Frequent
- Multilevel
- Focus on joint objectives
- Clearly understood by all concerned
- Provide relevant information
- Result in coordinated action.

Some of the attributes are obvious and need not detain us; others less so. Notice that the theme of alignment across multiple organizations and objectives exists—"joint objectives," "clearly understood," "relevant information," and "coordinated action." In other words, the initiative's success makes sense to all involved in terms that are relevant to them. They have skin in the game. A second theme is frequency and volume of communications so things stay fresh, urgent, and high on the list of things to focus on: "two-way," "frequent," and "multilevel." Multilevel means you have various organizations and different levels of management participating and supporting the decisions.

The appearance of strong working relationships is such a prominent best practice that it needs to be treated almost independently of communications although it is difficult to imagine working relationships without communications. Best practices companies demonstrate five attributes of working relationships time and again.

1. I/T executives participate in senior management committees and strategic decision-making activities. That means they also participate in decisions not strictly I/T in nature and their opinions on these matters are respected.

2. I/T enjoys an equal status with other functional areas, such as marketing, finance, and manufacturing. This means in a rapidly growing number of cases that I/T executives are reporting very high in the organization, often run divisions, and get their supervision from presidents and chief operating officers and not, as was most common in earlier decades, from the chief financial officer or one of his or her directors.

3. I/T and business units have integrated their operations in ways that make sense to line management. Manufacturing has its shop floor systems, stores their point-of-sale applications and I/T support staff assigned to them, and I/T is seen as being part of the team.

4. I/T has excellent working relationships at all levels of the enterprise, largely facilitated by the communications activities described above. This means I/T is part of many major projects, the key day-to-day activities, and participates in important communications events, such as line staff meetings and end-user planning sessions.

5. I/T's working relationships involve positive contributions at both the strategic and tactical levels. This means that over time I/T's quality operational support and leadership have been demonstrated repeatedly and, therefore, were given the opportunity to do the same on strategic issues and once again, proved competent.

Selection of the "right" I/T initiatives directly affects the level of business satisfaction with the information processing community. This is an extraordinarily important point since much of the assessment that goes on even in very well run companies relies on perception, not always on methodical fact-based analysis. In both good communications and working relationships perception of the overall capability and quality of performance of I/T are crucial in influencing the level of satisfaction line management and senior executives have with the selection and implementation processes.

Figure 3.2 is a simple representation of the four basic selection attributes evident today.

Again some themes continue to pop up: alignment and joint decision making. Companies are reporting that timely decision making is becoming crucial. As opportunities to exploit market conditions come and go quickly or technologies and their economics change at a rapid pace, the process for defining an initiative, building the business case, and then getting the go/no go decision made, make it possible to exploit speed, causing cycle time to become an important ingredient in "getting it right."

FIGURE 3.2

"Best Practice" Selection Attributes

- Linked to business strategy
- Decided jointly by I/T and business
- Timely decision making
- Fair and consistent selection process

Business Satisfaction

We all know of situations where I/T decisions may have dragged on for over a year or more. What well-run companies are doing is making decisions in weeks or, at most, a few months. They arrive at these decisions by using task forces, relying on the output of work done by process teams, or the recommendations of consultants on short evaluation engagements of several months duration. A combination of these, along with preexisting decision-making processes (e.g., opportunity or investment councils) speed up the process without introducing additional risk to the quality of the decisions.

The last point—fair and consistent selection process—speaks to many issues: politics, fact-based decision making, known decision criteria and where to go for decisions, and a true hunt for what is right for the enterprise. Best practices decision making is far from immune from these issues, but they are minimized through communications and joint decision making. While the list implies that they are negatives, in fact, they are quite the opposite. These are positive statements because they contribute to valued I/T practices. They cannot afford to do otherwise; I/T consumes too much of the budget for private little games to go on very long.

So what are the decision criteria most evident today? What gets monitored after the decision? Decision criteria focus on both efficient and effective deployment of I/T. The new news is that both are balanced in the weighing of a decision, not just efficiency as a regular course of action.

Historically, decision and monitoring focused on tracking costs of a project. Project budget estimates were developed and reviewed. Plans frequently looked like spread sheets. Well-run organizations link the decision to launch an initiative to a plan for subsequently monitoring it, through a combination of cost tracking with performance evaluation. Costs, therefore, can go up or down against an original plan in context with the performance of the overall value of the project. This makes it possible to take advantage of new market conditions (e.g., speed up implementation even if means spending more now but less later) or new technologies (e.g., switching to a new platform like client/server instead of implementing a centralized massive system).

In the past we did an initial benefit analysis and made our decision solely on those data. Today an increasing number of organizations couple that initial staff work with a rigorous verification of actual business results. How obvious, you say! But in reality, most companies in most situations never went back to figure out if they got their money's worth for an I/T investment. Best practices companies not only check after the fact, but also as the budget is being spent on the project! That is new.

How Monitoring of Progress Is Made

Another historical practice was to conduct some informal evaluation of customer satisfaction with a new I/T project. Customers in this case can be anybody: vendors, real customers, or end users. Given the enormous emphasis on customer feedback that we have all been party to over the past decade, it should be no surprise that a best practice is the formal evaluation of customer satisfaction with an I/T service. In fact, well-run I/T organizations routinely survey their customers on all I/T services. How you structure yourself for that will be discussed periodically elsewhere in this book and was the subject of extensive discussion in *TQM for Information Systems Management*. The point is that feedback becomes an influencer both in the decision to acquire another system and to monitor its performance.

By now you will probably have concluded that in the past there was no continuous improvement feedback loop being widely deployed. To get the feedback just discussed, the decision-making process includes measurements used to suggest how continuous improvements can occur in the overall performance of I/T.

No responsible I/T executive will argue today that they have figured out how to measure results and deliver compelling value every time. The fact remains that while some companies have been able to translate performance measurements into direct statements of value, they do not always have the data they want. The good news is that with all the major changes underway in how companies measure performance, they are creating sets of measurements that can be linked to the delivery of business value. Four primary strategies are in evidence today.

They define service quality indicators in customer or end-user terms so as to ensure that their I/T staffs maintain a customer focus, not an internal I/T focus. For example, availability of the computer is a common item measured by I/T organizations. The operations manager would historically look at how often the computer remained up and running—usually 99.999 percent of the time it works. The end user was at the other end of a telephone line from the computer on his or her terminal and might have access to the system only 80 percent of the time because of telephone line problems, or software issues, or out of ignorance of how to use the application. A customer-focused shop would look at the 80 percent and not the 99.999 percent and ask questions about how to move the 80 to 99.

Such I/T organizations solicit regular and specific customer feedback to ensure that I/T objectives are properly aligned to the business at large. Particularly in large corporations, rigorous new processes are being developed to understand what customers and end users want and need. Figure 3.3 illustrates what some of these are. This schematic is the result of ongoing research into the best processes and organizational structures of I/T that IBM has been conducting since the late 1950s. For those readers who grew up with IBM's "yellow manuals" on organization of data processing, this is an updated version of how I/T organizations poll their end users and customers. However, don't be muddled by it. This figure oversimplifies what is an enormous effort willingly undertaken by well-run I/T organizations today to make sure they are on track.

Notice that the language used to describe this function is heavily marketing oriented, not technical in tone. Marketing techniques are being adopted by I/T organizations to facilitate the process of monitoring progress on projects and daily service. In addition to the influence of marketing has been the growing adoption of quality management practices which also call for establishing baselines of external market comparisons—usually benchmarking one I/T organization's process against the same in other companies. This helps I/T management understand how productive or competitive they are versus their peers; they then report this kind of data back to the whole corporation. This marketing orientation is

FIGURE 3.3

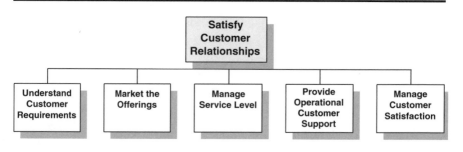

rapidly leading to the development of many formal processes in their own right to facilitate managing the delivery of I/T value to the business. How that process is emerging is illustrated in Figure 3.4. The figure is brief because under each of the five blocks are, on average, four to five other major activities that are performed. For example, under Justify Service Portfolio, criteria are set for selection analysis. Candidates for analysis are then routinely selected, analyzed, and recommendations are made to management. Since technical architectures often facilitate and influence such analysis, increasingly I/T organizations are viewing architectural issues as part of their strategy for managing delivery of I/T value to the business.

Finally, the establishment of balanced measures provides additional data for continuous improvement. Frequently now seen is the use of balanced score cards by process, application, and organization which we discussed in Chapter 2. We will have more to say about measurements elsewhere in this book because they are so crucial in instructing management about the value they receive from I/T.

How Value Is Perceived and Influences I/T

Perhaps the most interesting observation about value that has emerged in well-run organizations is that in general, higher satisfaction is achieved where shared I/T accountability exists. Figure 3.5 summarizes what best practices I/T organizations and their end users report. Common themes of joint communication and accountability appear once again. The hunt for value is therefore in the eye of the beholder, an end user armed with a fistful of facts about performance.

FIGURE 3.4

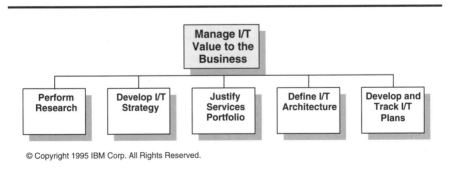

Figure 3.5

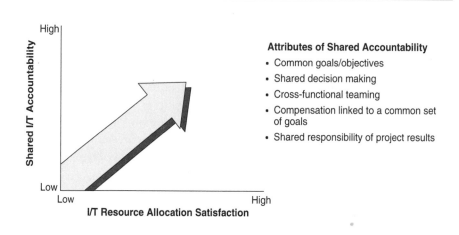

The drive for value, efficiency, and effectiveness is also leading to many new discussions about how to deploy I/T resources. The current wave of I/T restructuring is being driven primarily by the need to align the I/T organization with the business as a whole and to increase the value of computing services. One important trend associated with restructuring is the redeployment of resources to new business critical applications. That calls for new technical skills, assignment of personnel to end-user departments, and reliance on I/T resources outside the corporation. So what are the functions of these restructured organizations? Figure 3.6 suggests what is currently emerging today as the eight most important organizational components in the best-run I/T organizations. The primary driving force influencing the creation of this kind of structure is the need to deliver measurable value to customers, employees, and stockholders.

And what about outsourcing. What role is it playing? As with other functions in a company, I/T executives are turning to outsourcing when it can deliver greater value in efficiency or effectiveness. So far, most outsourcing has been looked at as a way of improving efficiency. However, some of the most dramatic improvements in end-user support have come by outsourcing Help Desks and software support (e.g., to the vendor of the application). There are three types of outsourcing going on in I/T today.

Ad hoc outsourcing: This is the use of supplemental staff to support one's own to provide specialized skills or handle peak workloads. Best practices required here are contractor/consulting management, broadening perspectives on available alternatives, and sharpening internal I/T competition.

Selective outsourcing: This is the use of outside resources primarily for low-risk commodity projects, such as migrating data from one system to another or doing data entry. The key management practices that well-run organizations focus on here are the management of longer-term contracts, risk, sustaining confidence and trust in working with external firms, and using those relationships to enhance internal skills.

Full-scale outsourcing: This is the use of contractors, long-term outsourcing agreements, and a combination of equity partnerships and alliances. It is this form of outsourcing that you typically read about in the *Wall Street Journal,* in which some company outsources the operations of a data center to IBM, for example, for a decade. The best practices these companies focus on the redefinition of internal competencies based on market forces, integration of internal and external human resource practices, and effectively managing partnerships.

FIGURE 3.6

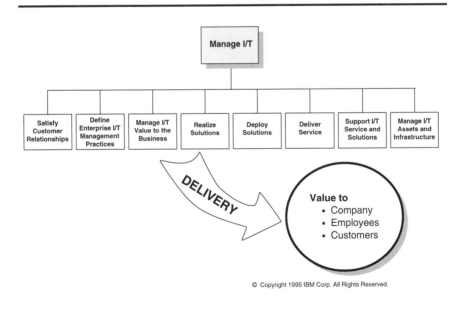

Outsourcing is one form of resource management; it happens to be a very popular option to explore today. The challenge is always to learn how best to manage the benefits and risks associated with external options. Typically, the risks associated with outsourcing are

- Dependency on someone else's skills
- Dependency on a vendor's performance
- Loss of maximum autonomy
- Effects of changing business environments.

On the other hand, there are some equally compelling benefits if you do it right:

- Flexibility in staffing
- Access to specialized skills
- Increased productivity
- Reduced costs
- Exploitation of changing business environments.

How you balance these risks and benefits, and which outsourcing strategy is adopted, is a function of how you deliver value to end users and customers. Best practices organizations do this through rigorous fact-based, cross-functional processes. There is discipline in what they do, not an informal or casual approach.

No book on management practices today is complete without the obligatory discussion about the role of senior management in causing change and positive performance. Best practices organizations all have senior management involved; this point will be made periodically throughout this book. But the best also have CIOs who are end-user focused, worry about customers, and act like business managers first. They must drive the development of a customer-focused culture within I/T. Harvey Shrednick, president of the Society for Information Management (SIM), recently put it in simple language: "I/T executives must be part of the fabric of the company so they are perceived as people who are involved in running the business, and this process of developing relationships with internal customers is not a one-time thing. It's ongoing." (*Banyan Computing*, January/February 1996)

Conclusions

It may seem almost trivial that we should discuss a best practice in the delivery of value to an organization by I/T. But the fact remains: I/T organizations, and the systems they support, become fixtures in companies and agencies through the passage of time. There is an entitlement that exists in the sense that I/T is a necessary expense in a corporation and that new things can't be done quickly because "the system won't allow it." No! Best practices I/T organizations, and the executives to whom they report, all comment how they are changing their structures, swapping out old skills for new (or using the old ways in clever new ways), and doing new things. In a study done by the SIM/IBM Working Group on reshaping IS culture, the group wanted to understand the role of high-performance I/T organizations. The group found that a variety of organizational structures were being used: radical decentralization, centralization, competency centers, decentralized ownership, and responsibility for the use of I/T. In other words, there is no cookbook formula. In response to changing needs of the business, well-run organizations viewed radical restructuring and constant change as normal and thus were learning how to do that as the norm.

Key messages from best practices companies are:

1. I/T and end users must jointly decide what initiatives to launch and why.
2. They should jointly be responsible for implementation and monitoring progress.
3. Management should be prepared to redeploy I/T resources of all kinds—organizational, personnel, systems, hardware, and software—to meet changing needs.

If there is a message it is that open dialogue, shared accountability, and a willingness to change are the hallmarks of best practices organizations that deliver compelling value to their companies and customers.

Any discussion about computers quickly and invariably evolves to a discussion about applications. It should. The reason we are interested in computers is because of what they can do for us. In the parlance of computing, we are talking about applications. After a half century of developing and using applications, are there some best practices in this area? Rules of the road? Things to go after, to watch for? The answer is yes. Well-run organizations have a process for going after these applications, and that is the subject of our next chapter.

Implementing Best Practices Now	
Action	**Why**
Define what value means to users of I/T for every project.	So you have a way of measuring what you are getting in return for I/T investments.
Get end users involved in assessing, measuring, and selecting I/T projects.	So that business considerations dominate all I/T decisions.
I/T should build a results-oriented measurement process that tells the business what it is doing for it.	So I/T can become less technology driven and more business focused.
Implement a formal cost-justification process for big I/T projects and use it now.	So you can define value in comparison to non-I/T investment opportunities (e.g., outsourcing).

References

1. Cortada, James W. "Balancing Performance Measurements and Quality," *Quality Digest* (December 1994): 48–54.
2. Hogbin, Geoff and David V. Thomas. *Investing in Information Technology: Managing the Decision-Making Process.* London: McGraw-Hill, 1994.
3. Landauer, Thomas K. *The Trouble with Computers: Usefulness, Usability, and Productivity.* Cambridge, MA: MIT Press, 1995.
4. Parker, Marilyn M. *Strategic Transformation and Information Technology: Paradigms for Performing while Transforming.* Englewood Cliffs, NJ: Prentice Hall, 1996.
5. Strassmann, Paul A. *The Business Value of Computers: An Executive's Guide.* New Canaan, CT: Information Economics Press, 1990.
6. Taninecz, George. "What's The ROI?" *InformationWeek* (October 7, 1996): 45–48.
7. Wakin, Edward. "The Customer-Centric CIO," *Beyond Computing* (January/February 1996): 42–48.

CHAPTER 4

BEST PRACTICES APPLICATIONS: FOCUSING ON THE ESSENTIALS

It requires a very unusual mind to undertake the analysis of the obvious.
—Alfred North Whitehead

*T*he purpose of this chapter is to describe basic qualities of best practices applications at a strategic level. This includes discussion about reducing labor content, role of cycle time, doing new things with I/T, and application of new information technologies.

Before we get too deep into this book with more chapters on how I/T organizations are best managed, let's deal with the obvious issue of applications. What are the best applications to implement? Management teams everywhere always want to know who is doing what with computers the best. There is a constant stream of articles and books appearing every month attempting to answer this question. Because the answers keep changing by industry, economics, and the effectiveness of evolving technologies, and as a result of growing experiences with applications, the key questions to ask should focus on results of applications. Are there some universal answers that can serve as guides for our actions and as benchmarks against which to measure the effectiveness of our applications?

Let's begin by understanding several tactical issues. Increasingly, specific applications, often called processes today, are being benchmarked within and across industries. The comparative data are often economic and financial, for example, what it costs to perform a specific transaction, such as cashing a check or answering a phone call. Benchmarks are readily available through industry associations, organizations of specific functions (e.g., suggestion processes, human resources), skills (e.g., training), and professions (e.g., accounting, marketing). More will be said about benchmarking elsewhere in this book, but suffice it to say here that there is a great deal of information about specific applications to give you a sense of how yours is doing in comparison to others.

If all you do is compare your existing applications with those of other organizations, you miss the boat because what well-run companies are learning are the universal lessons about the best uses of technologies. Alignment of I/T to business strategy, for example, requires that you know what effective uses of I/T at a strategic level are. From that base the best-run companies then decide what applications to implement, improve, or replace. The best start with application strategies. So our question really is, What are the best practices at the strategic level? It turns out that there are several topics to understand clearly because they are how we get to the answer. They are

1. Amount of labor content in work

2. Role of speed in doing work

3. Doing new things

4. Role of different types of technology

All four issues offer some best practices information. What is described below carries with it no editorial or moralizing, just the facts which you can then react to as you wish.

Reducing Labor Content in Work

The fact is, corporations since the early 1950s have attempted to expand productivity in all industries through the use of automation. Over the past five decades they have installed a vast array of machinery to do the work of people. It is a process that has continued and, according to the experts on labor, economics, and technology, will actually speed up. The intent is normally to displace human labor with equipment, much of which uses information technology. In recent years, economists have started to document dramatic increases in productivity which were finally achieved as a result of using technology. Those statistics can serve as best practices benchmarks for what you can do, industry by industry.

In a study for the *Annals of the History of Computing* (July 1997), I reported on a number of fundamental changes underway important to our discussion. At least 75 percent of all workers perform work which technologists believe can be automated in some fashion, ranging from robots welding to expert systems making judgments to phone systems, replacing receptionists and call takers in phone centers. If you take the U.S. work force of the early 1990s of 124 million, about 90 million are thus candidates for some form of automation. Perhaps the most dramatic examples of this have come out of manufacturing companies which, between 1981 and 1991, for instance, eliminated 1.8 million jobs just in the United States. When the automation process began in the 1950s, 33 percent of all U.S. workers were in manufacturing. By the early 1990s, that number had dropped to less than 17 percent. At the same time, manufacturing productivity rose. The most current data demonstrate that between 1979 and 1992 it rose by 35 percent; the work force producing that productivity shrank by 15 percent. A similar tale can be told about the service sector. Best practices thinking suggests that at a minimum you could expect similar reductions in labor content, similar levels of productivity gains, and, in fact, even more dramatic shrinkage of labor content. Peter Drucker thinks the U.S. manufacturing labor force will drop to 12 percent of the total work force while many in the banking industry expect that automation and reengineering will cause them to shed 30 to 40 percent of their workers by the first several years of the twenty-first century (see Table 4.1).

Table 4.1

Key Drivers of Productivity
Reduced labor content of work
Automation of tasks and data
Process simplification
Process reengineering for I/T optimization

This is not the book in which to debate the social virtues of technology in its effects on employment, or even its form and influence. I assume you are going to apply I/T wherever it can promise benefit to your organization. But we can make a very clear observation: Elimination of labor from work processes through the use of computers has been viewed by corporations and economists as a significant source of improvements in productivity and hence contributions to the bottom line. There are many distinguished observers who today see the real possibility of many near-workerless sets of processes. ATMs can and are replacing bank clerks, robots, blue-collar workers making automobiles, and now even robotics aid doctors in surgery! The farmerless farm may well appear in our lifetimes, perhaps the practical example of the ultimate intrusion of technology.

In the 1980s, American corporations invested over one trillion dollars in I/T to reduce costs of operation and to increase productivity. A great deal of this money was tied to reducing labor content of work. Over half of that investment was made in the service sector, responding to the best practices examples of manufacturing which had begun investing significantly in automation in the 1950s and 1960s. By the early 1990s, almost every corporate worker in America was backed up by an investment of some $10,000 in computing (Cortada, 1997). For years this investment appeared not to pay off very well, but then it began to in the early 1990s, suggesting a best practice. It did not help that all through these decades a good set of productivity measures were never deployed in business and government, thus probably adding to the strongly held belief of many executives, consultants, and academics (especially economists of technology in general) that a productivity problem existed.

In 1991, economists began to notice a rise in productivity in the United States, eventually determining that output per hour had risen by 2.3 percent; in 1992 by almost 3 percent, and so it has continued into the mid-1990s (Cortada, 1997). The data represent your company's benchmark hurdle against which to judge its effectiveness. Economists noted that in manufacturing, return on investment for computer capital climbed: Between 1987 and 1991 it achieved 54 percent. When combined with services, the increase climbed to 68 percent (see Table 4.2). Even the great critic of computer productivity, Stephen Roach of Morgan Stanley, had to admit that finally computers were contributing to productivity: "The U.S. economy is now entering its first productivity-driven recovery since the 1960s, courtesy of efficiency gains being realized through the use of information technology." (Roach)

Table 4.2

U.S. Productivity Growth		
Period	Average Growth	Comment
1950s	2–4%	Boom
1960s	2–3%	Healthy
1970s	2%	Flat
1980s	1–2%	Declining
1990s	2–3%	Expansion

U.S. Department of Commerce, *The National Income and Product Accounts of the United States, 1929-1982* (Washington, D.C.: GPO, 1986: *passim*) and James W. Cortada, "Economic Preconditions that Made Possible Use of Commercial Computing in the United States," *Annals of the History of Computing,* vol. 19, no. 3, (July-August 1997: *passim*).

What the most successful companies did was to delay their corporate structures, increase the ease and quantity of communications horizontally through the use of I/T (e.g., e-mail and groupware), use significant quantities of I/T on the manufacturing floor (especially numeric control [N/C], robotics, and data collection), and automation of repetitive tasks. That allowed them to implement many of the new management practices of the past 20 years: just-in-time, agile manufacturing, and lean production strategies, for example.

I/T made it possible to gather and display information in ways not possible before. The results were significant. For one thing, management did not have to distribute information through layers of employees so team-based organizational structures could be implemented, leading to a downward push in decision-making authority to the lowest level possible. Second, I/T made it possible to implement continuous improvement strategies—the heart of quality management—across the organization and even cross-corporations (e.g., to one's suppliers).

Businesses began to look at their workflows differently. The primary reason why computers did not deliver significant productivity gains in the earlier years is because they were used to automate existing processes and procedures and to do it within preexisting organizational structures. By the end of the 1980s, many companies had figured out that they had it backward; what they started to do then was to reengineer their processes and organizations to make them more computer friendly. That single action alone made it possible to apply computers more effectively by eliminating unnecessary steps, reducing cycle time, and off-loading essential tasks to computers which did the work cheaper and faster than workers. Whole layers of middle managers were eliminated; you have already read what happened to blue-collar workers. The results are now everywhere: agile manufacturing, quick response in retail, use of Electronic Data Interchange (EDI) in all industries, and immediate on-line access to information at the worker level.

You can find for each industry or function, benchmark levels of productivity as a result of these uses of I/T, which then can become your targets. Here is a short random list of measurable results you can expect. These kinds of "rules of thumb" are surfacing constantly now because of activities surrounding best practices, benchmarking, and cross-disciplinary studies (e.g., use of history, economics, and business).

- Every installed robot can normally replace four jobs, work 24 hours a day, and pay for itself in a year.
- Every industry that fully exploits technology can expect to reduce industrywide employment between 20 to 40 percent, with the larger number already the norm.
- Every industry that fundamentally automates can reduce the number of companies in it by a third or more.

Every industry has demonstrated the effectiveness of reducing labor content through the use of computers. In agriculture, less than 3 percent of the U.S. work force are farmers and some experts expect that we will halve that number in the next few years (see Rifkin, 1995). One of my favorite examples is Toyota because so many companies use it now as a model of reengineering using technology, organization, and process management. It cut labor content in car manufacturing down to 16 hours while GM needed almost 31; it used 4.8 square feet to build a car while GM needed 8.15 square feet; it had 0.45 defects per car while GM had 1.3. My intent is not to pick on GM—it too has made significant progress—but to demonstrate how much change one can implement in comparison to a competitor; not all companies in a particular industry do things the same way or have similar levels of productivity. Pick any industry—say steelmaking which was virtually dead in the United States by the end of the 1970s—

and you see that I/T even helps here. Labor saving automation between 1979 and 1990 reduced employment in steel about 1.7 percent per year. Similar experiences occurred in rubber, mining, chemicals, electronics, household appliances, and textiles.

While the services sector is just beginning to enjoy significant gains in productivity through the application of strategies similar to those applied in manufacturing, hard evidence is already available. Banks are shrinking in number—my forecast is that by the end of the century there will be 25 percent fewer than in the early 1980s—while 20 percent of their workers are expected to leave the industry due to automation and reengineering. ATMs are computer applications with well-defined productivity expectations that are best practices. A normal ATM, for example, costs about $22,000 per year, does 2,000 transactions a day, and works 168 hours per week. A bank teller costs between $8,000 and $20,000 per year, does up to 200 transactions daily, and works about 30 hours per week. See Table 4.3 for a list of new applications, all of which are currently under development or in pilot. Between 1983 and 1993, 37 percent of these workers were displaced by ATMs. Insurance examples of this magnitude also exist as they do for telephone companies as well with automated phone systems. And we have only just seen the start of the use of such new technologies as expert systems and imaging. Across all industries, low-skill work is disappearing, even for some functions that are perceived to have a higher order of work content, such as middle managers.

Table 4.3

Sample Best Practices Banking Applications
Community financial computer utilities
Networked consumer banking computing
Billess transactions
Moneyless transactions
Electronic check registers
Wealth management utility systems
Automated credit approval/management
Brokerless stock and bond trading
Agentless insurance

Nothing is escaping the eye of the best practices I/T organization when it comes to reducing labor costs. Take the ubiquitous secretary whose original entry into the work force in the late 1800s was due in part to such information process equipment as typewriters, telephones, and adding machines. Secretaries are shrinking in number. It turns out that about 45 percent of what they do involves the movement of paper, delivering messages, and waiting for work. Automation is beginning to demonstrate that half that time can be cut and, for some functions, up to 75 percent can be automated. Is it happening? Between 1983 and 1993 the number of secretaries in the United States declined by 8 percent while receptionists have become as rare as hens teeth thanks to voice mail and computerized telephone systems. Work force mobility with employees using laptops equipped with modems is reducing the need for office space. IBM, Dun & Bradstreet, and Ernst and Young are reporting savings of up to 30 percent of the cost of real estate by going mobile (Rifkin, 1995). That is your benchmark!

Another cross-industry application is warehouse management. IBM's own unpublished studies of those that were reengineered extensively using I/T are reporting labor savings of over one-third, space savings of 50 percent or more. Wholesalers are slowly being squeezed into oblivion through the use of I/T applications. The trend became dramatically evident in 1992 when U.S. wholesalers lost 60,000 jobs. Retailers in general are shedding jobs through the use of I/T. The large and venerable retailer, Sears, Roebuck, shrunk its employee base by 14 percent just in one recent year (1993), with more to come. Since 1990, U.S. retailers have shrunk their labor pool by some 400,000 employees through the use of point-of-sale technology because scanners could do the work 30 percent faster than previous technologies and required 10 to 15 percent fewer humans to use (Rifkin, 1995).

The best practices conclusion you can reach is that your I/T applications should, in general, lead to reductions in labor costs for an application of between 20 and 40 percent, with 30 percent, while good, is still below *best practices* levels. By the same token, broad-based applications can and often do contribute to the reduction in the number of companies in industries undergoing significant change. The shrinkages due to consolidations alone also approach or exceed 20 to 30 percent. New models of previous examples include the automotive, steel, telephone, and retail industries. Models currently being created through the trauma of change include utilities, telecommunications, movie and TV production, and a wide variety of professions. Look to education being next. With Internet, on-line query systems, and vast quantities of on-line data, we can also expect to see most of the 1,550,000 plus number of librarian jobs in the United States shrink sharply, just as we have seen farm labor in this country shrink from over 80 percent in the nineteenth century to less than 3 percent today.

Speeding Up Work

In one of those stunning moments when a book comes along that confirms in detail what we had suspected, George Stalk, Jr. and Thomas M. Hout published in 1990 *Competing against Time*, which has changed how senior management views strategy. Essentially what they demonstrated was that if you could increase your responsiveness and the speed with which you did everything—change, react, do work, deliver goods and services for example—you could be more competitive and more profitable. While how much varies by industry, on average you could have a 3x growth advantage over your competitors and a 2x advantage on profit. Best practices were performances that beat those. Stalk and Hout made the phrase "cycle time" popular. Through dozens of examples they clearly demonstrated the economic value of cycle time reduction. The book is must reading for any I/T executive who aspires to run an organization effectively because speeding up responsiveness can only be done by reengineering work and that, in turn, means making tasks I/T friendly.

The tactical consequences are clear:

- Productivity increases.
- Flexibility improves.
- Costs for In-Process Work (WIP) decline.
- Prices can be increased as time is compressed.
- Risks decline.
- Market share expands.

But why time? It turns out that if you can reduce complexity—which is what has to happen frequently in order to speed up work—costs go down. Second, customers will pay a premium for getting what they want when they want it, in other words, sooner rather than later. And, there is the traditional first entrant advantage. Time-based attitudes have been put on the short list of things executives worry about. Even with process reengineering projects, cycle time reduction is of major concern. Experts on reengineering have documented that today about 80 percent of executives expect results within 24 months while 60 percent expect results within one year (Cortada, *Quality Yearbook*, 1996)! Designing new processes to take advantage of I/T is emerging as the single fastest strategy for designing, implementing and obtaining results from reengineering! Table 4.4 summarizes key results that flow when you compress time. This is not theory. Many companies report they are enjoying these results today!

Closely related to time-based strategies is the need for agility or flexibility. Looking at applications of I/T that provide the corporation with these features represents some of the best practices today. Agility and flexibility allow companies to attack the problems posed by fragmenting markets, production requirements for small or individual lot sizes (e.g., mass customization), the requirement to treat all customers as individuals not as niches, shrinking product life cycles, convergence of products and services, global reach, and frequent and dramatic downsizing and other corporate restructurings (including acquisitions and mergers). An important study done by the Iacocca Institute at Lehigh University clearly demonstrates the economic value of agility approaching the same range as cycle time reduction and the benefits of reengineering (Table 4.5) (Goldman, 1995). Again, so there is no confusion about best practices, when the best reengineer, they achieve a minimum of 20 to 30 percent increase in productivity or quantifiable improvements. Every one of those success stories involved the extensive use of I/T.

High-tech Reps, Laptops, and Salespeople—Nordstrom Valve

Nordstrom Valve manufactures products used in the production and distribution of gas and oil. *Industry Week* reported that sales personnel used to manually calculate flows and types of valves their customers needed, often using three-ring binders of information to help in the time-consuming process. Today all the salespeople are equipped with laptops which they use in the presence of their customers to calculate rapidly what products to use, increasing productivity just for this one process—calculation—tenfold! Nordstrom Valve found a way to use information technology to improve an important process that resulted in higher-quality, faster, less-expensive service.

For further information, see Shari Caudron, "High Touch Plus High Tech," *Industry Week*, 243, no. 9 (May 2, 1994): 21–26.

Table 4.4

What Happens When Time Is Compressed?
Productivity increases.
Expenses drop.
Investments are recouped faster.
Prices can be raised.
Risks decline.
Shares increase.
Corporate culture changes.
Feedback on results come sooner.
Strategies are executed faster.
First entrant advantages are realized.
Competitiveness improves.
Agility becomes a reality.

Table 4.5

Sample Best Practices Performance (Iacocca Institute Findings)	
Activity	**Benefits**
Customer reject rates	0 to 3.8%
Percent of suppliers selected based on low bid	None
Work force operates in teams	20–100%
EDI links to suppliers and customers	70%
Average number of employee suggestions per year	50
Percent of payroll budget spent on training	2.5–6%

Source: Steven L. Goldman, Roger N. Nagel, Kenneth Preiss, *Agile Competitors* (New York: VNR, 1995): 355–376.

A simple example illustrates the value of merging I/T, reengineering, and cycle time reduction. One utility company in the Midwestern United States reengineered how it interacted with customers. It closed over a dozen small offices scattered in many little towns, centralized all its interactions with customers through a telephone call center, and linked all its customer files to the phone system so that a customer would call in whatever request or question they had. They no longer had to visit an expensive office; they now spoke to a clerk who had that customer's record in front of them. Whenever management wanted to sell a new service, they could broadcast information about the offering to the phone center which could immediately begin discussing (read selling) these with customers calling in or through outreach phone calls. As information about contract terms were collected through the system, it became possible to delegate decisions to the phone clerks. For example, the company learned that billing disputes of under $75 dollars cost more to resolve so it authorized its employees to use their judgment on whether to grant a credit real time based on previous customer-utility interactions and the clerk's perception of what was cost-effective and right to do. Customers could immediately be granted credits, documents and brochures shipped that night, and sales made on the spot. The system analyzed the types of calls that came in giving the company feedback on customer-related issues (Cortada, Hammer, Meeker, 1996).

Root-cause analysis on issues could be conducted immediately to resolve problems. For example, if billing complaints rose because of one line item in the bill, the system would flag that as a problem and, instead of equipping phone clerks with a clever response, I/T could go in and redesign the bill to eliminate the source of the confusion. Meter reading—the source of data for bills—was next to reduce labor content in reading meters, by moving to quarterly reads while in the intervening months estimated bills were generated based on a combination of history and recent weather conditions (e.g., temperatures).

Doing New Things

The third application area that has historically driven dramatic new uses of technology concerns the capability of using computers in different ways. Most of the management literature on how to use computing focuses on these kinds of applications. The well-worn best practices cases include American Airlines using computers to track inventory of airplane seats for its reservations process, Otis Elevator dispatching repair personnel, and Federal Express with its logistics processes. All three changed the marketing rules in their industries, gained significant market share, demonstrated the strategic value of computing, and forever transformed themselves. But each industry in each decade has had similar war stories to tell. And they continue to emerge today, based on mobile computing, the merger of telecommunications and computing and now, the merger of whole industries into possibly new ones (e.g., TV, cable, telephone, PCs, and entertainment). Are there some common features which can save us from reading hundreds of pages of war stories?

There are essentially nine major best practices evident in companies which are effective in the application of technology allowing them to do new things.

1. *They look for an application using a recently arrived technology to offer new services useful to customers.* The most obvious examples include use of ATMs to give customers greater access to banking services in the 1980s, use of credit-card sized modems and friendly networking software to make portable computers able to log into e-mail and Internet services in the 1990s.

Comparing Sales Performance—Duracell Case

Executive information systems have become quite popular and effective over the past decade. In the case of Duracell, executives can compare the performance of their sales organization in Europe and in the United States. Using this kind of data made it possible for management to learn how various sales teams went about their work. For example, salespeople in Germany focused heavily on small stores; management shifted to a distribution strategy of using dealers to do that, concentrating the Duracell sales force on larger, more profitable customers. Other data in this Executive Information System (EIS) on company Strengths, Weaknesses, Opportunities and Threats (SWOTs) help management make other strategic decisions.

For further information, see Christopher Koch, "Beating a Bad Rap," *CIO* 9, no. 21 (September 15, 1996): 28, 30.

2. *They combine technologies in new ways before their competitors do.* We are seeing this now in the trucking industry where logistical systems are being reengineered using databases, PCs, mobile telecommunications, and EDI between manufacturers and distributors (see Figure 4.1). The intent here is to make inventory and warehouse management a thing of the past; your basic 18-wheeler becomes your just-in-time warehouse!

3. *They form a very clear idea about how to apply a technology before they use it.* Several years ago image-based systems began to come on the market and were marketed to paper-intensive organizations like insurance companies. At first, most insurance companies looked at the technology, thought it clever, but did not know what to do with it other than stop having paper floating around their buildings. Furthermore, their lawyers did not like having copies rather than originals of signatures. Finally, they began to figure out that if they reengineered existing case management processes, this technology could offer the benefits of database market-driven strategies while improving operations. So today you see companies like USAA using imaging technology to reduce the cost and time to handle customer-related data and cases, while exploiting data

FIGURE 4.1

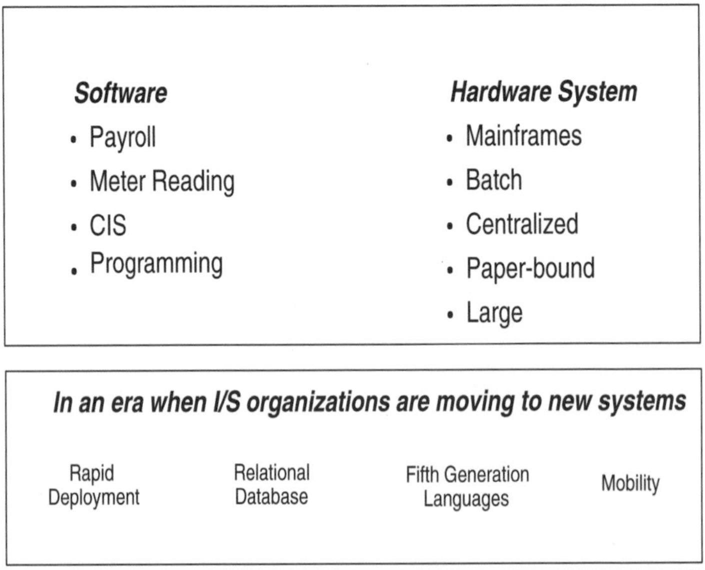

Software
- Payroll
- Meter Reading
- CIS
- Programming

Hardware System
- Mainframes
- Batch
- Centralized
- Paper-bound
- Large

In an era when I/S organizations are moving to new systems

| Rapid Deployment | Relational Database | Fifth Generation Languages | Mobility |

mining to figure out how to sell more products to each customer in coordinated ways. Instead of three different divisions of a company approaching a customer, you could now have one approach offering a comprehensive set of three products. Telephone companies now do this too and a few banks are beginning to demonstrate a similar approach. But in each case, specific expectations of functions, levels of performance, and results are established before installing these new systems.

4. *I/T executives ask themselves how I/T can be used to carry out a corporate objective rather than how a specific technology can be used to improve existing operations.* This may seem like a trivial point but it is not. If you apply some new technology to do what you have always done, the best one normally can hope for are improvements in efficiency. Yet we know that improvements in effectiveness often deliver far more dramatic results. Improving a process (e.g., simplifying it or making it run faster) normally yields improvements in the 10 to 20 percent range. Redesigning an application or process to make it exploit a new technology more effectively gives you the benefits of reengineering which have been clearly demonstrated to be in the range of 20 to 40 percent normally and sometimes far in excess of those numbers.

5. *They experiment with various technologies within their organizations and watch what others are doing.* The larger the I/T organization, the easier it is for management to try using every major new technology that comes on the market, learning its strengths and weaknesses and then applying the other rules of the road listed above and below. But they also watch what other companies are doing both inside and outside their industries to see what their experiences are. Migrating over a new use into your industry often becomes a best practice. For example, point-of-sale terminals were first used in the supermarket business but then spread into dry-goods retailing, drug stores, hardware stores, now even higher education. Mobile telecommunications came early to law enforcement and fire and health services. Now we all have pagers, mobile phones, and soon we will be buying Dick Tracy watch-like communication devices. The great drama of the move to portable communications is borne out by the sheer volume: There are 85 million cellular phones in use and 90 million pagers. Estimates suggest

that about 12 percent of the U.S. population today use cellular phones. Phone usage is expected to rise an additional 40 percent by the year 2000 (Price Waterhouse, 1995). Things are changing fast and in massive form! This happens with almost every technology that proves effective and today occurs usually within three to five years of its initial commercial introduction.

6. *New uses are most dramatic when they are industry specific.* Using a better spreadsheet or word processor does not do the trick. The major improvements have always come from industry-specific applications. The list is long: N/C on the manufacturing floor, Computer-Aided-Design/Computer-Aided-Manufacturing (CAD/CAM) in the design and manufacture of products, ATMs in banking, image in insurance, and Point-of-Sale (POS) in retailing. In each decade there are new technologies which lend themselves more or less to a particular industry. Network-based systems in the 1990s are drawing customers and retailers together in new ways. For example, telecommunications are generally beginning to alter how information and entertainment are being delivered to customers in the industrialized world. The enormous expansion in all things digital is making it possible to create industry-specific applications unavailable before, for example, entertainment and PC-based applications for the home, linking call centers with radio-dispatched repair personnel in the field, Geographic Information Systems (GIS) for infrastructure maintenance by utilities and municipalities. Table 4.6 lists a variety of I/T-based initiatives already underway in best practices companies, most in the United States.

7. *Technical architectures are increasingly becoming industry specific and are being applied to the selection and use of I/T.* Beginning about 20 years ago industries began to develop industrywide I/T-centric technical architectures to facilitate interactions electronically among members of the industry. The earliest example came in the 1950s with ERMA, the banking industry's agreement and process to have all lettering on checks be uniform and, closely related, the development of a uniform technical infrastructure to move money around the banking system. Manufacturing and clothing companies did the same in the 1970s by establishing technical standards for EDI and Universal Product Code (UPC). Today process and I/T architectures are either in existence or under

industrywide development across the board. The health and insurance industries are well underway, along with manufacturing. Cable companies came along and did the same in the 1980s. The point is, well-run organizations endorse, encourage, and exploit process and I/T-centric industry architectures.

8. *They use technology to form links with other companies and customers that can be expanded or decoupled fast.* Virtual organizations, partnerships, and other buzz phrases only become realities if multiple companies can find ways to work together. In practice, that usually means sharing information so that they coordinate and participate jointly in projects. Having a tire manufacturing company deliver each day exactly the right number and types of tires needed by a Ford, GM, Toyota, or Nissan plant to put on the cars built the same day requires sharing databases, EDI, and common I/T tools. Having retailers inclined to buy your products versus someone else's means having PC-based tools in their stores with convenient software installed that makes it easier to buy from you than from your competition (e.g., that's how American Standard sells a lot of product). It's AT&T announcing in late February 1996 that its long distance customers can have five free hours of Internet time every month and more at a discount if they are a long-distance phone customer. It's testing laboratories offering electronic links to hospitals so that health care centers give them all the business instead of spreading the work out among many laboratories.

Table 4.6

Sample 1990s Technology-Driven Applications
Just-in-time retailing
Shopping kiosks
Computer grocery shopping
Virtual shopping
Virtual work, virtual offices
Mass customization
Robotic manufacturing and services
Digital paper and communications
Do-it-yourself medical diagnostics
Bankerless banking
Robotic farming

9. *Use of industry-blessed best practices software remains a favorite way of adopting new applications.* Most industries have software packages designed for them that come to be considered the best and, in time, most players will use these. They design their processes around these packages because it is a fast, relatively safe way to get a useful tool. Best practices I/T organizations tend to participate in the development or enhancement of such packages, thereby reaping the benefits of their use sooner than their company's competitors. American Airlines' reservation system was an early example. A very current one is NIPSCO's customer service system in the utility industry. Others are competing at the moment for dominance in logistics within the manufacturing industry. We see the same kind of phenomenon at work with PC software: Microsoft Windows, DOS, OS/2, Lotus 1-2-3, and Excel.

Information Warehouse:
The Case of the McKesson Corporation

McKesson is the largest distributor of prescription drugs, various health- and beauty-care products, and a variety of specialty foods in North America. It supports some 16,500 retail pharmacies, along with 2,000 hospitals and another 2,000 home health-care dealers, not to mention thousands of retailers. This highly profitable corporation has developed a sophisticated information warehouse, created out of its electronic order process. This database contains over 200 million records which customers and sales personnel can access. The benefits: high levels of customer service and new sources of revenues. Sales personnel use laptops to access this information warehouse to do normal sales and marketing. Large retailers count on the system to make it possible to receive the right products in the right amounts at the right time. With these data, McKesson can help customers reduce their own cost of inventory while reconciling payments for third-party claims.

McKesson's information warehouse has become the key to how it runs its business. Its management of the information warehouse is a world-class example of using I/T well while enjoying the benefits of being a knowledge-driven corporation.

For further information, see Economist Intelligence Unit, *Global Telecommunications to the Year 2000* (New York: Economist Intelligence Unit, 1996): 68–72.

Role of Various Technologies

What kind of information technologies to use is a constant concern. If you use a technology too early, either it does not work well or your organization cannot exploit it effectively. On the other hand, if you are late in applying it, your company may lose the opportunity to gain market share, improve flexibility, or simply be cost-effective on a competitive basis. If you want to apply best practices in your I/T operations or in a process, the concerns remain the same. However, just using the latest and greatest does not necessarily result in best practices. As demonstrated in this chapter, a combination of the right technology, reengineering, and a clear sense of the value of labor and cycle time reduction must be balanced together. We see best practice applications, for example, that are mainframe based, client/server based, centralized, and decentralized. So there are many ways to arrive at a best practice. In the final analysis, a best practice is what gives your company the capability to outperform its competitors, grow market and profits, and provide compelling value to its customers, employees, and shareholders (see Table 4.7).

Table 4.7

Best Practices Technologies versus Uses	
Type	**Why**
Mainframes	Large databases Centralized applications Network switches
Client/servers	Distributed databases Dispersed users Team-oriented computing
PCs	Small applications Team-based computing Ad hoc applications
Networks	Large numbers of users serviced Organizations, companies linked together Data sharing Process outsourcing

So are there any "rules of the road" regarding what technologies to use? It turns out that the best answers are coming not from the business schools or the I/T professionals but rather from historians of computing. They are currently engaged in a large debate with other historians of technology (e.g., experts on railroad history, clocks of the Middle Ages, automobiles, and electricity) to define what technology is and its patterns of effective and ineffective performance. In the 1980s and early 1990s, their descriptions of when technologies make sense to use began to read like best practices lists relevant to I/T management and their staffs. Before listing some of these, note that these patterns of technological behavior are not unique to one form of technology versus another. They apply as much to bows and arrows as they do to pottery, plows, and computers. The list is not absolute; new lessons emerge continuously. But here are some of the more obvious ones.

- A new technology is not adopted widely unless it is at least as easy to use as its predecessor one.
- New technologies are never automatically adopted; users always have the choice of not changing, or to use alternative technologies.
- Users do not like to move to new technologies because change carries perceived risk of failure, unknown costs, or consequences.
- New technologies are adopted more quickly if they contain new function, perform faster, or cost less than predecessors. Eventually all three conditions must exist.
- Technologies and their use evolve incrementally over time; there is no such thing as a revolution in the evolution of a technology's value, though occasionally in its initial development.
- Speed of adoption is a function of product availability, clarity of what the benefits are, and availability of trained users.
- First to adopt do not necessarily obtain "first entrant" benefits, but the last to adopt hardly receive any competitive advantage.
- Murphy's Law applies just as much to new technologies as to well-established ones.
- The easier it is to use something, the more it will be used (the turnpiking effect).
- The more expensive the technology, the greater that risk assessment influences decisions to adopt; the less expensive the technology, the more functionality and features influence the decision to adopt.

- Reasons for controlling customers, markets, information, applications, or processes more often than not cause people to adopt a new technology.
- Some companies will adopt a new technology thinking it makes them look modern or scientifically correct; that is not an effective practice.
- All new technologies are ultimately used in ways never anticipated by initial users.
- Many technologies are applied in increasingly diverse ways over time.
- Some technologies remain in use long after other technologies supposedly superseded them.

In every case I have looked at where technology was supposedly very well applied, none of these rules were violated, including in the world of I/T. I/T managers involved in best practices apply them subconsciously. You will see examples of my observation at work throughout the rest of this book.

Having discussed the generic types of applications evident in well-run I/T organizations, are there some common ones evident in well-run organizations? In one recent survey conducted by IBM, the most critical areas dependent on I/T applications, ranked from most important to least, began with accounting, followed in descending order by treasury, administration, customer service, purchase and procurement, marketing and promotion, human resources, library, basic research, testing, sales, logistics, applied R&D, and distribution (Cortada, 1997).

Conclusions

The best practices applications vary industry by industry, decade by decade. There are no constants; they keep changing. That is why you will not see in this chapter a laundry list of the applications to install. But what you do see constantly are some basic patterns of behavior. I/T organizations seek to do things easier, faster, cheaper, and to provide their companies with competitive advantages as soon as it is technologically safe to do so. Second, because best practices applications keep changing, well-run shops are constantly searching for new ones, ways to change existing ones, and often look at what is going on in other industries for ideas to port over.

Software Packages versus Reengineering or Writing Your Own Software

When process reengineering came into its own in the early 1990s, an old debate renewed: Which is better, to reengineer a process or to install a software package and rework your processes around the software? The reengineering advocates argued that you should start with a clean sheet of paper, design the process that makes sense for you, and then either buy software that fits well into the redesigned process or write new software to do that. The software package advocates argued that if you had a tool that met 80-plus percent of your needs, why spend the time and effort redesigning—reinventing—the wheel? They argue that packages are less expensive and can be dropped in faster than a new process. What is emerging are best practices in all three areas: process reengineering, application development, and package selection and installation.

Best practices thinking has been slowly shifting in the mid-1990s to the use of software packages for common applications, such as spreadsheets, accounts receivable, inventory control, or logistics. You then modify packages to conform to your needs and design processes, training, and practices around the package. Many modern packages are designed to allow for modification. Most processes and packages deal with common activities in an organization. Only a minority of applications or processes are so unique that they require alternative strategies, such as reengineering or specially written software. The point is, regardless of which alternative is chosen, there are growing bodies of best practices for each. But the key message that the best deliver is that regardless of the path chosen, nothing happens in isolation. You will need to restructure work activities, how performance is measured and rewarded, and retrain people. The worst practitioners ignore one or more of these lessons.

For further information, see Thomas H. Davenport, *Process Innovation* (Boston: Harvard Business School Press, 1993).

Where do I/T organizations go today for information on what are the best practice applications? Normally, they turn to three sources. First, vendors and consultants are deep pools of information because it is their job to keep up with these and they talk to practitioners and end users all the time. Second, many important industry associations today routinely hold conferences on I/T practices which are industry specific or sessions on applications. These are sharing events in which end users, consultants, and vendors trade stories, information, and experiences. Third, best practices I/T organizations are constantly developing new ideas, and experiment with new technologies or old ones in different ways. They piece things together differently than other companies because they are attempting to support their corporation's business plans. Theirs are rarely "me-too" strategies.

Yet at the same time we are saddled with good and less-than-effective applications created over many previous years—delicately called legacy systems—which either continue to provide value or are a financial and strategic hindrance to growth. There is a whole body of best practices associated with these that we have to account for because legacy systems routinely take up over half the resources of any I/T organization. If we don't manage those well, well, you can stop reading this book and move on to something else.

Implementing Best Practices Now	
Action	**Why**
Create a formal cost-justification process for IT projects that define business value.	This ensures I/T investments are just that, investments of strategic value to you.
Reengineer processes with the expectation that the new ones will have very high I/T content.	Successful reengineering projects exploit I/T, thereby deliver value quickly to the business.
But don't just let I/T dominate major transformations, corporate culture change is critical.	Ensures major changes occur in the first place and on time, within budget.
Make sure major corporate process and organizational changes are I/T compatible.	That is how you get real productivity out of I/T.

References

1. Bradley, Stephen. *Globalization, Technology and Competition: The Fusion of Computers and Telecommunications in the 1990s.* Cambridge, MA: Harvard Business School Press, 1993.
2. Baumol, William J., Sue Anne B. Blackman, and Edward N. Wolff. *Productivity and American Leadership.* Cambridge, MA: MIT Press, 1989.

3. Cortada, James W. "Economic Preconditions That Made Possible Use of Commercial Computing in The United States," *Annals of the History of Computing*, vol. 19, no. 3 (July–August 1997): 27–40.

4. Cortada, James W. *Information Technology as Business History: Issues in the History and Management of Computers.* Westport, CT: Greenwood Press, 1996.

5. Cortada, James W., Donald P. Hammer, and Alana J. Meeker. "Down In the Trenches! Role of Procedures in Standardizing Processes," *Quality Engineering*, vol. 8, no. 3 (1996): 455–464.

6. Cortada, James W., and Thomas Hargraves. "Transforming Organizations," forthcoming.

7. Cortada, James W., and John Woods (Eds.). *Quality Yearbook* (New York: McGraw-Hill, 1996).

8. Goldman, Steven L., Roger N. Nagel, and Kenneth Preiss. *Agile Competitors and Virtual Organizations: Strategies for Enriching the Customer.* New York: Van Nostrand Reinhold, 1995.

9. Manganelli, Raymond L. and Mark M. Klein. *The Reengineering Handbook.* New York: AMACOM, 1994.

10. Mankin, Don, Susan G. Cohen, and Tora K. Bikson. *Teams and Technology: Fulfilling the Promise of the New Organization.* Boston: Harvard Business School Press, 1996.

11. Ohno, Taiichi. *Toyota Production System.* Cambridge, MA: Productivity Press, 1988.

12. Price Waterhouse. *Technology Forecast 1996.* Menlo Park, CA: PW, 1995.

13. Primozic, Kenneth, Edward Primozic, and Joe Leven. *Strategic Choices: Supremacy, Survival, or Sayonara.* New York: McGraw-Hill, 1991.

14. Roach, S.S. *Technology Imperatives.* New York: Morgan Stanley, 1992.

15. Rifkin, Jeremy. *End of Work: The Decline of the Global Labor Force and the Dawn of the Post-Market Era.* New York: Putnam, 1995.

16. Stalk, Jr., George, and Thomas M. Hout. *Competing Against Time: How Time-Based Competition Is Reshaping Global Markets.* New York: Free Press, 1990.

17. Stone, Alan. *How America Got On-Line: Politics, Markets, and the Revolution in Telecommunications.* Armonk, NY: M.E. Sharpe, 1997.

18. Wakin, Edward. "The Customer-Centric CIO," *Beyond Computing* (January/February 1996): 42–48.

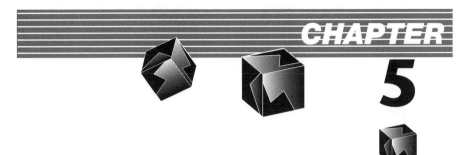

CHAPTER 5

MANAGING LEGACY SYSTEMS AND CHOOSING THE "RIGHT" ARCHITECTURES

What we call "progress" is the exchange of one nuisance for another nuisance.

—Havelock Ellis, 1904

*T*his chapter focuses on how well-run companies fold their vast collections of existing computer applications (legacy systems) into their I/T strategies. I then explore the role I/T architectures are playing today and the connections these have with existing applications.

Legacy systems are the combination of existing applications and technologies in our companies and agencies. The management of these is focused on ensuring that continuing value is derived from them and represents the single largest problem that I/T professionals face daily. These legacy systems are, for all intents and purposes, the sum total of existing applications. Best practices in this area are emerging very rapidly, especially on how to link these to I/T architectures and strategic plans. Yet the role of legacy systems frequently continues to frustrate end users while senior management fails to pay enough attention on how to squeeze additional benefits out of these systems. But all of that is beginning to change.

The Challenge Posed by Legacy Systems

We live in a business culture where anything that is not new is often considered old, even bad. In the world of I/T that is especially true. Executives are infected with the same idea, although not to the same extent as their I/T colleagues. But the fact is, many existing systems—perhaps most (it is hard to tell) return value to the corporations that installed them. Twenty-year-old payroll systems still generate paychecks. Airline reservation systems still get me tickets to where I am going. Most ATM software is a decade old and I can still get cash out of a money machine. So what's the problem? Just a negative attitude against what is not new?

First let us understand the size of the issue. In the mid-1990s, businesses globally were buying new and used I/T products and services at the rate of $300 billion a year. Over the previous four decades they had cumulatively spent over $3 trillion dollars, with some estimates closer to $4 trillion (Cortada, 1996). Those are only direct costs; add in indirect, hard-to-assign expenses, and you are probably looking at a figure twice the size! Some of these systems no longer provide what organizations need while many others still do. But the point is, there is a large body of legacy systems in excess of any you or I are going to add over the next few years. So any discussion about keeping, maintaining, or replacing legacy systems involves lots of money and all your currently existing software and hardware.

Second, let us understand the operational implications of legacy systems. Most I/T executives will tell you that their existing legacy systems consume 50 to 90 percent of their resources—people, hardware, software, and budgets— with the norm 70 to 80 percent. That leaves something less than 25 percent of all the resources you have invested in I/T to do the things we talked about in Chapters 2 and 3! If an end user has a complaint, it is not about a to-be-installed system; it is about an existing legacy application. If a retail chain doesn't know what its sales were for today, it is because a legacy software package or a machine did not perform today. Guess, therefore, what I/T management spends most of its time doing? You've got it! Putting out fires. The information processing world is a haven for vast quantities of Murphy's Laws and jokes about not being able to drain swamps because they are fighting alligators. Professors and consultants who have never run a data center glibly speak about focusing on the hatcheries to kill alligator eggs, while I/T professionals are out there fighting alligators, fires, vendors, and end users. The consequence is obvious: I/T does not have as much time, energy, or resources to focus on making your business competitive or strategic as you would like.

The "quick fix" has always been to fire the poor CIO. In fact, in the United States alone, the average job expectancy for a CIO has hovered at about three years over the past two decades while in well-run companies it mirrors more what we see in other functional areas—over four years. Some of these longer surviving CIOs have even been in their jobs as long as five to seven years. The problem with firing the CIO is that the problems existing in his or her organization don't go away; they just are passed on to the poor individual inheriting the position. What is very evident in well-run organizations, however, is a gradual but now obvious shift to a cadre of CIOs who are business oriented, often not having spent their full professional careers in I/T, and yet clearly understand how to exploit technology to benefit their companies and government agencies. To be sure they are very conversant with technology—often were the first on their block to put PCs in their homes—and have solid business credentials and know how to link I/T to the mainstream functions of the corporation as a whole.

The Document Company vs. Legacy Systems: The Xerox Corporation

This highly profitable corporation continues to teach managers how to do it right after a decade of corporate renewal. Today I/T strategy is developed with functional organizations, with senior management intimately involved since they consider technology strategic. They hunt for additional productivity through the use of I/T, outsource nonstrategic I/T functions, and learn how to apply technology to the core business of creating, manipulating, distributing, and printing documents. To a large extent, processes have and continue to be reengineered to better exploit I/T.

Legacy systems have been outsourced. EDS and AT&T play important roles in this strategy. Much of Xerox's networking systems have also been outsourced as well in various parts of the world. Xerox spends about 60 percent of its I/T budget on legacy systems infrastructure; hundreds of millions of dollars saved by outsourcing are reinvested in I/T. The remaining 40 percent is spent on new technologies that must deliver increases in productivity in excess of their cost. And the future? More work on upgrading and enhancing telecommunications.

The future for Xerox's I/T can be summarized by asking the question (as management here does): How do we converge I/T and telecommunications so that people can work anywhere while reducing travel, increasing productivity and shortening cycle time?

For further information, see Economist Intelligence Unit, *Global Telecommunications to the Year 2000* (New York: Economist Intelligence Unit, 1996): 59–63.

A third aspect of the problem with older software and hardware is that legacy systems can actually inhibit your ability to dart in and out of markets, reduce cycle time, change offerings, and so forth. Every senior executive has probably heard the speech about how some new system will take three years to deliver, when what they wanted was a new one in 100 days! This slowness has ensured that existing systems have survived for longer periods than executives might have wanted. Technology has evolved in some powerful and dramatic ways, but a lot of it is simply hard to change or replace. Our organizations have become so dependent on computers that there are just certain things you could not do tomorrow if you shut down a system. In fact, most factories, all major retail stores, every bank, and all mass transportation would stop immediately. The U.S. Department of Labor has estimated that over 80 percent of the work force directly uses computers in their daily work, while the rest of the population is indirectly dependent on them (Cortada, 1984). You can't even get food stamps or smuggle drugs into the country without some involvement of legacy systems!

Related to our dependence is the nature of our legacy systems. Our systems reflect what organizations look like and how they work. If you were operating in a company that had highly centralized decision making with command-and-control cultures, your computers were also highly centralized in big data centers with few options available to end users. If you implemented uniform practices and policies across the company, your systems were the same worldwide. Now, rush forward to the late 1980s and all of the 1990s, when companies want to be flat, decentralized, populated by empowered employees who also are I/T literate, and see what happens. Legacy systems begin to get in the way, and your employees want desktop computing fast and in forms that they dictate. What makes the problem thorny is that they, like you, know that the tools to do that now exist.

While you were installing systems in the 1970s and 1980s to be cost-efficient and to gain market share, technology kept improving and changing. The cost of a transaction continued to drop between 18 and 22 percent each year, while your organization kept acquiring more of it at rates of between 4 and 11 percent each year. Computers became more reliable, powerful, portable, and available. Telecommunications became practical, cost-effective, and ever so convenient. Now we all seem to have discovered the Internet! Software, which used to look like on-line Navajo or Egyptian hieroglyphics, now has English language interfaces and icons (little pictures of activities) that you can click on for action. And the technologists are promising more good things. That just makes you want more or, at least, different and better than what you have today.

So the problem for all major organizations is how to manage existing legacy systems while continuously moving to new applications that reflect the needs of today's organization. This is a balancing act between baby-sitting and exploiting existing I/T while implementing new systems. Figure 5.1 lists a variety of legacy-like software and hardware systems on the left and the world I/T is moving to on the right. We won't go into what these all mean. Suffice it to say that these are complicated, expensive, and usually important to have. Best practices companies are developing strategies for exploiting the old and moving to the new where it makes sense.

Strategies for Managing Legacy Systems

Let's briefly summarize the key realities of legacy systems.

- They are all of your existing applications.
- They represent millions and billions of dollars invested in them.
- They use up between 70 and 80 percent of your I/T budget.
- They still contribute value.
- They have received bad press as users and vendors have focused on the new.

FIGURE 5.1

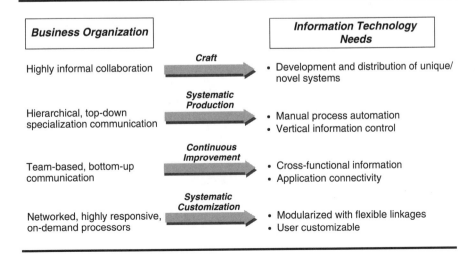

I/T managers will tell you almost universally that there are four problems any legacy management strategy has to contend with:

- They are too expensive to maintain as they are today.
- They take way too long to replace (usually years).
- They support and reflect outdated business strategies.
- They do not take advantage of newer, more effective technologies.

Thus they constrain the movement to new business strategies while generating greater expenditures than desired. Vendors, professors, consultants, and I/T professionals have spent a vast amount of time over the past two decades working on strategies for managing legacy systems.

Those who are most pleased with their strategies for managing these older systems tend to use one or more of five basic strategies. These strategies have stood the test of time and are particularly well suited to tackle the unique problems of systems developed in the 1970s and early to mid-1980s.

Strategy 1: Outsource stable and critical applications. If an application is not expected to change, companies will increasingly outsource these to someone who can perform them either more reliably or less expensively. The most obvious example is payroll. If, on the other hand, you absolutely have got to be the best now in an application and you know you cannot do that in a timely fashion, the related strategy is to outsource your most critical applications to someone who is the most effective.

Since this is a new idea, let's look at it more closely. In the 1980s researchers like James B. Quinn and Michael Porter—both at the Harvard Business School—began to argue the case for partnering with companies that had complementary competencies that both of you could take advantage of in the market (Quinn, 1992; Porter, 1985). Companies learned a great deal about forming partnerships, particularly in the early 1990s. As a result, they gained confidence in outsourcing major activities, all of which had some form of I/T attached to them. Thus you saw hotel chains and rental car companies taking reservations for each other and sharing databases. We saw gasoline vendors stuffing their credit card bills with offers to sell you vacations, stereos, and clothing. Now we are beginning to see a further step; the outsourcing of whole processes. In fact, this "little" enhancement to traditional I/T outsourcing will be $300 billion opportunity before the end of the 1990s!

Strategy 2: Assess the Relevance of Keeping Applications in the New Business Environment and Then Take Action. Essentially this strategy is one of asking forbidden questions such as: Why keep an application any more? Why not just stop doing it? They are rejustifying applications, in effect requiring a defense of their continued existence versus exploiting other options, such as stopping the work. This is a particularly useful strategy to pursue if your company has significantly downsized; you probably have systems you no longer need or which have more functionality than is affordable. It may be cheaper just to shut it down rather than enhance or continue using it. IBM, for example, after downsizing its employee population by some 40 percent in the early 1990s, quietly dropped a variety of systems that made sense to have when there were 405,000 employees but not with a population of 235,000. Very few people complained; it just made too much sense.

Strategy 3: Enhance existing applications to meet today's needs. This is very popular among healthy companies that manage I/T effectively. Essentially what you do is look at all your major systems, inspect their functionality, technology base, and the cost and value of redesigning them. Invariably the impulse is to enhance functionality by customizing what a system does; technology moves from large mainframe based to a combination mainframe and heavily client/server based; redesign goes from centralized databases, for example, to relational databases which provides more flexibility in changing systems in the future.

What makes this strategy attractive—assuming no impossible technical barriers—is that you do not throw the baby out with the bath water. You get to keep the best of the old that still adds value, thus continuing to reap benefit from previous investments in I/T, while adding functions that you need today. Thus you will use, for example, large mainframe systems that now send down information to PCs and allow local processing.

Strategy 4: Apply quality management principles to existing applications. One of the guiding principles of quality management which is accompanied by a very large set of effective tools and techniques is to continuously improve operations. Performance of systems are measured for results, and for finding ways to improve them incrementally. That strategy applies as much to software as it does to process improvement/reengineering. It is closely linked to strategy 3. However, what makes the quality approach effective is that it is very comprehensive. Companies that apply this strategy look for ways to improve operations (not just how a piece of software or hardware works), drive costs down on a continuous basis, and look for ways to speed conversions.

Strategy 5: Replace parts or all of an application with new software. Various tactical steps are often used such as upgrading databases, buying newer software packages to replace all or part of existing systems, writing modules in newer programming languages, linking to other systems inside and outside the firm to provide more function, and exploiting new technologies for some components (e.g., pen-based systems). A couple of quick examples illustrate the strategy.

Many corporations built their Customer Information Systems (CIS) in the 1970s so that their banks of telephone clerks talking with customers could have all the data they needed on-line to deal with issues. Over the years the smart ones moved their files, first to massive databases, then to relational databases, giving access first by terminal now by PC. They then added functions, such as links to service dispatch systems, and the ability of a worker in the field to update a work order via radio or to transmit an order over a telephone line. When these systems were first installed, they obviously did not have the ability to fax a letter to a customer in response to an order; today they do. Adding a telephone system at the front of the process whereby you, as the customer, hear a recorded voice, pick from one of several options, and then get plugged into a clerk's line who is an expert on your topic combines new off-the-shelf software, your old CIS application, some telephonic switching hardware (a minicomputer), and PCs.

Two more examples illustrate how you can reach outside the corporation to implement system improvements. Most large corporations have e-mail systems that were installed in the 1980s. Some of them were large centralized systems, like IBM's widely adopted PROFS software. Others were installed much later and could take advantage of radically different technology platforms, such as Lotus Notes. Either way, if your users were sales personnel, they probably asked for access to news clipping services so they could keep up with events concerning their customers. By the early 1990s, many of these e-mail systems had technical links that allowed end users to direct their systems to access databases owned by other companies (e.g., Standard & Poors) to look up data. The same occurred, by the way, with airline reservations systems. In the 1970s they were all independent ones. Now through one terminal you can look at just about anybody's reservation file. In both cases, software and databases of different types and ages are used from multiple companies right off the same screen employees use for accessing their own company's applications.

A mixture of all five strategies are often used. Legacy transformation activities exist; nobody is simply staying with what they have. These changes vary from minor ones to radical redesigns, both, however, are based on tactical and strategic business needs. If the motivation is strategic, I/T organizations are usually trying to facilitate the transformation of an existing system or technology platform to a new architecture required to support the business. If management's intent is more tactical, you typically see a set of activities underway to enhance the existing system to reduce complexity and increase the adaptability to change while reducing cycle time. Either approach—strategic or tactical—invariably maximizes return on investments already made.

How Transformation Strategies Are Implemented

Companies serious about transforming legacy systems are merging four separate sets of activities together. First, business management teams are defining business strategies if they did not exist before. Second, working with business management, I/T professionals are understanding what in their existing systems fits the new business plan and what then become candidates for transition. Third, they are developing system transition plans—the five basic strategies we just reviewed—and fourth, they are developing a plan for what technical platforms they want their systems to reside on. The important message is that *together they are integrating their technology architecture and legacy system strategies.*

The first step after a formal business plan has been created is to assess the functional effectiveness and efficiency of existing applications to gain insight into future investment opportunities. To put it in a phrase, they perform a classic gap analysis. Most companies today think of all their applications as parts of a portfolio so they review the investment attractiveness of these just as you and I would periodically look at whether to buy a new car. The questions are similar: Which applications remain I/T assets and which are I/T liabilities? Well-run operations invariably include this kind of exercise as part of their annual strategic planning. It is a regular and proactive assessment.

The second step is to calculate the full cost of operating and maintaining existing systems. With the growth in popularity of ABC accounting systems over the past decade, many I/T organizations have gone through the exercise of learning how to do this and are beginning to develop a base of knowledge about these kinds of expenditures.

Third, they develop an architectural blueprint (about which I will have more to say below), that serves as a basis for assessing old and new applications. Finally, a formal financial analysis of options is documented, usually for those few systems which have profound strategic implications. It appears most are not analyzing the entire portfolio of applications, only those that are big, consume a great deal of resources, and help or hurt the company carry out its business objectives.

This whole process (see Figure 5.2) is increasingly becoming evident as a recognizable pattern in many I/T organizations. It copies from the best practices of traditional market gap analysis in which you look at what business you want to be in, what the market and customers say about you, and then at the gap between how you perform and how you must perform across processes, organization, skills, information, and financial strength, selecting a short list of candidate projects or initiatives to take on. These are ranked by desirability on the basis of which give you the best value; then you develop detailed implementation plans.

FIGURE 5.2

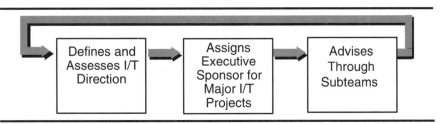

So what is the best practice on implementation? For about three decades now the best practice has been to create detailed implementation plans for each initiative, one by one. The best examples of migration plans all have very similar features, confirmed in study after study. They can be boiled down to a half dozen attributes.

1. Management does not hesitate to invest in appropriate tools to do the job.

2. Projects are phased to ensure both a continuing stream of improvements and to avoid overtaxing the ability of an organization to deliver results.

3. Software packages are purchased for noncritical functions, major packages if they are truly the best solution for a particular initiative.

4. Clear objectives and expectations are set by executive management

that are described in terms of cost improvements, enhancements in specifically described functionality, all of which are measured for progress in very precise terms (e.g., in numbers by date with specific names of those responsible attached to each step).

5. Dedicated teams are assigned because part-time projects are rarely finished.

6. Rigorous project management practices are emphasized and adhered to.

These practices borrow heavily from project management methods that have evolved over the past four decades for the development of major systems. In fact, the SIM/IBM study demonstrated that skills learned years ago to write COBOL projects—which placed a premium on both project management and structured analysis—are exactly the same kinds of skills required today to implement many of the new technologies and applications. The chairperson of the committee, Janet Caldow, director of IBM's Institute for Electronic Government, was quoted on this very point: "These guys have taken it in the ear over the past few years during the rapid transition to distributed environments. But we are now seeing 'Cobblers' moving into key leadership roles in applying the rigors of COBOL-era legacy systems to global, client/server roll outs."

They also borrow heavily from quality management practices, bringing process design and management methodologies to the table, along with more rigorous measurement disciplines. They build into their plans, and then management of newly installed applications, the various quality disciplines associated with continuous improvement. What you see in I/T shops at Motorola, Xerox, IBM, Ford, Toyota, GE, and others is clearly part of this newly adopted heritage. Interestingly, many quality management techniques have long been the bread and butter of I/T organizations and engineering departments; they are now fashionable to apply across the entire enterprise. The value of this recent development is that an I/T manager can now stand up with a migration plan, use concepts long in use within the technical community, and have an understanding audience. Without that new development of the past decade, all suggestions about cross-functional cooperation, teaming, and so forth, would simply be impractical, as it had been prior to the adoption of quality management practices.

The one very tough issue that all companies face, regardless of how well they approach the management of legacy systems, is that of costs. The problem is simply stated: It usually costs a fortune to replace a strategically critical I/T system and invariably it has to come out of the I/T budget, although today best practice is increasingly for business funding of the initiative, not out of the I/T department's budget. Those companies that feel they have figured out how to get around this problem address it through proactive assessment of the issues, hone in on exploring options, and then apply outstanding project management to contain the risk of cost overruns—often the biggest fear senior executives have about the cost of major conversions or new systems. At the end of the day, costs need to be balanced against strategic value of enforcement, for example, opportunity to change the playing field to one's own company's advantage.

On the assessment side of the equation, the key question to ask is: When should a system be replaced versus enhanced? Well-run organizations routinely respond with four answers applied at the same time:

1. Business units and I/T conduct regular and proactive assessments of their portfolios. Regular means at least once a year, and usually more frequently if done division by division in which case it is going on all the time.

2. Full costs of maintaining and operating existing systems are identified, often using ABC accounting methods but, regardless of technique, no gaming of the numbers!

3. The company's architectural blueprint for I/T forms the basis for assessing the value and quality of existing systems.

4. Executive management insists on and gets in-depth financial analysis of all the obvious options. The analysis is comprehensive, taking into account development costs, ongoing support expenses, and includes collateral infrastructure investments. In short, the total costs are included—again no gaming of the numbers to avoid additional levels of review!

On the migration side of the equation, the key question asked is: What can be done to address the time and cost it takes to migrate? In addition to the obvious issue of cost, is time. Executive management in the industrialized world has bought into the concept that cycle time reduction is really a fantastic strategy for improving business results. They may not have paid attention to many other management fads, but this one they did.

Almost all the surveys, testimonials, and published accounts clearly support that statement. They have also learned to ask how one can speed all
projects, including I/T's. The most common answer to the question is to do
three things:

1. Adopt tools and techniques to ensure a smooth and rapid migration. If the company needs to use new programming languages or
   Rapid Application Development (RAD) techniques, it is done. The
   old ways are set aside; people are taught the new and given the
   necessary tools.

2. Break up large projects into smaller ones and thus deliver a steady
   stream of measurable improvements that provide value. There is
   more value to be gleaned from ten $1 million projects than from
   one $10 million one because of the time value of benefits and the
   reduced risk of failure or delay. That strategy may cause the technicians fits since it could require a very different implementation
   plan, but go for it. It's usually safer and faster.

3. Have I/T exercise outstanding project management *and* manage
   end-user or customer expectations. The second point cannot be
   emphasized enough. Recall Figure 3.3 (page 54) describing how to
   deal with end users and customers. It made the point that managing relationships was a major process, one even outstanding I/T
   organizations do a poor job at. Well here is a situation where that
   function can help as I/T migrates to new applications.

The Role and Value of I/T Architectures

Yes, technologies have architectures, just as buildings have styles. When
you tell an architect that you would like a house built in a certain style,
such as a colonial or modern, you just have to use the adjective describing
the type you want. Implied in an architectural style are so many other
assumptions and decisions: size, nature of the woodwork, type of doors
and window moldings, decorations, floor layout, and so forth. Architectures also give you a direction in which to plan the kind of furniture that
goes into the home, and the look and feel of additions and redecorating.
Use how you want to live to plan and drive the appropriate architecture.
And so it is with technologies of all types.

In the world of information technology, architectures are of extraordinary importance. Sadly, most I/T executives do a terrible job in explaining the significance and strategic value of architectures to general management, leaving behind, therefore, a wonderful opportunity to collaborate jointly on the exploitation of computers for strategic purposes. They also fail to seize occasions to ensure practical alignment with what the business wants to get done. So let's discuss architectures because the best-run companies in the world pay very serious attention to the subject.

What is an I/T architecture? Gargols on an ornate computer? Center hallway layouts in overcooled data centers? More mundane. Architecture in I/T is a blueprint for delivering the application structures and data availability needed by the business. Put in less formal language, an architecture is a collection of guidelines, software and hardware components that work together, and features of technology desired by an organization. Architectures (also called platforms) are means to ends. The reason we care about I/T architectures is basically very simple: By managing architectures I/T organizations facilitate the delivery of computing resources to the enterprise quickly, cost-effectively, and of the right kind. Get the architecture wrong and the opposite occurs: New applications and functions come on-line too slowly for your taste, are often too expensive, and may not deliver the value desired.

As Figure 5.3 illustrates, there are essentially three sets of issues that good I/T organizations focus on because these cover the bulk of the concerns that they realistically face both on a daily basis and when debates about strategies and plans come up.

FIGURE 5.3

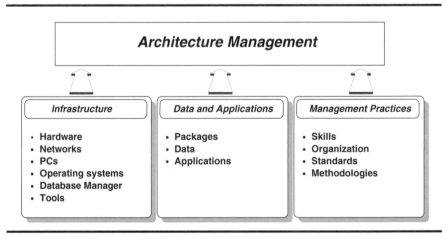

Infrastructure is the stuff of which computer systems and networks are made of. It is in this realm that we speak of types of hardware, operating systems (the software that allows various machines to work together and to coordinate the activities of applications), and the other toys and tools of technologists. Take it seriously. Collectively we all spend about $300 billion each year on such things. Making these work together is a very important part of any I/T organization's role. I/T executives spend a great deal of time—if they worry about how to deliver services in the future—trying to understand what sets of devices to standardize on. Such decisions are conditioned by a variety of important variables, such as,

- Technical flexibility of a family of devices
- Support computer vendors provide for their architectures
- Age of the technology (Will it be obsolete sooner or later?)
- Availability of people to baby-sit this equipment and software
- Availability of software application packages to run on it
- Ability to link it up with systems and data files of other companies (otherwise forget partnering!)
- Cost considerations (The older stuff is cheaper to buy, more expensive to run and take care of.)

Technologies should be chosen to mirror the culture of an enterprise. One way I/T executives align their operations with corporate goals is to "get it right" when it comes to having the right technology architectures. Most frequently the discussion is about infrastructure considerations that facilitate various parts of any organization to perform whatever they need to with technology.

This serendipitous view of the role of technology is strongly reinforced by considerations of data and applications. Packages refers to software you can buy; applications, to uses to which computers are put (e.g., writing a paycheck to you, paying the company's bills); and data concern how machine-readable information is gathered, housed, managed, and regurgitated as information in a timely and relevant manner. Since enormous strides have been made in the past 20 years with architectures and products in the areas of data management and applications, this area today is subject to blueprint strategies. Thus you will see well-run I/T organizations worry about "object-oriented" technologies, "client/server" systems, "relational databases," and so forth. If your I/T organization does not even use these kinds of buzz words, worry, because no well-run organization would be caught dead without a blueprint for the software side of their infrastructure.

Then there is the myriad of management practices. The idea is simple enough: Let's pick the best ways of writing, acquiring, and maintaining software to match our hardware and software, our I/T objectives, and those of the corporation. But this is where the best part with the average. The average can be counted on to worry about hardware and software architectures—you can count on I/T vendors to at least make sure of that—but the best also integrate skills strategies, organizational structures, technical standards, programming, and design methodologies into their blueprints. It is here, for example, that holy wars are waged over what programming languages to use, what design methodologies to insist upon (there are over a dozen), and what management methods to apply (e.g., TQM, centralized vs. decentralized). In the final analysis, the best link all this back to corporate business plans.

Open Architectures and End Users: It's Not Hot Air at Air Products & Chemicals, Inc.

With a proud record of revenue and productivity growth in the 1990s, this leading supplier of industrial gases and chemicals has figured out better than most how to allow I/T to operate in an open group environment with centralized I/T management while application development stays within the business units. An I/T steering committee chaired by the CEO makes it possible to link I/T strategy to that of the corporation as a whole.

Key to I/T's operation are the development and deployment of an architecture strategy. I/T management has evolved in thinking to the point where it will give up functionality on a machine or software in exchange for conformance to its architectural standards—an enormous change in view for any I/T management team! The hunt is for applications and services that provide seamless support of employees around the world. Open architectures are important tools for increasing productivity across the company. Key platforms include Microsoft NT, UNIX, and IBM's MVS. Processing at the desktop has been increasing from about one-third in the mid-1990s to an anticipated 50 percent by the first few years of the twenty-first century. At Air Products & Chemicals, mainframes are seen as servers!

For further information, see Economist Intelligence Unit, Global Telecommunications to the Year 2000 (New York: Economist Intelligence Unit, 1996): 78—82.

This effort is often expressed as models of behavior. Figures 5.4–5.6 are some sample architecture models. Figure 5.4, for example, is one widely used by IBM consultants to explain linkage between I/T and business strategies. Figure 5.5 reflects what most I/T organizations do with a heavy emphasis on the command-and-control part of their work. Figure 5.6 reflects the result of my own findings while doing research for my previous book *TQM for Information Systems Management*. They are all fine; you can find many others as well. The point is, well-run I/T operations have one that reflects how they want to operate and make decisions in support of the model.

Cats and Dogs: How Legacy Systems and Architectures Relate

The ugly reality is that architectural blueprints and legacy systems have to coexist because on your way to the future—what the architectural blueprint is supposed to help you do—you still have to rely on existing applications and hardware. As Figure 5.7 suggests, there is a relationship that must be accounted for as you move into that future. The key lesson you learn from well-run I/T organizations is that they have a plan which acknowledges the symbiotic relationship between the two. There are six interacting facets to this relationship that they account for.

FIGURE 5.4

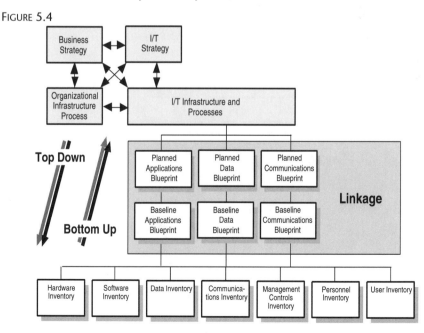

FIGURE 5.5

General Characteristics	Organization

• Target: Productivity
• Quality reactive
• High volume usage
• Maintenance vs. new development
	• Task specialization
	• Repetitive activities
	• Workflows —serial, linear, executed to plan
	• Defect removal oriented
	• Postprocess measurements
	• Project management
	   – Estimating discipline
	   – Commitment discipline

People/Cultural	**Technology**
• Hierarchical —top down • Departmental task specialization • Management directed • Positional/level oriented • Separate doers and thinkers • Large investment in legacy code maintenance • Vision —"Don't rock the boat." • Value —stability • Culture —highly formal • Skills —narrow, doer oriented • Establish baselines	• Structured programming • Innovation via tools • System stabilization, system monitors, backup, recovery, performance monitors • Automation of manual process for efficiency • Job schedulers

FIGURE 5.6

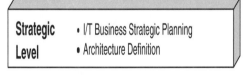

Strategic Level	• I/T Business Strategic Planning • Architecture Definition		

Tactical Level	• Application and Data Planning • Human Resource Planning	• Systems Planning • Capacity Planning • Skills Planning	

Operational Level	Control	Development & Operations	Support
	Development & Maintenance Change Scheduling Performance Problem Resolution Inventory	Applications Software Aquisition Facilities Maintenance Operations Help Desk Enduser Relation	Budget Staff Evaluation Training Recruitment Quality Assessment

FIGURE 5.7

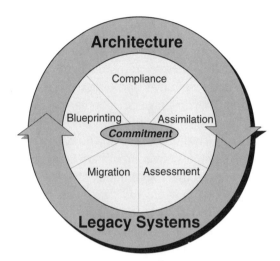

Compliance: This is the requirement to maintain a proper balance between flexibility and control while you are building an infrastructure designed to make possible a smooth transition to some future state.

Blueprinting: As discussed above, it is the act of defining a technological vision of the future.

Migration: This is the process by which you manage the transition from the past to the future.

Assessment: As you see in all well-run organizations, the process by which one evaluates the ability of past investments in I/T to support future needs.

Assimilation: This is the series of actions that enable an organization to use new technology to position itself for the future.

Commitment: The glue that holds it all together, the act of gaining funding and organizational commitments to make the changes necessary for the future.

I have found that leading-edge organizations always close the gap between their architectural blueprints and legacy system capabilities by developing a strategy and then skillfully managing migration efforts. This sounds so obvious but, in reality for many I/T organizations, migration to the future is done with little or no planning and some legacy systems either absolutely block change or linger in some cases for decades! In fact, even I/T organizations that have a nice crisp plan, commitment, and work on the items just listed, also face stubborn technical and organizational problems associated with migrating from existing platforms and legacy systems to some other new world. But some organizations are enjoying success by implementing an organized approach. The point is to plan migrations and to spend money where the business benefits the most.

That approach calls for attention to detail and absolute tenacity in the management of end-user, executive, and customer expectations while going through the migration. They leverage development tools by dividing projects into manageable pieces with valuable deliverables, while treating project management with as much discipline as any human organization is capable of doing. I/T executives in this environment are fanatical on the need to use disciplined project management techniques to ensure constancy of focus and progress in overcoming problems. They also proactively assess gaps between their architectures and blueprint legacy systems, using that analysis, combined with business strategies and cost information, to drive their I/T investment strategies. These investment strategies are driven by the need to support and implement the business strategy of the company or agency.

The first step is to begin by creating an architectural blueprint for the company designed by taking into account the enterprise's strategy for I/T. As suggested in Chapter 2, some organizations will focus, for example, on improving productivity while others on marketplace differentiation, using I/T as a tool. Figure 5.8 answers the question: What attributes are identified with either approach? The chart is self-explanatory. However, let me add that in either strategy, you have to address each of the four attributes because they will crop up in the course of day-to-day activities, forcing you to deal with them.

Architectures: Lessons from Client/Server Systems

Benchmarking more than 50 I/T professionals revealed that client/server was not less expensive than mainframe systems. In fact, these expenses ran 20 to 30 percent higher because of troubleshooting, need for GUI experts, and higher support costs. Those CIOs who were most pleased suggested three best practices: Think enterprisewide and extended enterprise (your company and others linked together) when implementing a client/server architecture; have a design and strategy for implementation that is comprehensive; control how LANs and software releases are implemented across the entire enterprise.

For more information, see Sidney Diamond, "Client/Server: Myths and Realities," *Journal of Systems Management* 46, no. 4 (July/August 1995): 44–48.

In order to determine how much progress I/T managers are making with either strategy, benchmarking becomes a useful tool. Invariably it begins with financials, as suggested by Figures 5.9–5.11 but then moves on to the other components of the selected strategy.

FIGURE 5.8

Productivity
(Operational focus)

- Focus on improvement
- Lower existing operating costs
- Concentrates on automation of existing activities
- I/T picks its projects

Differentiation
(Strategic focus)

- Focus on new services, market share growth
- Invests in new applications, services
- Business units determine I/T investments
- Also lowers overall costs

FIGURE 5.9

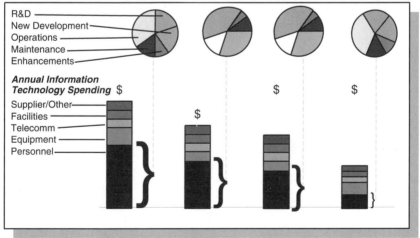

Technology Spending Relative to Personnel Spending

FIGURE 5.10

Estimated I/T Investment

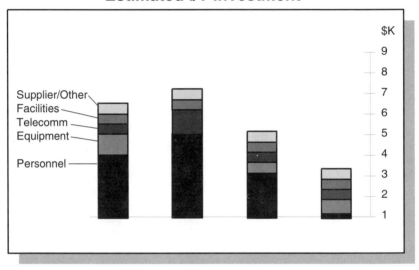

FIGURE 5.11

Estimated Annual I/T Operating Costs

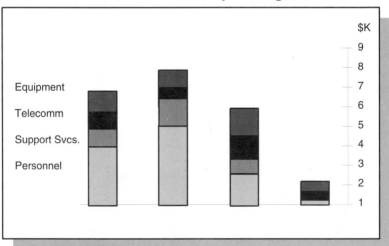

But one characteristic of the leaders is that they also look at changes in technology. This is particularly the case with differentiation-focused I/T organizations because they are more dependent on exploiting changes in technology sooner than either their competitors or firms interested in optimizing productivity. Typically those interested in weaving technology benchmarking and blueprint strategies together look at three issues: required new technologies, roles of these new technologies, and the capability of competitors to exploit these. Figures 5.12–5.14 illustrate the kinds of data such firms look at. Figure 5.12, for example, demonstrates the innovation curve which has been widely adopted since the mid-1980s. The key to the role of new technologies is in understanding what makes for a follower, provides parity, or creates value through technological leadership. Understanding one's relative position to competition influences what technologies to adopt and the probability of seizing the high ground or being stuck in the mud.

Churn and Change, The Case of Telecommunications

Books like this one are very clinical and sanitary in their neat descriptions of what is or should be. Yet reality is quite messy with chaos and massive change a reality for every I/T organization. We like to speak of changing markets and global competition but drop down a few feet to the ocean bed of I/T and you see vast churn that challenges even the most egocentric, confident I/T executive. Since telecommunications is today often at the center of the churn and often also an integral part of the collection of legacy systems, it illustrates the order of magnitude of what is happening.

IBM completed a study in February 1996 on the nature of the convergence of telecommunications and I/T, a major area of concern to the I/T community (Economist Intelligence Unit, 1996). The authors of the study concluded that this merger would profoundly influence the way companies conducted much of their business by the early years of the twenty-first century. Some of the key findings were

- Voice and data will explode in volume over the next five years.
- Companies are already looking at area and wide band area network technology to link these together.
- Much computing will travel through networks.

FIGURE 5.12

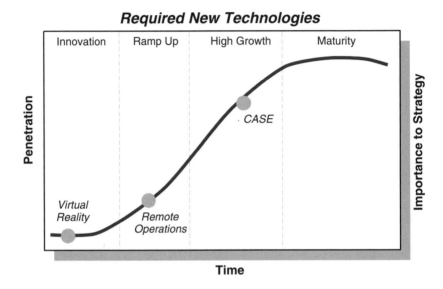

Required New Technologies

FIGURE 5.13

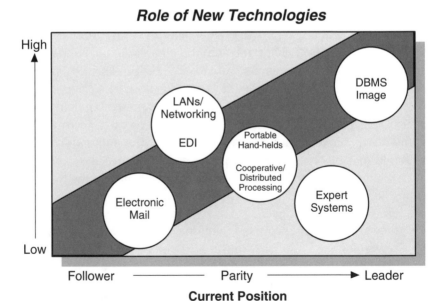

Role of New Technologies

Figure 5.14

Competitor Capability in Use of Technology

Business Area	Rating vs. "Leading Competitors"	Leading-Edge Competitor Capability	Win New Competence
Marketing/R&D	1	• On-line data access/DSS tools • Product attribute database	7
Sales	2	• On-line order processing • Hand-held terminals (initial stages) • Computer-to-computer ordering	5
Manufacturing	6	• Manufacturing systems • Process control	6
Distribution	8	• Network planning models	8
Financial		• Decision support models/tools	7
Executive Information Sup	2	• Performance indicators • Responsibility reporting	
Office Tech	3	• End-user computing	5
Overall			

One hundred twenty companies across the world reported that they had much work to do to link all of these together. As of 1995–1996, 24 percent reported that telecommunications and I/T were still managed separately but might change, while 38 percent said that this circumstance would continue into the future. However, a best practice was emerging in the form of a strategic intent: Over 80 percent reported that they would integrate both the management and strategy of these two functions. Furthermore, the vast majority spoke of developing architectures and plans to make these seamless across their enterprises, around the world, and into their customers and vendors.

Complicating this picture—already a challenge due to the complexity of the two collections of technologies involved—is the churn. By that I mean the amount of change organizations are already experiencing anyway. Turnover and change have always been a constant, and the data simply suggest that churn will continue. So the data has to be managed effectively. The same IBM study illustrated that 60 percent of the companies already had local and wide area networks; 97 percent would within five years. The Internet was looming large—an example of integrated use of I/T and telecommunications—and would move from 66 percent to 90 percent using it. Best practices firms were already going down the path to this new merged and massive set of changes. Not covered by the study but looming is the effect of using intranets, the consequences of which are not clear as of this writing.

The corporate commitments to these new technologies are so big that senior non-I/T management is involved. In this particular study, for example, respondents reported that their spending, just on telecommunications, would rise by 24 percent over the next five years, with spending as a percentage of annual revenues rising from 3.7 percent to 4.6 percent. I/T spending would increase 14 percent with the leading firms moving up nearly a whole percentage point of their annual revenues dedicated to I/T. Small companies were reporting even larger shifts of percent of budgeted dollars to I/T, exceeding 9 percent. Both large and small companies were trying to hold the line at 5 percent of revenues being spent on telecommunications. Voice traffic was growing for all on average by 20 percent, internal and external data traffic by 56 percent and 49 percent, respectively.

Looked at by industry, we see dramatic uplifts in change as well. Financial services, historically a heavy user of all forms of I/T and telecommunications, expected to experience growth in internal data traffic of nearly 100 percent and of 83 percent in external traffic. Companies in retail and wholesale industries projected 78 percent growth in internal traffic, 73 percent in external data traffic.

Several other statistics suggest the degree of churn. For example, 70 percent of the firms reported that Local Area Network/Wide Area Network (LAN/WAN) technology will more profoundly influence how they deliver telecom and computing services; much of that technology is only just now coming on stream. Distributed processing will shift from 60 percent in 1995 to 97 percent by the end of the decade—as big a sea change as I/T has experienced since the early to mid-1960s! Perhaps the largest cultural change, and one already in evidence in very well run organizations, is the increased use of outsourcing of services which they anticipate. These companies predicted that 40 percent of them would deploy that strategy; many were already laying out their plans for accomplishing this. Even if you cut the forecasts in half or even by 75 percent, the sea change is still massive. Historically, however, most companies have underestimated the degree of change they have experienced with I/T. What this IBM/Economist Intelligence Unit 1996 study suggests—and what history hints at—is that migrating to new technologies will be a massive, expensive, and critical set of activities. The best-run organizations argue that they cannot, indeed will not, attempt to deal with these issues in a casual manner; this is not like herding cats.

The Promise of Object-Oriented Applications

Today, well-run I/T organizations are flirting with a new way of writing software, much of it to replace legacy systems with new ones that can be changed in the future much faster than in the past. Perhaps the most sought-after new technology is the use of object-oriented computing so we must deal with the issue. But first some definitions. An object is the representation of any thing, be it real or conceptual. In practical terms, an object is often a set of work procedures, or a piece of software that can be reused, bolted on or detached from some application, can include its data handling tools, and/or the data needed to do something, all in one little package. The idea is to create software that is both highly modular and reusable. The idea is to write software that is independent of any programming language, operating system, or hardware.

This approach is causing whole new programming methodologies and tools to be developed. It has led, for example, to the fast expanding use of C++ as a programming language. New careers are being created for "object fabricators" and "object assemblers," people who can write objects. Designers of operating systems and other software tools are making them compatible with this approach. The question that arises with any new approach is, When does a new technology move from concept to vaporware (hype) to actual reality, and finally to best-of-class tools? It appears that we are now just moving out of the vaporware phase into usable code. *Market Perspective* in 1994 did a survey on why people were beginning to apply Object-Oriented (OO), as it is known, and discovered that the primary reason was to improve programmer productivity with cycle time reduction running a close second (*Market Perspective* unpublished White Paper 1994).

But we are just at the start of the application of OO. Worldwide revenues for OO tools in 1996 ran at about $1.5 billion, but International Data Corporation (IDC) predicted it would reach $4 billion by the end of 1998 (Price Waterhouse, 1995). The majority of these expenditures were going to programming tools, with object databases a close second. This technology is being applied mostly to information retrieval and reporting applications. Since the best practices I/T organizations always focus on such issues as programmer productivity, cycle time reduction in meeting end-user requirements, and cost controls, we can expect to see these centers of excellence lead the way in using OO. It is my expectation that by the end of the decade we should have a healthy collection of best practices in OO to discuss in future management books.

Wrestling with Issues, Leading with a Plan

Regardless of which strategic direction one takes, what tools and technologies one adopts, or the volume of anticipated change, leading-edge companies consistently report that some issues have not changed in several decades. Some are timeless in their universal relevance to architectures or blueprints. The degree of anticipated change simply intensifies the need to implement the kinds of best practices some companies already display. The primary thorny issues concerning architecture are

- Commitment
- Compliance
- Assimilation

With regard to commitment, the basic issue is how to get commitment and funding for infrastructure. The problem is that there is rarely a direct and immediate payback. This is like the contractor who tells you your roof leaks and you have to get it replaced or that your home's foundation is cracking and is affecting the safety of the entire house! Good infrastructure but not a whole lot of return is going to come out of that this year. Probably, however, it will make it possible for you to sell the house or, at least keep your things dry and your family from being injured.

Concerning compliance, the question to answer is, How can we encourage effective compliance with the architecture? The chances of people making short-term decisions that may conflict with the architecture are enormous. Politics alone might cause management to want to deviate from some sense that such a strategy avoids Big Brother I/T controlling things. Economics could play a similar role. The real problem is analogous to the person on a diet. You know you have to lose weight and someone is constantly putting a plate of ice cream in front of you. There are many reasons why, in that particular case, you should not eat it but . . .

Finally, the issue of assimilation is at work. The question is, How can we effectively adopt technology and meet business needs? Emphasis is on effectiveness in providing the most value to the business; otherwise what is the point? We don't want technology for technology's sake.

So what are the answers? The best-run organizations will tell you there is no cookbook answer; it depends. It depends on what your existing legacy and platform systems are. It depends on what fundamental I/T strategic path you are committed to. It depends on what the business wants to do. It depends on your capabilities and your access to needed skills. In short, it depends on many things. But what the best do is to ask, research, and answer the questions. Then they gain the commitment of senior management, along with the resources to implement, and apply rigorous project management methodologies.

The point is, the successful ones are methodical. They take a systematic approach in the development and maintenance of architectural blueprints. For each of these three sets of issues, there are some common best practices behavior evident. So what are some of these?

Commitment in this kind of circumstance requires a healthy dose of vision and focus: vision as to where the company is going and focus in the form of many forms of corporate resources being committed to it. With regard to computing, the key is having powerful senior executives armed with a vision of I/T as a key or *the* key to future company success. That comes from a deep understanding of how I/T can help the firm. That understanding has to be brought about largely through the initiative of the computing community showing the way. Communication of that understanding is also key for it brings insight and context for decisions. Trust is also closely related, trust in various parts of the business making decisions that support the overall strategy and cause investments to be made in support of it. A second evident pattern involves R&D funding which permits I/T to conduct very targeted research on technology. This can range from people attending seminars on new technologies to actually having in-house projects to experiment and gain insight. Common targets today include the use of object-oriented programming, limited projects involving the Internet, and advanced forms of data mining.

Compliance is the collection of tactical steps taken to enable the vision. Normally, one sees four patterns of behavior among outstanding organizations. First, I/T organizations develop architectural blueprints that support business processes. Second, I/T and end-user management conduct systematic evaluations of new technologies and processes. I/T then regularly updates architectural blueprints to take into account these new technologies and processes. Third, I/T management is very tactical on the delivery of services based on these platforms, keeping them manageable so they can continuously deliver unique functions to specific business units. Finally, there always seems to be at least one grass-roots champion, invariably in the end-user community, although often I/T has the advocate who then acquires allies at his or her peer level. The best always have senior executive sponsorship for major projects. I/T management must have the vision to see the possibilities, but the business has to want it.

Concerning assimilation, the issue is deployment of the blueprint outside the I/T organization, not just within it. You normally see among the great performers a series of steps taken to encourage business units to support and use hardware and software that are within the blueprint. The same applies to applications that support the I/T strategy. But the other key feature of such organizations is the clear propensity of employees to create management processes to support the maintenance of the technology blueprint. The plan is not left as an intent, a wish; people sit down and figure out how to implement it, with all the normal process management trappings required: tasks, responsibilities, assessments, measurements, owners, and so forth.

In such companies you will find an enterprise model has been developed to serve as the key link between business processes and the major components of the architectural blueprint. Figure 5.15 is an example of a very high level model illustrating the business of I/T. Structure and perspective (context) are important in helping I/T professionals understand their role. The basic message of this model is that business requirements drive I/T's agenda and that I/T's capabilities influence business activities. Competitive and technology trends influence business strategy, demonstrating how the business works. Supporting those are the various applications and their required data. Below all of that are the infrastructure management and maintenance activities, where most of I/T is housed: skills, organization, standards, methodologies, and so forth. To the far left of the chart from top to bottom are the various fundamental business activities: definition of business needs, management of applications, and infrastructure. To the far right are the domains of the business units, activities focused on effectiveness (results) and the infrastructures designed to deliver efficiencies.

The model could just as easily be something radically different and with a smaller emphasis on technology and a greater one on process or data. Figure 5.16 is an example of a measurement-centric model. However, this one also places emphasis on the centrality of data which we can read to mean I/T since most operational data required to support how this management processes are usually in machine-readable form.

Models are simply tools that well-run organizations use to describe how they function and what they produce. They have become increasingly popular over the past decade, particularly after PC-based graphic tools became available and easy to use.

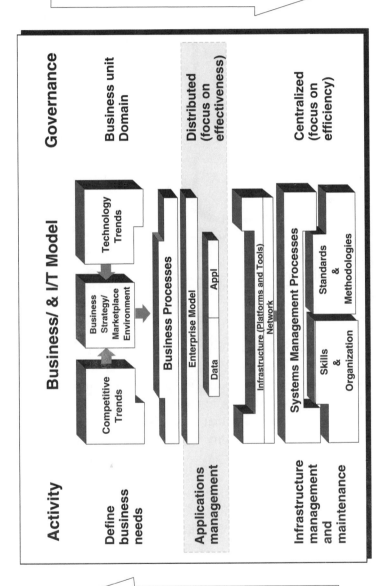

© Copyright 1995 IBM Corp. All Rights Reserved.

Figure 5.15

115

FIGURE 5.16

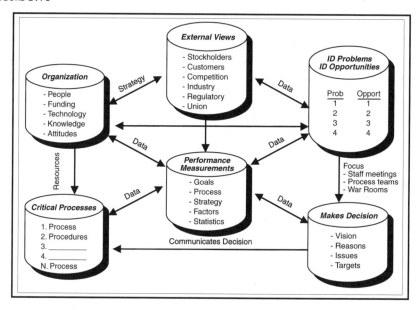

Conclusions

Well-run I/T organizations are not new enterprises; they have been around for years, decades in most cases. Some trace their lineage back to the late 1800s with their initial use of punch card equipment rented from Herman Hollerith! So they all have massive investments in legacy systems, some of which are very productive and others that they wish would go away. But what they have in common is a commitment to exploit remaining value in these legacy systems and to implement a plan that gradually migrates less-effective systems to new ones which conform to technological blueprints in support of the corporate business strategy. Sounds simple, doesn't it? Well, to explain it, yes, but in reality the key ingredient of success is organization, laying out plans for strategy, organization, applications, people, and hardware and software.

Popular tools include blueprint architectures, infrastructure investments and business models both to clarify thinking and with which to construct communications strategies. Laced around all this activity is sharp attention to changes in technology that influence the degree of value delivered by legacy systems, what new or different technology platforms to deploy, and strategy for implementing them.

By now you have probably started to worry about the internal operations of the I/T organization, regardless of whether you are a general manager or a member of the I/T community. Legacy systems, architectures, and corporate strategies need more than just buyin from I/T. We need I/T to think and act in a way that "fits" the rest of the corporation. Thus we face the issue of aligning business and information processing cultures, the subject of the next chapter.

Implementing Best Practices Now	
Action	**Why**
Decide which legacy systems to keep and which to outsource.	It may be cheaper to let someone else do it and this causes you to focus more on the value-delivering applications.
Expect to outsource or replace applications that are not core to your business.	This allows your I/T organization to build new systems relevant to your business today.
Understand what legacy systems you have and ensure you have a comprehensive strategy for maintaining and replacing them.	This makes it possible to control costs and to address the year 2000 problem now.
Get a handle on telecommunications; know what you want and go get it.	So you can derive value from the use of Teleprocessing (TP), not letting it sweep you along by its force.

References

1. Behan, Maria. "Wise Choices: Leveraging Your Legacy Systems," *Beyond Computing* (January/February 1996): 58–61.
2. Cortada, James W. *Strategic Data Processing.* Englewood Cliffs, NJ: Prentice Hall 1984.
3. Economist Intelligence Unit and IBM Consulting Group. *Global Telecommunications to the Year 2000: The Impact on Corporate IT Strategies and Applications.* New York: Economist Intelligence Unit, 1996.
4. Foster, Richard N. *Innovation: The Attacker's Advantage.* New York: Simon & Schuster, 1986.
5. Jacobson, I., et al. *Object-Oriented Software Engineering: A Use Case Driven Approach.* Reading, MA: Addison-Wesley Publishing Co., 1992.

6. Lorin, Harold. *Doing IT Right: Technology, Business and Risk of Computing.* Greenwich, CT: Manning, 1996.
7. Porter, Michael E. *Competitive Advantage.* New York: Free Press, 1988.
8. Putnam, Lawrence H., and Ware Myers. *Controlling Software Development: An Executive Briefing.* Los Alamitos, CA: IEEE Computer Society Press, 1996.
9. Quinn, James Brian. *Intelligent Enterprise.* New York: Free Press, 1992.
10. Stalk, Jr., George, and Thomas M. Hout. *Competing Against Time.* New York: Free Press, 1990.
11. Weizer, Norman, et al. *The Arthur D. Little Forecast on Information Technology and Productivity.* New York: John Wiley & Sons, 1991.

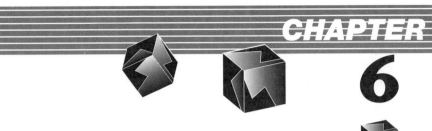

ALIGNING BUSINESS AND INFORMATION PROCESSING CULTURES IN A TECHNO-CENTRIC AGE

Excellent firms don't believe in excellence—only in constant improvement and constant change.

—Tom Peters

*T*his chapter looks at how corporate and I/T cultures are linked together to serve the common purposes of the business. Examples are drawn from application development, organizational models, skills management, and rewards.

The rationale for developing an I/T culture consistent with that of the rest of the enterprise has long been to ensure cooperation. In an age when teaming has come into its own, the arguments in favor of aligning business and I/T cultures seem more urgent. Clearly how an organization operates, and the values it cherishes, are important. Surprisingly, with all the attention being paid to the subject in print and at conferences, we are really still learning the basics about the value of such an approach. What we do know is that the answers are unclear. The evidence still being collected, and circumstances are changing. Whole schools of thought have emerged that sweep I/T and the rest of an enterprise before it with theories and strategies. What they all have in common, however, is one central theme: All parts of an organization influence each other and management must approach improving efficiencies and effectiveness holistically.

The machine model of organizations is rapidly being discarded for a new one that is biological in form. If your toe hurts, the rest of you feels pretty miserable. If your overall physical condition is excellent, all parts of your body work well. Your nervous system tells your brain how to deploy all parts of your body to handle negative or positive situations. That analogy is rapidly being adopted by companies and government agencies in all industries around the world.

The World of I/T

The most widespread image of I/T organizations is that they are different than the rest of the company. The bit twiddlers in I/T are more interested in their technology than in delivering business value; I/T management grew out of the ranks of data center managers or applications programming and thus are more interested in feeding their iron monsters than in making their companies competitive. While the senior executives still wear analog watches, the techies have digital time pieces that look as if they were going to go scuba diving. Do these images hold true in high-performance I/T organizations, or do they march to a different drum beat?

The evidence to answer this question remains scarce. The most important recent study on the subject was done by IBM (introduced in the previous chapter). It looked at such household firms as Aetna Life and Casualty, Cigna, Home Depot, ITT Hartford Life, Merck & Co., Texas Instruments, and UPS—all considered within the I/T community to have some of the best-run information processing organizations in the world. Here is what that study team uncovered.

1. Frequently I/T organizations have a culture different from the rest of the enterprise. In part this was because the rest of the company saw I/T as different, as outsiders. In several cases, I/T had expanded rapidly in recent years, hiring many new employees who had not yet had time to adopt the local corporate culture.

2. There seemed to be no correlation between how a department was organized and its performance. Organizational structures range from centralized to highly decentralized. In one instance, I/T personnel are considered so different that they are sheltered from the

rest of the company. Another organization deposits its I/T staffs in competency centers, by skill types, using them like supplies from a skills supply cabinet for projects. In general, the patterns evident are various balances between decentralized ownership and centralized provision of services.

3. Skills developed in the "good old days" of large systems development are still valuable as project management expertise is required to make fundamental changes in how organizations deliver services to end users.

4. Constant and dramatic organizational changes within I/T are frequent and are seen as normal within the I/T community.

5. Extraordinary emphasis is placed on current skills. Management urges everyone to continuously upgrade their skills. Executives and managers viewed their staffs as pools of skills to move around, apply, improve, and discard.

Another way of looking at this study is to list what the expectations were that did not appear to be evident.

1. I/T's culture and that of the enterprise as a whole has to be the same for I/T to be a high-performance value delivery organization.

2. The best-run I/T organizations are generally organized the same way.

3. Mainframe-era skills cannot be applied to the "new" I/T world.

4. I/T organizations are stable and secure.

However in retrospect, none of this should be a surprise. One of the hallmarks of all highly successful organizations, regardless of functional department, is their flexibility in adapting to the world around them. This study suggests that well-run I/T organizations are simply following that path.

Links between I/T and the Corporation: The Case of Application Development

We can see that process at work, for example, when looking at how best practices organizations approach the creative process of writing new software. Highly effective organizations, as judged by the end users or receivers of I/T services, clearly indicate that the method for application development changes dramatically depending on the nature of the supported business. The approaches may also vary from one set of applications and end users to another.

There are essentially four cultural styles applied by I/T departments in the development of applications. Well-run organizations are flexible in applying more than one, but clearly at least the most effective one, within their company. The four styles are

- Craft
- Systematic production
- Continuous improvement
- Systematic customization

Figure 6.1 documents one kind of business organization using one type and the kind of I/T needs delivered by a particular approach. If an end-user organization is highly informal and has a collaborative culture—like a consulting firm, for example—a craft approach appears very common. That is to say, I/T develops and distributes unique or novel systems and tools.

FIGURE 6.1

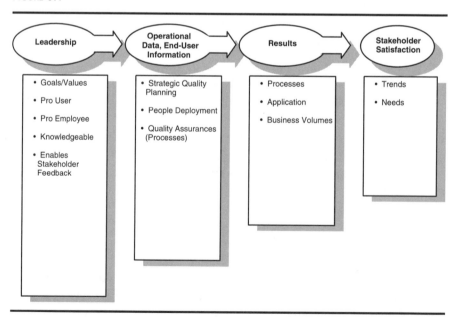

**Spreading the Word of Good Practices:
What Makes You Effective?**

After looking at the experiences of 45 firms, propagation of best practices varied all over the lot. It is not uncommon for performance of various business units to vary tremendously because companies are not transferring best practices effectively from one business unit to another. The critical success factors are how well a particular best practice is understood; the quality of contact and relationship between the business unit communicating the best practice and the recipient of that information; capability of the recipient to take in the information being imparted; and the degree to which the recipient organization is willing to learn and apply the good news.

For more information, see Richard Pastore, "Preach What You Practice," *CIO* 8, no. 19 (August 1995): 14.

On the other hand, if one is dealing with a hierarchical, top-down organization—for example, accounting in a large corporation—manual systems are being automated and information moved up and down the organization. Frequently, information must be created and moved about systematically and in some repeatable fashion. In companies where team-based, bottom-up approaches apply—as in a factory that applies TQM and process management techniques—application development for these people focuses on cross-functional information delivery, connecting applications, and developing ways to continuously improve applications and the quality of services delivered. In this world, I/T probably also has to have a bit of the craft mentality since end users want to tinker with existing applications.

Networked, highly responsive organizations typically require systems and work habits from I/T that lead to systematic customization. In this world, application development has to be modularized with flexible linkages among departments, data files, and applications. In this kind of environment, end users also want the capability to modify files and applications.

If you look at how each of these function in well-run I/T organizations, we quickly can understand the value of flexibility in responding to corporate business strategies. A look at general characteristics, organizational patterns, cultural considerations, and the role of technology indicates what best practices are emerging.

The infrastructure associated with a *craft organization* must enable the development and distribution of unique or novel systems (see Figure 6.2).

Figure 6.2

CRAFT CULTURE

Business Organization ➤ *I/T Needs*

• Highly-informed collaboration	• Development & distribution of unique/novel systems
• Team based	• Innovative, imaginative solutions
• Change oriented	• Collaborative
• Value creativity	• Prototypes used
• Cowboy approach	• Experimental

They have to be highly creative, change oriented, and deal with high risk. Organizationally they normally have the ability to do multitasks, are very adaptive in order to deliver results, and create independent workflows. It is an ad hoc environment. The organization combines craftsmen and professional project leaders/managers into small specialized groups, operating in a collaborative environment. If you had to pick a vision for them, it might be "to go where no person has gone before." The coin of the realm is creativity in a world that is unstructured, what we like to call the informal "cowboy approach." With such a high premium placed on skills, everyone develops expertise, keeps skills current and operates with a professional work ethic. You live and die in this world based on how your creativity is perceived by colleagues. These people like to tinker with new technologies, create or experiment with new concepts in I/T architecture, and will build one-of-a-kind systems.

In most cases, an entire organization will not have the same culture; a culture will develop to support the work being done. In many companies we have examined, I/T must be able to respond to different user communities with different cultures driven by differing work demands. Thus, while we can speak about various organizational and cultural models—useful in helping to identify what characteristics are needed—invariably the best have combinations of these that change over time.

The infrastructure associated with a *systematic production organization* must enable the automation of manual processes to achieve cost-justified efficiencies (see Figure 6.3). Four characteristics define this world: the hunt for productivity, quality in responding to requests, building systems that can handle large volumes of transactions, and maintaining legacy systems as the primary function. Quick response between identification of customers or market opportunities and the ability to deliver based on recombining parts which already exist is the real competency of this kind of an organization.

While new applications are always under development, this is the archtypical shop with 70 to 80 percent of its resources going to the maintenance of existing systems. Everyone is organized by task where they do repetitive functions all the time (e.g., produce payroll every Thursday). Workflows are highly structured and routinized. Like a manufacturing operation, they hunt for defects because they cut into productivity and disrupt the routine. This is the kind of organization that will adopt process management practices and create innovative measurements. All projects in this kind of environment are managed with great discipline. These are the bastions of structured programming methodologies, where high-tech tools are used, and in which operations managers apply a broad range of practices to ensure consistency and reliability of service.

The culture of this organization is quite different from that of a craft shop. Hierarchical command-and-control management is in evidence, while departments are organized by specialty (e.g., operations, programming, end-user support). Management drives activity and rank is important. Managers think, nonmanagers do. If you had to pick a vision for this crowd it would be "We don't rock the boat." The coin of the realm is stabil-

FIGURE 6.3

SYSTEMATIC PRODUCTION CULTURE

Business Organization  I/T Needs

Business Organization	I/T Needs
• Hierarchical, top-down control	• Manual process automation
• Specialized communication	• Vertical information control
• Emphasis on productivity	• Repetitive tasks
• Separate doers and thinkers	• Structured programming
• Formal outline	• Job schedules

ity, not creativity as we saw with the craft shops, and folks are formal, with lots of memos and documentation and meetings with presentations. Skills are highly specialized and benchmarking is a popular sport.

The infrastructure associated with *continuous improvement organizations* has as its purpose to enable cross-functional information and communication systems (see Figure 6.4). In this I/T organization a learning culture thrives with strong overtones of quality management values and formal TQM programs. Connections with end users, customers, and people in other companies are quite high. Workflows are carried out by teams made up of end users and I/T professionals. These people are also on the constant hunt for defect prevention, measure everything in sight, and are effective process managers. They use benchmarking as a critical tool, fold in their work with those of end users, and value the involvement of the end recipient of their work (e.g., end users or customers). Such people are heavy users of imbedded intelligence applications, user-friendly software (e.g., icon/Graphical User Interface [GUI] based), break up software into modular packages (hence their interest in object-oriented code), and are extensive users of groupware like Lotus Notes.

The central organizational tool they use are teams operating in a highly collaborative environment. If you had to pick a vision for this team, it might be "Quality is free." Their coins of the realm are efficiency and quality. They too are formal because of the process-management and team-based best practices which emerge in this kind of world. They strongly emphasize communications, intrapersonal/team skills as essential, along

FIGURE 6.4

CONTINUOUS IMPROVEMENT CULTURE

Business Organization **I/T Needs**

Business Organization	I/T Needs
• Team-based, bottom-up work	• Cross functional information
• Top/bottom communication	• Application connectivity
• Internalized quality practices	• Defect avoidance
• Highly collaborative	• Imbedded intelligence
• Values efficiency & quality	• Classes and objects

with the normal technical skills required to do their jobs. They measure results on the basis of defects, refinements, improvements, and performance against baselines.

The infrastructure associated with a *systematic customization organization* is one that enables the integration of constantly changing networks, information, and communications (see Figure 6.5). Three characteristics are evident when you walk into this organization: A focus on differences in end user needs and wants, very few standard offerings, and responsibility for using an application lies with the end user. The organization looks at in-process measurements and how an application is doing against preestablished goals. End users play a major role in the design of services to be delivered and great emphasis is placed on design and planning before execution; often one-third of the effort is devoted to this task alone. These folks like the same kind of technologies and software tools and have stable processes.

They create highly developed cross-functional networked teams and work with facts and detailed analysis of issues. They focus on customer satisfaction and both efficiency and effectiveness of all processes. In fact, they believe they already have these. If we had to create a vision for this group, it might be "Variety is the spice of life." Their coin of the realm is adaptation and their world is flexible. You can order any kind of food for their working lunches. They value cross-training in skills and identify themselves as knowledge workers, not as techies. They measure performance on speed with which things are done well, and the degree to which their end users are satisfied with their work.

FIGURE 6.5

SYSTEMATIC CUSTOMIZATION CULTURE

Business Organization  *I/T Needs*

Business Organization	I/T Needs
• Networked, highly responsive	• Modularized with flexible linkages
• On-demand processors	• Users can customize
• End-User focused	• Object oriented
• Informal	• High reuse
• Values adaptation, skills	• Imbedded intelligence

I have just described four absolutes. In reality, well-run I/T organizations often mix and match many of these models of behavior. But then again, so do the organizations of which they are a part. What I/T executives will point out, however, is that they consciously understand that there has to be some sort of cultural fit with the rest of the enterprise. That does not mean they need to be organized or operate like the rest, they just need to be able to connect or plug into it in a way that delivers value across the enterprise. That is why, for example, the SIM/IBM study can report a variety of differences in how high-performance I/T organizations operate. In all four models, they would advise: Be flexible, nobody has *the* right answer. My own historical studies of both European and North American I/T organizations demonstrate that organizations also change how they manage and deploy I/T as business circumstances dictate.

How are we to make sense of these organizational models? In fact, well-run companies consciously or even subconsciously apply the one or more models that reflect how the I/T organization can work best with the rest of the business. Those executives who are very sensitized to the use of organizational models will consciously apply one or more of these on either a project-by-project basis within the I/T organization or as a way of linking project teams together made up of individuals from multiple parts of the corporation. The point is, these executives do not see organization as either an absolute cast-in-concrete structure or as something that is simply there. They exploit different ways of organizing people and resources to squeeze the most value out of I/T.

The Crucial Role of Training and Skills Management

Well-run I/T organizations are constantly changing and despite the fact that many of the people who work in such departments live with change, it is hard. Companies making significant changes in I/T report that the "soft" issues of corporate culture are the "hard" issues. It is well recognized today, for example, that you can redesign (i.e., reengineer) a process faster than you can change an employee's behavior. Business transformation is not a consultant's cute phrase, it describes the hard reality of the holistic, comprehensive nature of change that I/T executives share with their colleagues in the rest of the enterprise. As Figure 6.6 suggests, nobody is immune from the large and tough-to-deal-with list of variables.

FIGURE 6.6

VARIABLES AFFECTING I/T ORGANIZATIONS

• Vision	• Morale	• Values
• Structure	• Tolerance for change	• Communications
• Compensation	• Leadership	• Employment contract
• Decision making	• Performance, Evaluation	• Management changes

Despite whichever one of the four models described above you are attempting to build, one common practice all leading-edge companies exercise is the construction and deployment of a human resources strategy based on leveraging I/T competencies. Many have had to move from a static human resource strategy based on I/T core competencies and little change to one characterized by an organized human resources strategy that is systematically reviewed to ensure alignment with the business. They look at what necessary skills are being developed or hired to carry out the corporate business plan, they judge execution against plan, and they deploy people based on their measurable skills. Many companies that have downsized have also "rightsized," a euphemism for swapping out "surplus" people in exchange for critically needed skills.

A second pattern is the move away from the development of just technical skills in the organization and toward a world in which technical skills and consultative skills are acquired. This is necessary as I/T organizations become increasingly linked to customers and end users through daily activities. Consultative skills include questioning and listening, using analytical capabilities to determine what problems and needs are being addressed, and the ability to devise solutions and have the courage to recommend them. The technical skills required to implement these are acquired.

A third pattern now evident is a move away from having reward systems which fail to reinforce attainment of business objectives and toward a strategy that synchronizes measurements and rewards with business objectives. I/T human resources programs continue to reward technical skills of decreasing value. Others, however, are paying more for results that can be linked to what the company is attempting to do as a whole. Shops of all four types described above are implementing these three classes of changes.

If we step back from day-to-day activities of highly effective I/T organizations and ask what the best practice pattern is, the answer is probably close to what is depicted in Figure 6.7. People are valuable and expensive assets who need to be aimed, like a good rifle, at the right target. Second, effectiveness of performance against corporate targets is constantly being measured. I/T executives want to know how their team is contributing to the business as a whole. All training, activities, and rewards are then linked together. Sound difficult? I/T executives say yes, but no more difficult than preexisting processes that do the same thing. All they are telling you is that you have a choice: Focus on your internal values and activities or those of the corporation. They choose to focus on those of the whole enterprise.

In order to leverage I/T competencies, well-run organizations appear to face the same issues. For example, they ask and answer the question: How do we develop a human resources strategy that supports the business and I/T strategies? Regarding policies and practices, they ask and answer: What skills do we need? How do we reward good performers? Concerning assessing performance, the basic question is: How do we manage our people as assets? It is important to begin by asking the right questions. Once asked, most I/T managers can find good answers.

FIGURE 6.7

KEY ACTIONS

1. Know what you need.

2. Know what you have.

3. Understand the gap.

4. Do you hire or rent needed skills?

5. Continue matching skills in-house with skills needed.

6. Train, train, train.

As they move through these questions toward answers, the good news from the battlefield is that human resource strategies which deliver I/T competencies needed by the business as a whole provide the greatest value. "Best practices" attributes in evidence today are clearly unmistakable and very uniform across many types of organizations:

1. Human resource strategy is aligned to the business and I/T strategies *by design.*

2. I/T competency requirements are based on the technology needs which provide the best business value, not what the I/T organization happens to be good at today.

3. Internal resources are focused for maximum business advantage, not the convenience of departments, within I/T.

4. Less critical activities are candidates for immediate outsourcing.

5. Vendor relationships are managed to minimize risks.

Human resource policies are shifting from an emphasis on just technical skills to balancing technology with consulting and business skills. The best-run organizations are developing an impressive list of best practices for which positive results have been turned in. For all employees, for example, individual short- and long-term skill development needs are balanced. Second, skill development is sourced from internal and external organizations. People learn in-house and from other companies; internal talent and consultants and other software/hardware firms are brought to bear on projects. I/T organizations are appreciating the benefits of tracking their inventory of skills and planning for new investments in hiring and training based on the needs of the company as a whole.

In the past several years we have seen a growing emphasis being placed on understanding business issues and terminology in addition to technical expertise. This is probably the biggest change to occur in how skills are developed and rewarded in the world of I/T. Closely tied to that change is the growing value being placed on consulting skills which make it possible for I/T professionals to interact with end users in an effective manner. That requires probing for problems and issues, and then applying analytical business skills in arriving at proposed recommendations. A third set of consultative skills—the art of persuasion, otherwise known as communications—is essential both to get buyin from end users on proposed solutions but also in order to keep everyone informed as projects move forward. Remember from

Chapter 3 a key success factor for delivering value to an enterprise is good communications skills. It is within the context of skill development that I/T organizations acquire the know-how to get that job done.

Technical skills are just as important as ever. In fact, there is a growing application of technical experts to maximize the value of core technologies. But that does not mean that these organizations are wedded to what they have today. Rather, it calls for you to acquire the right technologies appropriate to support the business plan and that means more frequently than in the past a willingness to own or buy specific skill resources based on the needs of the business. Consultants and software houses, outsourcers, and vendors are increasingly being woven into a more comprehensive strategy to ensure the right skills are available to an I/T organization. The advantage of this approach is that you have great flexibility to quickly change skill types and quantities.

A practice increasingly appearing in well-run I/T organizations is the use of certification programs as a way of giving management empirical proof of the creation and availability of specific skills. For example, at Depository Trust Company in New York, vendors certify the skills of client/server experts in the company so there is no misunderstanding about who knows that technology. The evidence so far suggests that employees who are certified tend to outperform their noncertified colleagues because to get certified one normally has to undergo a defined amount of training and have gained a certain body of experience. Independent testing organizations are also used to validate skills, through formal testing programs such as those administered by Sylvan Prometric or the American Society for Quality Control (ASQC). Vendors help out with programs as well, for example, IBM's Client-Server Integration Specialist Certification.

Making Your Practices the Same as the Rest of the Company: Federal Express

Federal Express Corporation became an outstanding performer because across the entire organization it implements best practices, often with a heavy dose of I/T. It focuses on human resources, logistics, customer satisfaction, quality management practices, and exploitation of I/T. It will standardize a process across the firm when it has figured out that it is a best practice. Teams can change practices when better ones are found.

For more information, see Richard Pastore, "CIO 100—Best Practices: Special Delivery," *CIO* 8, no. 19 (August 1995): 32–42.

**Having the Right Skills at the Right Time:
The Texas Instruments (TI) Way**

TI uses a simple PC to match an applicant's skills with open positions in the company to identify the right candidates. It uses this same information to improve its recruiting process. Human resource managers in well-run organizations look to match a candidate's skills and values with the needs, goals, and values of the corporation. I/T organizations that are well run excel in training and education processes because these are vital to their success. Like TI, they see enormous synergy between their practices and achieving corporate goals when the right skilled people are hired and subsequently nurtured.

For more information, see Megan Santosus. "CIO 100—Best Practices: Personnel Best," *CIO* 8, no. 19 (August 1995): 62–68.

Formal human resource assessments are beginning to be implemented as a way to manage the impact of changing competency requirements. Beginning about 1991–1992, I began to notice such assessment processes appearing in I/T organizations. Many were modeled on the Baldrige criteria which include a chapter devoted to human resources. It asks many probing questions about skills, results, and other personnel practices based on satisfying the strategic needs of the business and the tactical requirements of customers. Five best practices attributes are evident in well-run I/T organizations.

1. These organizations survey regularly to define their training requirements.

2. They formally design and develop training curriculum not only for internal use but also in support of end users who want to acquire key I/T skills. Invariably this training of end users is part of the overall support process (e.g., Help Desks).

3. A broad variety of training delivery options are used, such as internal training, self-training, on-the-job training and mentoring, access to commercially available courses, and time and budget to attend seminars and conferences.

4. These departments implement formal training assessments and feedback from end users and senior executives. Those data are then used to improve training and skills development.

5. Regardless of the model of organization that exists, all have increasingly formal processes for improving training programs.

Role of Rewards

One of the chronic problems faced by most I/T organizations is the fact that what businesses in general value from information processing departments is not what those technical organizations normally reward. The best-run I/T communities have stepped up to the problem. But let us understand the problem in more detail before looking at how organizations address it. Information systems organizations historically have valued three things:

- Technical skills
- Technical elegance
- Loyalty to the profession

All three are variations on a theme: an identification with a profession's own values.

Technical skills is fairly straightforward: The more technical you were, the more social status you had in the department and consequently the more you were rewarded. Salaries rose steadily for technical heavyweights all through the 1970s, 1980s, and into the 1990s. There was less regard for the strategic type of skills being rewarded and more emphasis placed on the skills needed to run existing applications and hardware.

Technical elegance refers to the nature of the solutions developed internally within the I/T organization with little or no regard for the effects these might have on end users. Thus we might see a very sophisticated application written with vast quantities of functionality built in and with pointers to all kinds of files, and so forth but not meet the needs of end users. Yet it may be an application that from a technician's point of view is a *tour de force.*

Loyalty to the profession continues as a chronic problem. The world of I/T has long been filled with industrial gypsies. It was, and continues to be, very common to see technical staff having worked in five, ten even fifteen companies during the course of their careers. This has long been the case because with I/T not linked to the mainstream of companies, incentives for company loyalty were rarely there. The result has been technologists who know that their real worth is their technical ability which they can sell down the street. During the period of very rapid growth in information processing that began in the mid-1960s and has continued for thirty-some years, the lack of an adequate supply of technicians in the industrialized world simply facilitated this loyalty to the profession, not to the company.

Businesses in general valued other attributes, the most obvious of which were and continue to be

- Financial performance
- Service
- Innovative products.

This is quite a different list from one the I/T organization would have come up with even though I/T professionals also value innovative products, for example. But as I/T became an increasingly central part of what businesses at large were attempting to do, that dichotomy could no longer be tolerated. Soon many companies, those considered well run today, began the long process of changing I/T values to conform more to traditional business ones while not giving up those which had made computer-based services productive in the first place or, in some instances, to make I/T aware of how closely both communities valued the same things. The dichotomy was often one of emphasis, with I/T professionals valuing technical innovation while other parts of the business focused on product innovation. Yet both valued innovation.

How are they doing this? Leading human resource practices all have several attributes, but the one to really focus on is their use of rewards and recognition to motivate I/T professionals toward an agreed-upon set of services needed by the business. The mechanics of the process are straightforward. Shared company objectives are set in the areas of employee satisfaction, customer service quality, and profitability. That leads to the development of roles, responsibilities, performance plans, and training programs intended to deliver business results. The results these companies seek vary all over the lot. Some examples are

- Being nationally recognized as outstanding in customer service.
- Delivering over 40 percent annual growth in a new service line.
- Making the firm the acknowledged quality leader.
- Nurturing high employee satisfaction.
- Being the industry low-cost provider.
- Being the industry high-value provider.

Again, as with everything else reported in this and in all previous chapters, the fundamental strategy is one of alignment of I/T to a business-wide plan of action. The human resources role works only if there is a real corporate strategy; otherwise, you have only posters, rhetoric, and dys-functional reward and recognition programs.

Conclusions

What leaders tell you today is that the underpinnings of corporate and I/T cultures have to be the same. They work on it, aligning rewards, recognition, skills development, training, roles, responsibilities, and measurements, but not necessarily organization. Second, this does not happen by accident. The effort is conscious and organized, treated as a process much as application development and service delivery are also processes. Third, I/T organizations leading the pack display several common patterns of behavior. They view themselves as integral parts of the company. No enterprise realistically oper-ates as the sum of its parts, yet they are all holistically linked to each other, helping and hurting depending on how effective they coordinate across the enterprise. Skills and services change, expertise is developed and changed iteratively. I/T organizations do not look simply to themselves for resources. They use end users, customers, outsourcers, vendors, and consultants to build core competencies and to deliver services quickly to their parent com-panies. IBM does it, Shell does it, GM does it, Cigna does it, NationsBank does it. The leaders are similar in their behavior.

So much for grand theory and war stories. Reality consists of keeping the system up, getting payroll run every Thursday. If we don't do these things, alignment, strategic fit, and competitive advantage will not happen. So the question arises: Are there best practices developing in the area of day-to-day operations? It turns out that of all the possible topics we can address concerning I/T, this one has the longest heritage of sound practices of any. It is well documented and clearly understood. It is to these that we will now turn our attention.

References

1. Cortada, James W. *Information Technology as Business History*. Westport, CT: Greenwood Press, 1996.
2. Davenport, Thomas H., and Larry Prusak. *Information Ecology: Mastering the Information and Knowledge Environment*. New York: Oxford University Press, 1997.
3. Hersey, Paul, and Ken Blanchard. *Management of Organizational Behavior: Utilizing Human Resources*. Englewood Cliffs, NJ: Prentice Hall, 1992.

| Implementing Best Practices Now ||
Action	Why
Make sure the senior I/T executive is a full-fledged member of the senior management team.	So he/she can apply their knowledge of I/T to basic business strategies in a timely manner.
Assign either I/T professionals to line organizations or functional department representatives as contacts to I/T.	This improves the dialogue about what I/T projects to work on and better defines the value needed in return.
Develop a clear strategy for skills development in I/T, such as a mix of training, acquisition, and outsourcing.	Because you need the right mix of skills to have I/T do the best job possible and to contain the costs of more traditional training approaches.
Insist that all I/T activities be measured by outcomes.	So you can identify what to stop doing, outsource, or do more of.

4. Keen, Peter G.W. *Business Multimedia Explained: A Manager's Guide to Key Terms and Concepts.* Boston: Harvard Business School Press, 1997.
5. Kotter, John P. and James L. Heskett. *Corporate Culture and Performance.* New York: Free Press, 1992.
6. Longenecker, Clinton O., Jack L. Simonetti, and Mark Mulias. "Survival Skills for the IS Professional," *Information Systems Management* 13, no. 2 (Spring 1996): 26–32.
7. Moschella, David C. *Waves of Power: The Dynamics of Global Technological Leadership, 1964-2010.* New York: AMACOM, 1997.
8. Pastore, Richard. "CIO 100: Best Practices: All for the Best," *CIO* 8, no. 19 (August 1995): 26–30.
9. Rouse, Ann, and David Watson. "Applying TQM to Information Systems Quality: The Role of Culture," *Asia Pacific Journal of Quality Management* 4, no. 1 (1995): 12–23.
10. Schulmeyer, G. Gordon, and James I. McManus (Eds.), *Total Quality Management for Software.* New York: Van Nostrand Reinhold, 1992.
11. "Stamp of Approval: Employers Seek to Certify Information Technology Employees to Gain Confidence in Their Abilities," *InformationWeek* (April 15, 1996), p. 58.

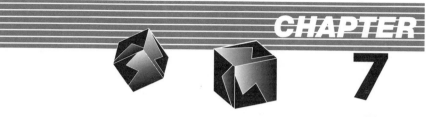

CHAPTER

7

MAKING DAY-TO-DAY OPERATIONS WORK EFFECTIVELY, ALWAYS

Winners in business must learn to relish change with the same enthusiasm and energy that we have resisted it in the past.

—Tom Peters

T his chapter explores how well-run I/T organizations approach daily operations, particularly in regard to data centers and then explores the power of measurements as a way of understanding thoroughly how effectively these responsibilities are carried out.

Daily operations are the major activity of any I/T organization. It is the stuff of which legacy systems are made. But making changes to applications, swapping in new hardware for old, and writing new applications are what I/T organizations do. It all has a project management quality about it. For that reason it should come as no surprise that project management was the first I/T function to undergo significant changes, becoming in most departments the most mature and robust of all I/T processes. This was especially the case in well-managed I/T operations, no matter what decade you pick. It is the one that frequently experienced the latest thinking about project control and was one of the first areas to be influenced by process management thinking in the 1970s and 1980s. As Figure 7.1 suggests, in the 1960s and 1970s many of the disciplined work habits of the U.S. Defense Department and those of the software development community seeped into most I/T organizations, regardless of how effective these departments were. In the 1970s and 1980s the introduction of many new tools, including hundreds of new programming languages, database management tools, and personal computers were added to the repertoire of project management. In the 1980s and 1990s more technology, but most important, the introduction of statistical quality control practices and quality management, added more influences to the process, reinforcing I/T mindsets that life is a series of projects.

FIGURE 7.1

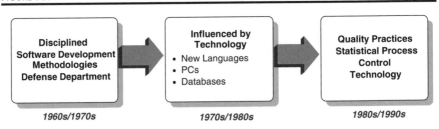

In the case of applications, these I/T organizations learned that it was especially important to practice rigorous project management with large applications. As Figure 7.2 illustrates, project management practices are valuable in every phase of an application life cycle, particularly in conducting analysis, design, and testing. The operations side of the organization, however, also applies the same techniques for operating and evaluating these applications. The difference between the run-of-the-mill I/T organization and world-class operations is not that they use these techniques, but rather how well they deploy them.

Best Practices in Project Management

Seven major software quality components are invariably the focal point in well-run operations. Figure 7.3 lists widely evident components in these organizations. As a group they address basic business issues: efficiencies, effectiveness, end-user concerns, containment of risk, and exploitation of technology. The components match very neatly with similar concerns evident in manufacturing, engineering, and a wide variety of I/T activities: daily operations, systems design and implementation, application coding,

FIGURE 7.2

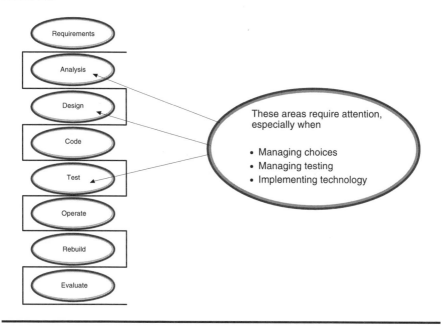

FIGURE 7.3

Component	Definition	Importance
Flexibility	Continuous evolution and changing needs	Response to users
Maintainability	Quick repair and replacement	Improves customer service
Reusability	Optimal productivity and quality of software	Lowers development cost
Integration	Coupling one product to another	Easier to use applications and get access to data
Consistency	Ease of learning and use	Reduces training needs
Usability	Optimal user productivity	Exploits power of applications and reduces user technical training interface
Reliability	Optimal system productivity	Supports end-user processes

benchmarking, and outsourcing of functions to mention a few. Most data centers have lists similar to Figure 7.3; the best constantly refer back to them and try to have a list that is applicable across the entire organization.

The top I/T organizations around the world have taken the extra step of aligning their project management practices with those of the rest of the enterprise because they have to work with other parts of the company that may have different project management philosophies and techniques. Outstanding organizations have even gone so far as to lay out on paper the interactions that are now familiar across functional departments. Figure 7.4 provides a conceptual construct of how that looks. The two boxes with the heavy borders, for example, come back to our arguments in Chapter 2 about the need to link business and I/T architectures. The same thing occurs in linking what computing people want to invest in and I/T's responsibility to find out what technologies there are to invest in. Project phasing, systems organization planning, and management controls work very well across organizations, providing the language and scope are similar and agreed to, in other words, another form of linkage.

Any crusty technical manager will tell you that most project management methodologies are very similar, almost a management commodity. What they must do, however, is focus attention on delivering services. Project management methodologies over the past decade have continued to evolve, acquiring a more customer/end-user focus. We can see that focus demonstrated, for example, in IBM's own findings about what some of the best practices are in how services are delivered. A close look at Figure 7.5, for example, shows that resource commitments, actual performance of work, delivery, and then maintenance are not independent, discrete events. Rather, the I/T community has worked hard to integrate these various functions. Poorly run organizations know that they have all these tasks to perform and treat them independently of each other; the best do the exact opposite; they link them together tightly.

Listen to what your end users have to say about project management as well. *Computerworld* conducted a customer satisfaction survey of the 25 largest systems integrators, firms that routinely manage large projects. What they learned is just as applicable to what organizations do well or poorly when they manage projects internally. When asked what their most important criticisms of large integration projects were, end users said inflexibility of the project management methodologies, inadequate training of end users, and never-ending expansion of the project scope published (February 26, 1996).

FIGURE 7.4

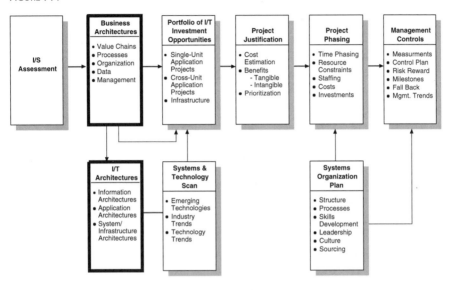

FIGURE 7.5

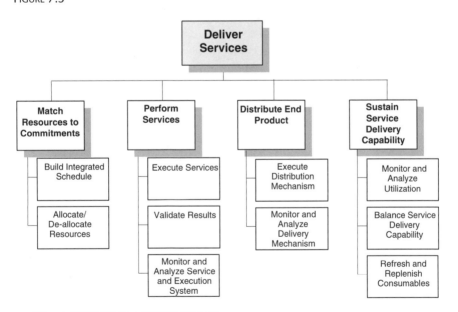

The Changing Data Center

The heart of most I/T organizations is the data center—the glass house—the place where the computer resides. We all know what the place looks like: raised floors, lots of air conditioning, security cameras, locked doors, everyone walking around with identification badges conspicuously displayed; the place looks almost like a hospital. Even in small companies that rely on networked PCs, you find clusters of hardware together. In very large companies you may see one or two dozen data centers each with hundreds of employees and millions of dollars invested in hardware and software. For many companies in numerous industries this is about as close to the heart of the business as you can get physically.

Data centers are primarily responsible for the actual delivery of day-to-day services. They keep the networks and computers going so you and I can log onto a terminal and do our work. They operate the Help Desks and the telephone hot lines you and I call when we have problems. They buy equipment and software. They maintain databases and often perform software maintenance on legacy systems. They are the information factory of the company, spewing out paychecks, reports, and data on-line. To a large extent, they are run like manufacturing sites. What has become very evident during the 1990s is that data center operations are adopting formal process-based approaches, just as factories did. And like their manufacturing counterparts, they were drawn to the same issues: efficient automation, quality management practices, just-in-time strategies, and cycle time reduction.

Part of that discipline has been for managers in data centers to define clearly their role versus those of other I/T departments and end users. The hallmark of well-run organizations is that they have taken the time to set expectations within I/T and with their customers. Service-level agreements are quite common, joint reviews of performance, customer surveys, and documented reviews are everywhere. Data centers post their performance on their walls and send copies to end users. Companies like IBM, Appleton Paper, and Motorola, to mention a few, use sophisticated measurement processes to track a wide variety of performance characteristics which they then broadcast to their stakeholders. Figure 7.6 illustrates a best practices type of communication that appears in many organizations with only slight variations. Real-world examples also contain many more names and telephone numbers and are published on paper and exist in databases accessible by end users.

FIGURE 7.6

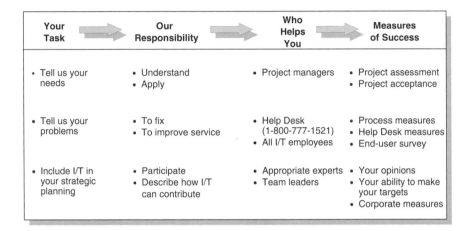

Your Task	Our Responsibility	Who Helps You	Measures of Success
• Tell us your needs	• Understand • Apply	• Project managers	• Project assessment • Project acceptance
• Tell us your problems	• To fix • To improve service	• Help Desk (1-800-777-1521) • All I/T employees	• Process measures • Help Desk measures • End-user survey
• Include I/T in your strategic planning	• Participate • Describe how I/T can contribute	• Appropriate experts • Team leaders	• Your opinions • Your ability to make your targets • Corporate measures

The number of processes required to run a data center is staggering (see Figure 7.7). IBM's own count is 35 megaprocesses clustered around eight groups of activities. The documentation accumulated over the past 20 years on these processes far exceeds the amount of material on all other processes in I/T. Of all the sets of processes in any I/T organization, these are perhaps the most widely implemented. Put another way, even the worst I/T shop views most of its data center operations as collections of processes and have good, fact-based appreciation for the quality of its performance. I call this point to your attention, however, to reinforce that this is where many information processing professionals live. Best practices companies work very hard to make sure these employees don't forget all the issues discussed in the previous five chapters.

Buying I/T Equipment and Software: The BuyIT Campaign

For many I/T organizations the acquisition of I/T is expensive and the way decisions are made to acquire is risky. The BuyIT campaign is a campaign decision to promote and facilitate best practices in the acquisition of technology. Purchasers and vendors of I/T in the United Kingdom are joining together to develop a best practice in this area.

For more information, see "BuyIT: Taking the Risk Out of IT Procurement," *Purchasing and Supply Management* (February 1995): 4–5.

FIGURE 7.7

8 FAMILIES OF I/T PROCESSES

- Satisfying customer relationships
- Defining enterprise I/T management practices
- Managing I/T value to the organization
- Realizing solutions
- Deploying solutions
- Delivering services
- Supporting I/T service & solutions
- Managing I/T assets and infrastructure

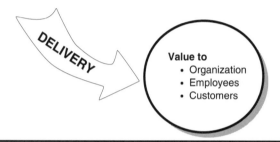

Value to
- Organization
- Employees
- Customers

Does this mean there is nothing unique about well-run data center operations? In fact, one of the most important developments of the late 1980s and early 1990s has been the creation of formal processes to maintain I/T management practices (see Figure 7.8).

There are essentially three basic tasks involved:

- Establishing an I/T management systems framework
- Planning and developing the I/T management system
- Executing the I/T management system

The first one involves identifying those variables and guiding principles essential to I/T, laying out a management framework for how I/T will make decisions and judge performance. Typically it is at this point when management decides how baselines and desired frameworks are to be defined and a strategy for communicating across the organization. Planning and developing a management framework takes you to the next step by actually developing such things as the key measures of performance (e.g., departmental report cards), creation of the management model, and documented statements about roles and responsibilities. Execution involves reviewing and analyzing key performance indicators, identifying and changing management practices, and assessing how the organization as a whole works together.

FIGURE 7.8

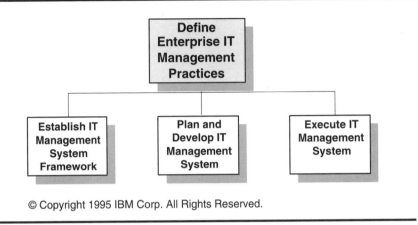

So far in this book, we have jointly looked at what people do well. There is one area that most everyone seems to be struggling with, namely the management of I/T assets and infrastructure *as a whole.* The reasons are not completely clear. But first, let us understand what the tasks to be performed are (see Figure 7.9). First, there is the budget; second, buying hardware and software; third, pricing I/T services to customers and end users; fourth, managing assets like hardware in the data center, on order, and in the warehouse; fifth, providing data and physical security; sixth, all the people management issues; and seventh, managing the portfolio of skills. In many cases tasks are being done well, such as training and implementing human resource plans. But the rest is spotty.

The problem can be largely traced to a wide variety of activities that need to be performed. I think most readers understand good and bad budget management practices. But these are also linked to acquisition of equipment and services. If PC vendors keep lowering the cost of computing by close to 20 percent a year, how do you take advantage of that both in terms of prices paid and how you depreciate the equipment? If yours is the kind of organization that charges expenses back to end users—and well-run shops both do and do not do this—what effects do your charges have on encouraging or discouraging use of computers? Managing software licenses is currently also a nightmare for all I/T organizations. So is keeping track of all the hardware. Walk around your company or agency and you will see discarded PCs, old printers, and unopened outdated software in closets; go to the company

Figure 7.9

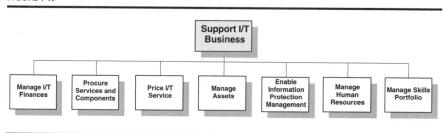

warehouse and you will see more hardware piled up in corners. In the data center there is always the debate of when to swap out installed equipment for newer devices. And so the problems go on and on.

One best practice that is beginning to emerge is to outsource desktop technology, their networks, and overall management and support to an organization that does this for a living. Under such an arrangement, you could also contract with such a company to refresh your desktop technology from time to time in an organized way. They key is to outsource to a company whose core competency and support infrastructure is desktop technology and its associated management practices. The rationale is that this is a huge area of responsibility for any normal I/T organization and a monster for a large corporation that might have 10,000, 30,000 or even 100,000 desktop devices installed. Do you want to manage something like that, especially if it is not a core competence of yours or even a strategic part of what you do for a business?

For any individual issue just listed, there is a body of best practices in print. Many of them were the subject of my previous book *TQM for Information Systems Management* and some of my earlier publications. We have known about these things for a long time. Practicing them remains a challenge, even though well-run organizations are now attempting to lash these specific asset and resource deployment practices together. There are several good reasons for this. For one thing, about a third of a company's I/T bill is spent on the acquisition and disposal of hardware, software, and related services (such as hardware maintenance). Just managing those three sets of assets more effectively can save a lot of money. But linking replacement of hardware with newer devices means you have to make sure your training plans take that into account.

Planning for asset swaps has to be carefully done if you are to install quickly and thus take advantage of this equipment. Budget management is difficult because it is linked with corporatewide budgeting processes and at a time when there are fundamental changes that bode well for I/T. For example, many companies are expressing strong interest in applying ABC accounting to various functions; that requires looking at budget data in new and different ways. A piece of them always seems to include I/T. If you are pro-ABC, you immediately subscribe to the notion that lashing asset management together is a good idea; if you are not a fan of ABC, you still have to understand what value hardware, software, and services renders the corporation. Regardless of your accounting practices, the best always make the link between I/T expenditures and increased value delivered to the business. Benchmarks of state-of-the-art data centers demonstrate that they have great capacity and leading-edge capabilities and are also rated high on cost/millions of instructions per seconds (MIPs) and other technical measures but have done a poor job in teaching programmers how to utilize effectively such software tools as database managers, consequently driving costs of applications too high. In some data centers with this problem, the centers were great while the organization's ability to utilize these were poor. So are dollars well spent in this environment? The point is, to implement best practices, you must ask, for example, what value does a computer upgrade return to the business?

How Hardware Is Selected Today: The Decision Criteria

An IBM survey in 1995 looked at the process by which companies selected what hardware to acquire. Done in context with understanding the role of strategic applications of I/T, researchers noted that the key selection criteria were most frequently reliability, performance, compatibility with existing installed technology in the organization, adaptability to changing application needs, and conformity to "open" standards. Cost and vendor support remained high on the list but not to the extent they were a decade ago. Respondents to a survey said that today and for the next five years, the decision about what technologies to acquire would largely remain centralized. Only a third had distributed or anticipated distributing the acquisition decisions to the business units. The larger the company, the more centralized the architecture and technology acquisition decisions became. Companies with I/T strategies most frequently centralized key strategic acquisition decisions.

For further information, see Kevin Burden, "Reputation, Price Catch User's Eyes," *Computerworld* 29, no. 46 (November 13, 1995): 126.

The Power of Measurements

One of the most obvious developments to occur in well-run I/T organizations is the revolutionary changes made in measurements. Many of the problems just discussed, for example, concern measurements: accounting for how things happen and cost. There are a great deal of exciting new best practices emerging in well-run I/T departments. To make a long story short, customer focus has come to I/T measurements. Looking at performance from the point of view of the end user is having a renaissance unlike anything we have seen since the 1960s. As management practices have changed, so too has the need for different measures. Process management styles now call for process measurements. Value-add activities require measures of value, and so forth. Measurements are becoming more comprehensive and not limited to speed of equipment, amount of uptime for hardware and software, or expenditures versus budgets.

Perhaps the most obvious best practice evident today is a fundamental shift from looking at performance by internal criteria to viewing them from the point of view of end-user communities. As Figure 7.10 demonstrates, asking different questions yields new answers. In this case, the Information Systems (I/S) organization looked at skill levels from its perspective. In the second chart, end users were asked, along with I/S to compare the quality of application delivery. End users were not as generous in their assessment as were I/S professionals. Well-run I/T organizations look at the end-user assessments quite seriously, want to know what their people think to see how realistic their views are but then take action primarily motivated by end-user perspectives.

A second pattern currently evident is the attempt being made by I/T executives to close the gaps between what they know and what they need to know from measures. For example, they are now developing measurements that document the degree of cultural change in their organizations, defining rates of progress. Figure 7.11 (p. 152) is a sampling of some of the new measurements being implemented. Executives are becoming students of measurement processes, a relatively new field, an outgrowth of quality management operating strategies. The most advanced are now trying to understand the relationship and effects of one measure on another. Executives outside and above the I/T department are increasingly focusing on customer satisfaction data and such business measures as I/T dollars spent

FIGURE 7.10

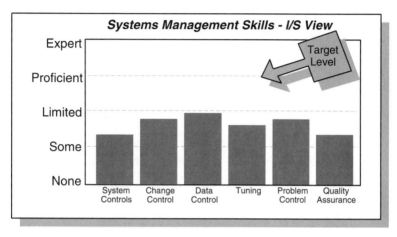

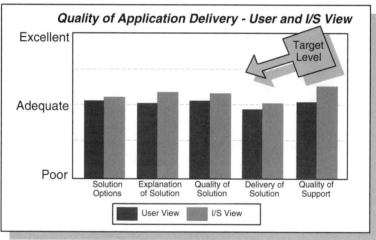

as percent of revenue or number of I/T projects aligned to corporate strategy. The measures in Figure 7.11 thus become second-tier indicators of operational effectiveness within the I/T organization. My own research, and that of others, is leading to a better understanding of the relationship between various types of measurements. Figure 7.12, which I explain in greater detail in the companion volume to this book, defines nine types of measures and which ones influence each other. This is the way you read it. Waste affects the speed (cycle time) with which an organization can perform. The speed at which you perform makes it possible or not possible for you to be more flexible in responding to changes in market conditions and customer needs. Flexibility influences productivity and customer satisfaction. Customer satisfaction will affect the amount of business growth you can enjoy and what happens with your vision.

The bottom line, however, for I/T organizations, is that they are adopting a wider collection of measurements than they have used in earlier years. Departmentwide report cards are particularly popular. They are typically published monthly, are posted on bulletin boards, and mailed to end users. Figure 7.13 (p. 154) is a sample of such a report card.

The best begin with measures that link the performance of the I/T department to corporate goals both through the actual measures and a clearly communicated explanation of how those measures demonstrate progress toward contributing to the success of the business as a whole. The best organizations always use corporate goals to drive I/T measures.

FIGURE 7.11

Type	Format	Why
Size (# of Lines, Modules)	Numbers	Size Drives Cost
# / Type of Defects	Sigma (Errors per Million)	Quality of Software, Performance of Developers
Error Density (Pages/Hour)	Logorithmic Chart	To Understand Quality of Review
Resource/Plan Expended	Bar Graphs	To Understand How Effective is Planned Application of Resource
Customer Feedback	Bar Graphs, Pie Charts	To Understand Types to Eliminate
Review Rate	Bar Graphs	To Understand Quality of Review Process, Speed of Work
Ranges of Errors	Control Charts	To Understand Pressure on Workers to Speed Up Production
Inspection Errors, Intensity	Logorithmic Chart	To Understand Effect of Speed on Workers, Quality of Work
Customer Detected Defects	# and Type Bar Graphs	Quality, Level of Customer Satisfaction
Production Failures	# Control Chart	To Develop Predictability
Application Size at Time of Delivery	Lines of Code or Modules	To Improve Project Predictability
Development Costs/Time	Table, Trend Charts	To Improve Predictability of Costs and Effort
Trouble Spot Density	Control Charts/Bar Graphs Scatter Diagrams	Project Control

FIGURE 7.12

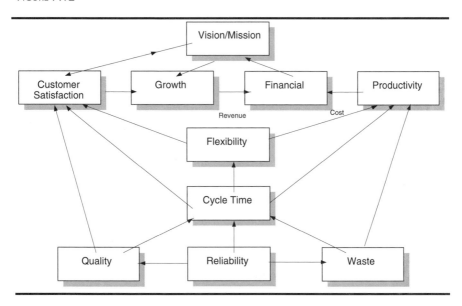

Conclusions

The key best practices in running day-to-day operations involve the implementation of formal project and process management techniques for daily operations. These techniques are heavily end-user/customer focused and are linked to corporate business objectives. Measurements are broadening to take into account the new types of information operations managers and their stakeholders' needs.

This area remains the most difficult part of I/T to innovate in because of the broad scope of activities involved. Operations is also the one area that first of all adopted many of the practices now seeping out into other parts of I/T and the corporation as a whole. Such practices as procedures documentation, performance standards, and benchmarking have long been hallmarks of how most operations functioned. Their techniques are the ones being adopted by others. Thus operations managers, in order to innovate from their point of view, often go beyond what everyone else is appearing to be adopting for the first time. However, the net result is that by linking closer to the needs of customers, end users, and colleagues in the department (e.g., programmers) and to the corporate business plan, these departments are becoming more visible. They

Figure 7.13

Customer Satisfaction -	Index %
Quality -	Baldrige Points
People -	Opinion Survey
Revenue & Market Share -	Money & %
Financial Performance -	Number & %
Corporate Goals	
IS Measures	
Programming Related Incident Reports -	IRs
Cost of Service/End-User -	Money
Cost per MIPS -	Money
Gigabytes per MIPS -	Ratio
MIPS per Data Center Headcount -	Number
MIPS per Systems Support Programmer -	MIPS
End-User Satisfaction Surveys (Performance, - Timeliness, Attitude, Communication)	Percents
Trends in End-User Satisfaction -	Percents/Time
Skills Training -	Average Hours/Employee
Baldrige Assessment -	Points
Time Spent on Quality -	% of IS Div's Hours
Suggestions -	% Implemented
Abandoned Call Report -	% of Sigma
Problems Resolved -	% of Sigma
Response Time MeetingTargets -	% of Sigma
Network Response Time Meeting Targets -	% of Sigma
DASD Growth -	% Y-T-Y
Total Defects by Group -	Number/Week
Availability by Systems -	Minutes Downtime

are also being seen by end users and customers as being more responsive, a clear example of the role of end-user and customer perceptions about value delivered that we discussed in Chapter 3. Surveys of end users and customers also suggest that the better support increases business management's support of information systems, user satisfaction, and ultimately their job satisfaction in general.

Our next chapter folds in many recent developments of a general management nature because in our continuing quest to align I/T with the rest of the corporation, practices in management are essential. For that reason, we will review the role of quality management practices, changing corporate cultures, and even what we still don't know because we must not think that I/T is the silver bullet, the black magic of the late twentieth century. I/T organizations are populated with people just like those in the rest of the enterprise, so we need to appreciate what works in creating a culture that hunts for value.

What's the Best Way to Measure Software?

For two decades now there has been a significant debate about how best to measure the productivity and effectiveness of software development, maintenance, and use. Popular measurement systems have included Factor Criteria Metrics (FCM), Quality Function Deployment (QFD), Constructive Quality Model (COQQUAMO), Goal Question Metric methods (GQM), Application of Measurement in Industry (AMI), and a wide variety of maturity-based techniques. Evidence suggests that AMI is one of the most flexible but that GQM may be the best measurements practice because it produces consistently high ratings from users. AMI does not have a terrific track record but it is one of the most popular approaches so far. The most mature measurement processes are FCM, QFD, and COQQUAMO. The big move in many of these systems is incorporation of process measurements.

For more information, see John Roche and Mike Jackson, "Software Measurement Methods: Recipes for Success?" *Information and Software Technology* 36, no. 3 (March 1994): 173–189.

Implementing Best Practices Now	
Action	Why
Outsource those portions of data center operations which are stable or can be done better/cheaper by someone else.	Because you want your I/T organization focusing its resources and energy on making the company more competitive.
Link day-to-day I/T operations to day-to-day activities of the company through use of review boards and end-user surveys.	This will help ensure that I/T operations remain "end-user" focused and responsive.
Benchmark stable operations regularly.	So you can be as efficient as is humanly possible.
Implement a broad range of measurements that are results oriented and tie back to corporate business objectives.	Focuses on "where's the beef?" and not just on fluff and "going through the motions."

References

1. Boynston, Andrew C., Gerry C. Jacobs, and Robert W. Zmud. "Whose Responsibility Is IT Management?" *Sloan Management Review* 33, no. 4 (Summer 1992): pp. 32–38.
2. Grady, Robert B., and Deborah L. Caswell. *Software Metrics: Establishing A Company-Wide Program.* Englewood Cliffs, NJ: Prentice Hall, 1987.
3. Guimaraes, Tor. "Assessing the Impact of Information Centers on End User Computing and Company Performance," *Information Resources Management Journal* 9, no. 1 (Winter 1996): 6–15.
4. King, Julia. "Big Britches," *Computerworld* 30, no. 9 (February 26, 1996): 17–18.
5. Lee, Sang M., Yeong R. Kim, and Jaejung Lee. "An Empirical Study of the Relationships Among End User Information Systems Acceptance, Training, and Effectiveness," *Journal of Management Information Systems* 12, no. 2 (Fall 1995): 189–202.
6. Oman, Paul, and Shari Lawrence Pfleeger. *Applying Software Metrics.* Los Alamitos, CA: IEEE Computer Society Press, 1996.
7. Putnam, Lawrence H., and Ware Myers. *Industrial Strength Software: Effective Management Using Measurement.* Los Alamitos, CA: IEEE Computer Society Press, 1996.
8. Tapscott, Don, and Art Carson. "IT: The Sequel," *Journal of Business Strategy* 14, no. 4 (July/August 1993): pp. 40–45.

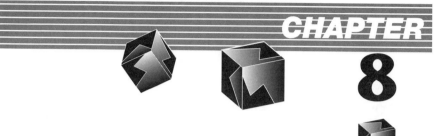

CHAPTER 8

Staying in Top Management Shape, Winning the Culture Wars

The great law of culture is: Let each become all that he was created capable of being.

—Thomas Carlyle

T *his chapter is devoted to a brief discussion of three issues: the role of quality management practices, the nature of the current cultural changes being experienced by companies, and what we still do not know about best practices in the world of I/T.*

I/T organizations are not immune to the waves of management fads and practices that wash over companies and government agencies. Best practices companies clearly demonstrate that I/T departments reflect the same patterns of behavior evident elsewhere in the enterprise. If corporate values emphasize the significance of employees, you see the same in I/T. If the company manages its business by applying such quality management practices as process improvement and TQM, then you will see the same in the I/T part of the business. What well-run I/T organizations demonstrate, like their companies, is a greater than normal interest in such issues as quality management, customer focus, measurements, results, continuous improvement, corporate culture, and employee well-being.

Role of Quality Management Practices

This is not the place to discuss in detail the role of quality management practices in I/T; that was the subject of my last book. However, what is very evident is a continuing adoption of such practices without necessarily heralding any endorsement of "TQM." We have already described many of the new practices of the past decade in earlier chapters. The key elements that are being adopted include

- Implementing continuous improvement management philosophies and strategies
- Linking I/T strategies to business plans
- Responding to or providing what customers and end users want and need
- Performing quality assessments
- Applying statistical process control
- Deploying process management
- Organizing around teams

These are all driven by a customer- and market-based focus. Learning strategies are enterprisewide, cutting across all organizations. Assessments are increasingly standardized across the enterprise too, relying on Baldrige-centric or ISO 9000-centric approaches. Statistical process control is leading to a richer set of measures of performance that do far more than simply describe financial conditions. Process management is helping companies decide what to reengineer or simply to improve and why. Team-based personnel practices are expanding a long-standing tradition in I/T of positively exploiting the expertise of employees.

While enterprises have taken actions over the past decade, customer and end-user needs and wants came to dominate decisions about what I/T is to do. Four trends support this observation.

First, information processing departments have been moving from an environment in which they knew "what's best" to accepting what end users want. Joint committees, shared decision making, and cross-functional teams are some obvious signs of this type of change.

Second, I/T organizations are moving from only delivering services one way to their customers to a strategy of delivering services many ways. This often represents a profoundly different approach, particularly when it comes to how large systems are developed, delivered, and supported. This change has radically altered who makes decisions, from I/T only to joint I/T end users.

Third, I/T managers are moving away from being the people most responsible for cost-justifying I/T projects to supporting end-users' efforts. While this process is perhaps the newest trend, it signals several basic changes. I/T organizations are being folded more fully into the mainstream strategy and operations of the business; end users are enhancing their power over I/T; and everyone is becoming more dependent on "getting it right" when it comes to deployment of computers.

Fourth, companies are expanding the net covered by I/T from just simply providing services to other employees within the firm to forming links with customers and suppliers as intimate as any you might have with your company's various departments. That process is having the profound result of making it difficult to define where your company ends and mine begins. Some people even speak of whole industries eventually beginning to look like one massive company! The implications are profound, not just interesting!

Corporate Culture Is Changing

The implications of these kinds of changes for corporate cultures are profound, just as they have been for the companies of I/T departments. A key dependency that well-run operations have discovered is the critical requirement to rely on a motivated, properly skilled work force. As employees are more empowered, both by management practice and through availability of I/T tools (such as e-mail and access to databases), they are taking the initiative to decide what gets done and why. That process is enhanced by the confidence that comes out of working in well-formed teams. As companies invest more in skill building, even more momentum for change is created. As a result, management teams in well-run companies are dropping old ways of commanding and adopting new ones, sometimes willingly and other times as a desperate last measure. Either way, corporate cultures are changing. Figure 8.1 catalogs some of the most obvious types of changing management practices which are resulting in the creation of new corporate cultures both within I/T and across the enterprise. Technology drives much change throughout this process. At GE Information Services, for example, careful attention is paid to the impact of telecommunications on staff. Here management has learned that the use of communications in a networked environment is incompatible with a command-and-control hierarchical culture. Lotus Development learned the same lesson as it adopted its own Lotus Notes software to link all its software programmers from around the world (EIU, 1996).

FIGURE 8.1

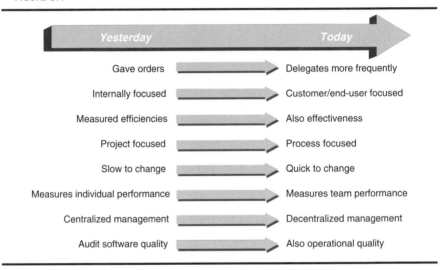

Yesterday	Today
Gave orders	Delegates more frequently
Internally focused	Customer/end-user focused
Measured efficiencies	Also effectiveness
Project focused	Process focused
Slow to change	Quick to change
Measures individual performance	Measures team performance
Centralized management	Decentralized management
Audit software quality	Also operational quality

Teaming and group decisions are making it very difficult to run a command-and-control world, so direct ordering is declining. As I/T organizations measure success based on what customers and end users believe are results and value, department-centric politics and perspectives are slowly giving way. We may come to look back on the 1990s as a period when effectiveness finally became equal to or greater in importance than efficiency. Projects are becoming processes to design, build, manage, and improve—a strategy for improving both efficiencies and effectiveness. Cycle time reduction is now one of the premier strategies being deployed across the entire industrialized world. It is leading to enormous change. Go to a PC trade show two years in a row and you won't see the same products displayed twice! Even the speed of design and manufacturing move fast. Measures of individual performance, while they have not gone away, are rapidly being accompanied by looking at the results of teams as well. In this decade, decentralization is back but not just where hardware is installed; it's in how everything is done. The old software quality audits have not gone away; they are now one of many quality audits being performed on such issues as personnel practices, end-user support, customer focus, continuous improvement, financial performance, and how a department learns and applies its knowledge.

These best practices companies are, with their I/T organizations, increasingly coming to view information processing operations as collections of processes to be led, not controlled. We have seen examples all through this book. Figure 8.2 suggests how broad lists of processes can get within any department. The point is, just about everything done in an I/T organization can be managed as part of a process and some well-run I/T departments are already doing so. Figure 8.3 demonstrates at a macro level how these various assortments of processes are generally managed when they are viewed as processes. What is important to note is that activities are linked to corporate strategies, and measures tie back to the values of the enterprise as a whole, not just to some peculiar needs of I/T.

FIGURE 8.2

Strategic Planning	Compensation
End-User Support	Personnel Management
End-User Feedback	Employee Feedback
Supplier Relations	Recognition
Communications	Facilities Management
Skills Development	Application Design
Service and Repair	Application Development
Budgeting	System Support
Telephones	Software Maintenance
Measurements	Hardware Conversions
Resource Deployment	Software Acquisition
Organization	Technology Acquisition
Quality Assessments	Database Management
Systems Assurance	PC Administration
Complaints	Case Tools Use and Application
Telecommunications Support	

FIGURE 8.3

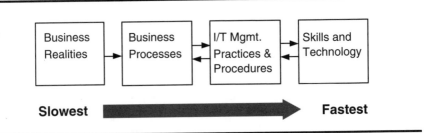

One important key ingredient mentioned throughout this book is the broad adoption of many new types of measures. There is no one right set, but they are broad and constantly changing. Figure 8.4 is a collection of measures that I have seen in well-run I/T organizations just to look at application development! Recall that earlier I argued that most I/T organizations spend less than 30 percent of their time and effort on this activity. So you can imagine the variety of measures that are emerging from the other 70 percent of the enterprise! The point to keep in mind here is that best practices organizations are looking at their businesses in many different ways. They have found it necessary to do so because who participates in I/T decisions has changed at least as much as what I/T is expected to do.

IBM's own research on the topic confirms the change occurring in corporations as they link I/T and business issues. In a joint IBM-American Express benchmarking study done in 1992, the two firms reported on the value of culture and commitment as the two most important elements underlying excellence in I/T. The alignment of I/T (and its culture) to business strategy was important because it ensured that the I/T strategic process would remain effective. This study confirmed what we reported in Chapters 1 and 2: Well-structured and communicated I/T planning efforts, goals, and culture increased effectiveness (Prairie, 1993). Subsequent research done by IBM's consultants in 1994–1996 indicated that the issues and findings remained the same as in 1992. Since basic changes in such findings occur slowly, these studies suggest that alignment remains a basic "rule of the road." My own research on the history of computing during the 1950s–1970s indicated the same lesson. For those who think that the management of I/T is revolutionary, sorry, it is conservative, very practical, and changes at the speed that management practices across a company or industry change (Cortada, 1996).

	Growth	Stakeholder & Customer Satisfaction	Productivity	Cycle Time	Waste	Reliability	Quality	Flexibility	Financial
System Requirements Analaysis/Design	# Preventative Processes, Files Needed	% of End-User Involvement (FTEs) in Design	% of Total Project Spent on Design		# End-User Design Changes	Complaints	Actual vs. Planned ROI		Planned vs. Actual Cost
Software Requirements Analysis	# New Changes to Design	Enhancements by Module	# Interfaces with Existing Software	Time to Acquire Requirements	# of Changes Required	# Omissions Noted in Review of Objectives		Speed of Changes	Cost of Phase as % of Total
Preliminary Design		End-User Satisfaction	# Data Items Passed between Modules		# of Changes to Specifications Due to Design Requirement	# Changes to Project Plan, Test Plan after Review	# Changes to Design after Review Due to Error	# Screens / # Required User Interfaces	Cost of Phase as % of Total
Coding and Tesing	Modules or Lines of Code in Excess of Original Design	% Grade by User	% of Time Spent on Coding	Time to Code a Module and by Type	% of Code Changed Due to Reliability Errors	Errors/Module	Defect Rates (Improvement vs. Plan)	# Lines of Code Reused	Estimated Hours vs. Actual
Integration and Testing		# User/Tester Misunderstandings	# PTF Steps Reduced	Time to Train User, Tester of Documentation	# of Recoded Modules	Problem Rate	Errors in Coding Problems/Month	Rate of Speed to Change	Defect Fix Time
End-User Acceptance Testing	# of Modifications by Type, Module	Time Spent on Walkthroughs	% Features Tested at Alpha Sites	Time to Performance vs. Planned	# Defects Total	Complaints	% Grade from Usability Lab Testing	% Resolution of Defects	# of Delivered Errors
Overall	Growth in Customer Acceptance of End Product	Complaints, Customer Satisfaction	Ratio of Man Days per System/Lines of Code/Module	Time line of Finished Code	Defects by Program	% of Missed Deadlines	% Improvement in Inspection Effectiveness	% Changes Mode/Man Day of Effort	Cost of Executable Instructions

FIGURE 8.4

The third trend in I/T culture is the expanded use of formal assessments of an ever-widening set of I/T practices. Of increasing popularity in the United States is the use of the Baldrige criteria for assessments. While many national quality awards around the world use similar criteria, it is not clear how much these criteria influence I/T assessments. At least in the United States, they are gaining in popularity. International trade and a more closely linked world economy have given the adoption of ISO practices great momentum, leading to widespread adoption of ISO 9000 standards. Adoption causes I/T to play an assessment role. Western Europe led the world in the adoption of ISO and only recently has the United States finally bought in. So if we take the United States as a worst case, we can still see that adoption of ISO standards is massive. In the U.S. case, ISO registrations went from just over 2,000 in 1992 to over 17,000 in 1994. In 1995, registrations were running at over 6,000 per quarter (Cortada, 1995)!

Assessments increasingly take into account such broad management issues as leadership, use of information, quality planning, deployment of human resources, application of quality management practices, business results, and impact on customers. Emphasis is placed on the use of information to continuously improve all operations and to gain feedback from customers and end users which is applied to additional improvements. Best practices organizations thereby institutionalize improvements with methods to learn how to perform better. These improvement strategies are documented and communicated to all interested parties. Figures 8.5–8.8 are examples of improvement strategies. The direct and not so subtle consequence is the emergence of a culture and set of management practices that demonstrate value from the application of continuous improvement strategies.

The Hunt for Improvements Using Assessments: Appleton Papers' Way of Life

Appleton Papers, a manufacturer of highly specialized paper products, is a strong believer in using the Baldrige criteria for measuring performance across the company. The I/T organization measures all its key processes, communicates them to the entire company, and coordinates its annual assessments with those of the rest of the company. It has been doing this for so many years that measuring, assessing, communicating, and focusing on quality practices has become a way of life. Today, Appleton Papers' I/T organization is a model of how to understand a department's contribution to the rest of the corporation.

For more information, see James W. Cortada, *TQM for Information Systems Management* (New York: McGraw-Hill, 1995).

FIGURE 8.5

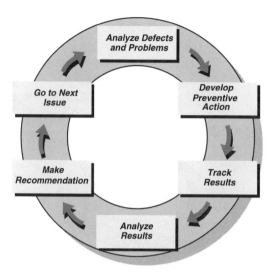

FIGURE 8.6

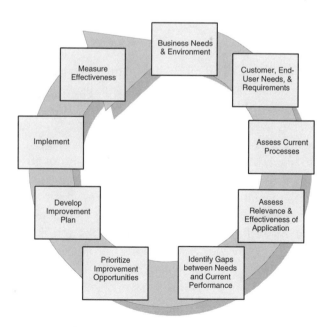

FIGURE 8.7

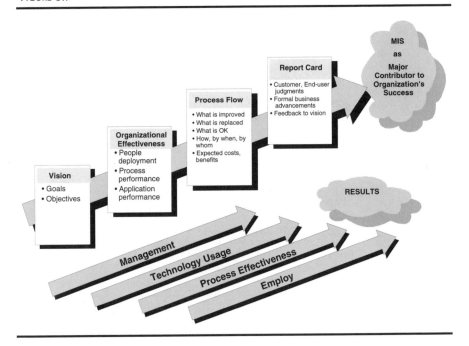

What We Still Don't Know

At this point in the book you must be thinking to yourself, "Gee, these best practice I/T organizations have got all this stuff figured out." Wrong! Every best practices survey I have seen in the 1990s indicates the exact opposite. While successes are frequent and commitment strong to these new ways of doing things, I/T managers are also complaining about how much more they have to learn, how much is so uncertain. This is not false modesty. The problem they face is that once they bought in to their role to support and facilitate implementation of corporate objectives, these managers can no longer hide behind comfortable old ways and previous tasks. Their world is changing rapidly and they stand to lose their jobs and departments if they do not produce. Put another way, unless I/T professionals buy in, they are replaced. This is not a situation where I/T is leading; it is I/T being driven. Remember, most corporations today have a generation of end users and senior management that is very computer literate. They increasingly know what to ask for and what to expect!

FIGURE 8.8

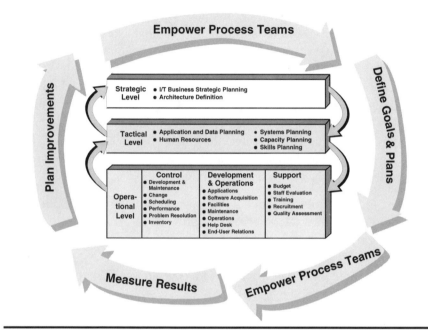

So what don't we know? The successful CIOs would be the first to tell you that the perfect I/T organization and the optimum use of technology do not exist. Like Diogenese, the Greek seeker of an honest person, you could walk around a long time with a lamp and be as frustrated as he was. However, move yourself toward truths that work, those that function realistically in your environment. The first truth is that there are never ultimate "best practices." There are practices that work very well today and when you see them in a specific I/T organization you can learn things from them that can be applied in yours. But a 100 percent transplant is not only unrealistic, it is also simply bad management because no two information processing operations are the same. Tools without thought fail!

That said, what keeps us all churning? For one thing, technology keeps changing, causing "ideal" solutions to shift. Hardware comes out in new versions every year and prices fluctuate. Software appears in new releases almost as frequently, and definitely so for PC tools. All the forecasts, from industry gurus to such major vendors as IBM and Microsoft, speak about continued massive increases in the use of personal computers and networking. Early in 1996, for example, one widely quoted survey claimed that 9 million Americans were using the Internet, half of them for less than one year. Another survey spoke about 35 million Internet users worldwide. Cellular phone users were coming on stream in North America at the rate of over a 125,000 per month. Sales of PCs were running into the tens of millions each year in the 1990s (Cortada, 1996). The point is, technology is churning and being implemented at the fastest rate we have seen in the 50-year history of the computer. The rapid pace of marketplace change compels companies to face changing realities. They need I/T support to be successful in meeting new market demands so they too are adding to the phenomenon of churn. That churn has three effects on best practices:

- New technologies, products, and capacities make new applications possible, old ones candidates for improvement.
- Pricing dynamics make uses of technology either more or less attractive right now.
- Process reengineering or business transformation is increasingly relying on this changing technology.

A second dynamic at work is change in many industries. In fact the change is often so great that the "ideal" company is constantly under construction. Some industries are too, for example, whatever is currently emerging out of the mix of telecoms, movie studios, and television industries. Yet even that as yet unnamed industry has strategies which I/T has to support. In fact that same industry would not be possible to put together if it were not for computer and telecommunications technology!

But what are the gaps in our knowledge? Actually, the questions usually asked by well-run organizations tend to hover around key issues associated with the best practices they have today. The most obvious areas of concern are

- Benchmark data on performance
- Results of quality practices
- Network management
- PC usage
- Strategic I/T applications
- Personnel development (skills focus)
- Metrics and assessment practices

A Learning Culture:
The Best Don't View Learning as a Distinctive Strategy

In a study done by the IBM Consulting Group and the Economist Intelligence Unit, they found that the best have learned to share knowledge as an instinctive part of their daily lives, often driven by historical tradition in the company. Tools to facilitate learning grow naturally out of a "genetic" inclination to do so. AES Corporation, which produces power, and 3M have long been best practices examples of this phenomenon. By having such a heritage, they have had to do less work in renovating their cultures to continue to thrive as learning organizations. As in other learning organizations, senior management, leading by example, proved essential in fostering this kind of culture. Asian executives in a broader study demonstrated a greater interest in collaboration—listening, experimenting, and using life-long learning—than their counterparts in North America or Europe. What problems do they routinely overcome to be best practices in this area? They say negative cultural influences, corporate politics, and pressures of time.

So what do I/T and other functional areas do to stay on top? The keys include reinforcement of goals and values that transcend immediate profit targets, learning as a strategic goal, performance measurements that set and track learning objectives, rewards for collaborative behavior, sharing ideas and achievement in daily work, a profound respect for corporate history and company traditions, frequent and open communications up and down the corporate ladder, teamwork, and organization of people into teams and work groups.

For further information, see Economist Intelligence Unit, *The Learning Organization* (New York: Economist Intelligence Unit, 1996): 45–50.

We touched on many of these in this book, but the fact remains these are topics that are receiving significant amounts of attention by users, I/T departments, consultants, professors, and vendors. The bad news is that we do not have as much "best practices" data here as we all would like; the good news is that there is a great deal of information and research is being done on these topics. Key I/T publications deal with these on a regular basis. These include most of the major ones such as *ComputerWorld, Datamation, PC Magazine,* to mention a few examples.

But after all is said and done, changes outside of I/T increase our overall sense that we are in a period of profound change which in turn makes it difficult to reduce the list of what we do not know. For example, the very nature of work in all jobs appears to be changing. The rapid migration to electronic commerce, and away from traditional retailing, puts I/T right in the middle of how companies sell and governments work with citizens. Whole industries are being created, others destroyed, and traditional borders among each are changing. As with work and electronic commerce, a primary driver of change is I/T. These are new circumstances and new situations create whole bodies of issues and questions which have yet to be answered.

But answers are being sought. In addition to academics thinking about the future, companies are experimenting as they invent the future—a best practices already noted in earlier chapters—and vendors of computers are looking at the issues as well. For example, the IBM Consulting Group and IBM's basic research laboratory—Watson Research Center—have undertaken extensive studies of the issues surrounding the changing nature of work, commerce, and industries. Their research is less about technology and more about business issues, implications for best practices, and, most important, how management in general runs corporations and public institutions. Ultimately, it is change that is the primary driver of uncertainty and the list of topics that we know too little about. Interestingly, however, best practices strategies serve as a way to navigate through issues about which we know too little.

Conclusions

Despite constant change in the world of I/T and in the broader arena in which their companies play, well-run I/T operations do well, exploiting opportunities present in a coordinated fashion with their parent enterprises. The keys are integration of a wide variety of business and technical methods. Business strategies lead to business organization (the classic form follows function idea), with I/T supporting business processes. I/T's strategy is in support of those and below that I/T's own form (structure, processes and assets). As Figure 8.9 suggests, it is those things that drive what methods and assets are used, what applications and data are offered the business, and what applications and information projects are launched.

Companies that exploit I/T the best have some common characteristics evident in their cultures and processes. We can boil these down to a short but powerful list of six actions that they take.

FIGURE 8.9

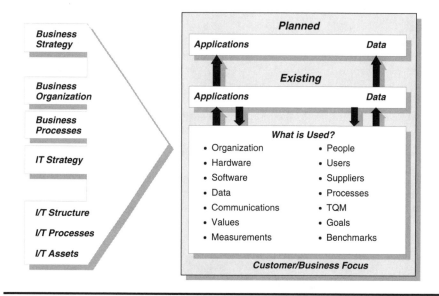

1. They align I/T with the corporate business plan.

2. They apply continuous improvement techniques.

3. They take a process view of operations.

4. They invest in their employees.

5. They take very seriously customer's views of services.

6. They experiment and innovate constantly.

My own research suggests that most I/T organizations that have been around for a decade or more display some or all of these characteristics. No one I/T operation is outstanding or awful. They have smatterings of greatness, average performance, and things that should embarrass them. Where your organization is in this spectrum of performance and how you get on the "best practices" train are the subject of our next chapter. This chapter is crucial because the best-run I/T organizations will tell you that their success depends on two things: Taking a holistic approach and continuously improving and changing. That is why we have to deal with the whole issue of developing and applying a strategy designed to hunt for value using I/T.

Implementing Best Practices Now	
Action	**Why**
Take a holistic view of the use of I/T; it is not simply to handle data.	Because 40 years of I/T experience suggests you can compete by integrating I/T into key functions.
Work to link the culture of the I/T organization to that of the corporation as a whole but learn from the technical community, too.	Because they know how to apply rigorous analytical techniques to problem identification and solution and make these stick.
Make I/T measurements of performance very broad and comprehensive, use report cards and balanced measures.	Because that aligns focus with corporate objectives and gets everyone pulling the oars in the same direction at the same time.
Meet regularly with peers and attend conferences that tout best practices.	Because silver bullets are being made every day and your company deserves to use them when they become available.

References

1. Anonymous. "Nontechnical Staffers Flourish in I/T Shops," *Information Week* (June 6, 1997): 146

2. Beer, Michael, et al. "Why Change Programs Don't Produce Change," *Harvard Business Review* (November-December 1990): pp. 158–166.

3. Blumenthal, Barbara, and Philippe Haspeslagh, "Toward a Definition of Corporate Transformation," *Sloan Management Review* 35, no. 3 (Spring 1994): pp. 101–106.

4. Cortada, James W. *Information Technology as Business History* (Westport, CT: Greenwood, 1996).

5. Cortada, James W., and John Woods (eds.). *Quality Yearbook* (New York: McGraw-Hill, 1995).

6. Economist Intelligence Unit and IBM Consulting Group. *The Learning Organization: Managing Knowledge for Business Success.* New York: Economist Intelligence Unit, 1996.

7. Fried, Louis, and Richard Johnson. "Gaining the Technology Advantage: Planning for the Competitive Use of IT," *Information Systems Management* (Fall 1991): pp. 7–13.
8. Gertz, Dwight L., and Joao P.A. Baptista. *Grow to Be Great: Breaking the Downsizing Cycle*. New York: Free Press, 1995.
9. Hopland, Jan. "I/T Strategies for Profitability Providing High-Level Customer Service," *Information Strategy: The Executive's Journal* (Winter 1997): 17–18.
10. Kaplan, Craig, Ralph Clark, and Victor Tang. *Secrets of Software Quality: 40 Innovations from IBM*. New York: McGraw-Hill, 1995
11. Kuczmarski, Thomas D. *Innovation: Leadership Strategies for the Competitive Edge*. Chicago: American Marketing Association and NTC, 1996.
12. Prairie, Patti. "The American Express/IBM Consortium Benchmarks Information Technology," *Planning Review*, no. 1 (January/February 1993): pp. 22–27.
13. "The Search for the Organization of Tomorrow," *Fortune* 125, no. 20 (May 18, 1992): 92–98.

CHAPTER

9

A Strategy for Managing the Hunt for Value: The Focus on Best Practices

A fool can learn from his own experience, the wise learn from the experiences of others.

—Democritus

T his chapter is devoted to describing how to create an environment in which you deliver value to your end users and customers on a continuous basis. The process for continuous delivery must operate at both the organizational and personal levels. Both are described.

We live in an age when we are so dependent on computers that no responsible senior executive will long tolerate an I/T organization that is not seen constantly delivering compelling value. At a minimum the CIO can be replaced and, at the other extreme, the entire I/T organization. These two extremes can be accomplished today in less than 30 days. As the need for businesses to transform themselves increases, speed of delivery is as valued as the end product itself. Management teams in well-run I/T organizations understand the need to constantly look for ways to improve, apply techniques to ensure they are delivering value, and to report on their contributions to the organization at large. "Selling upwards," as a salesperson might put it, means making sure your stakeholders clearly recognize that I/T is about delivering value, hauling its own weight, contributing its fair share, and making sure you get credit for it. These things do not happen by accident.

The Organization's Game Plan

The process required to deliver value has been suggested throughout this book—it is the heart of what best practices is all about—but now let's pull it all together. There is a process, often well documented, that outstanding I/T organizations invariably have. It is characterized by a profound concentration on what end users and customers of the company want from I/T. This customer-centric focus also invariably includes the classic quality management strategy of Plan-Do-Check-Act (PDCA) made so obvious by the late Dr. Edwards Deming. These organizations also judge their success by what their stakeholders think and know. Inputs come from many sources, but assessments are organized. Finally, such organizations intend to remain in business for a long time—stay in the hunt—which means they invest in infrastructure and in the hard work that it takes to be out front.

Figure 9.1 is a high-level model of the strategy. All the variations I have seen essentially have the same seven steps.

FIGURE 9.1

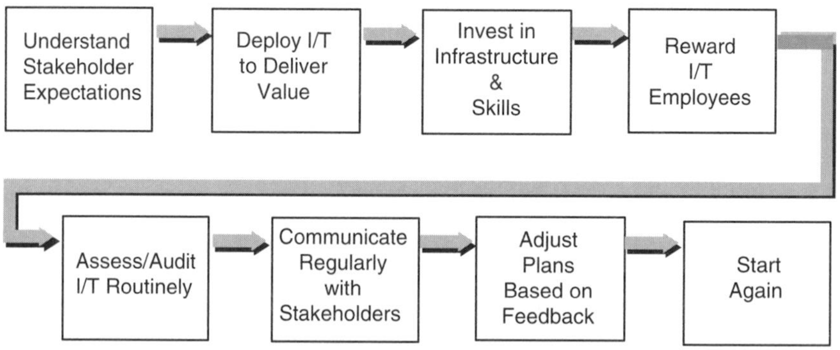

Step One: Understand What Your Stakeholders Expect and Need from You

These range from customers to suppliers, from senior management to end users. They all have expectations of you—information and services that they need to have from I/T in order to be successful in their work. Understand them by asking constantly what they want and how they define success. Negotiate the definition of win/win if necessary. Then take it to the next level: Anticipate what they will need before they request it so you can build the infrastructure required to deliver. To a large extent, those within your company who survey customers can help you with the mechanics of the surveying and analysis process. This process has best practices associated with it and a large body of literature. It is a process, however, that has not been fully documented when applied by I/T to its end users, so a little invention is always required.

Step Two: Organize I/T and Deploy Resources to Optimize Your Ability to Deliver Compelling Value

Increasingly, delivering levels of service as we knew them in the 1980s and early 1990s won't cut it anymore. Yet our I/T processes, and the organizations developed to support these, are invariably structured to meet the needs of an earlier age. A quick way to test this is by comparing your I/T processes with those illustrated throughout this book; mine reflect mid-1990s forms, do yours? What complicates the problem is that organizational structures have to change constantly, with continuous tinkering a way of life. A good step here is for I/T personnel to become experts on virtual or agile organizations because how they deploy technology is central to their success. Agile organizations have methods which focus on delivering compelling value to end users and customers and the number of case studies of such organizations is growing rapidly. (A good source on these is Goldman, Nagel, Preiss in the references at the end of this chapter).

Step Three: Invest in Technical Infrastructure and the "Right" Skills

This too is a continuous process as described in Chapters 2, 4, and 5. The challenge is to balance supporting legacy systems—many of which you would prefer sat on different technical platforms than they do today—while investing in skills needed to support future I/T needs. That requires a clear commitment to align with what the business as a whole needs and with technical platforms that will provide future value, not just results today. Here the key ingredients are

- Clear understanding of the corporate business plan.
- Exact inventory of existing I/T skills person by person and organizational.
- Solid understanding of existing and emerging technology trends and their economics.
- Good application knowledge of how I/T is being applied within processes.

Step Four: Reward Your Employees for Aligning I/T with Business Objectives and for Taking Care of Stakeholder Wants Today and Needs for Tomorrow

That means customer-centric employee behavior is rewarded while skills development is made part of everyone's job. While we have discussed these issues in some detail elsewhere, particularly in Chapters 5 and 6, most organizations do not execute this step well. Even well-run I/T shops are sloppy on this point. Invariably the best at rewarding and aligning people's behavior in an organization is the sales department. I suggest you benchmark how you align and reward people with how your peers in sales do it. Yes, the type of employee is different, but the issues management faces are not. At IBM, for example, it is not uncommon to see I/T executives who, at one time or another, did a stint in sales. That experience spills over into personnel practices.

Step Five: Routinely Assess and Audit All I/T Operations in a Formal Manner

Just as the accounting and finance departments regularly check their own work and hire outside accounting auditors to inspect their workmanship, some rigorous and formal process is invariably in use by well-run shops. We will review in more detail below how to apply a Baldrige-based approach. If your company is using ISO 9000, build your assessment around ISO standards and language. The point is, by assessing how you are doing against the overall business, I/T strategies, and annual plans, you can get very specific about what is working well and what needs to be improved or radically changed. That assessment can also be the foundation for step six. Well-run organizations frequently do some sort of formal assessment about once a year, often linking this exercise to their strategic planning process.

Step Six: Communicate with Key Stakeholders What You Are Doing, How, and Results

A poorly executed communications plan simply leaves your stakeholders in the dark. And we know what happens then: They assume you are not doing as good a job as they think they need to have you do. The newsletters, departmental report cards, bulletin board scores by process, and Baldrige assessments are all actions taken to communicate what I/T is doing. Well-run I/T shops also make sure that they conduct formal presentations to major stakeholders and participate in cross-functional planning sessions and staff meetings on a regular basis. These communications vehicles can serve double duty when you have to present benchmarking projects to other I/T organizations outside of your company. This kind of communication becomes absolutely crucial if your company is attempting to become a key supplier to some other firm that practices quality management, has been recognized with a quality award, like the Baldrige or Deming, or is an ISO 9000 certified enterprise. It will be crucial in these situations for I/T to demonstrate in a compelling and rapid manner its best practices and level of performance across a broad range of services.

Step Seven: Adjust Your Departmental Plans Based on Feedback from Stakeholders and Data from Your Key Process Owners and Implement the Changes

This last step closes the circle on continuous delivery of value. The plan-do-check-act approach is a never-ending process that has been proven to be very effective in many organizations, not just in I/T. In I/T best practices shops, invariably they are part of other departments' PDCA process. As corporatewide modes of operating emerge with PDCA inherently imbedded in their modus operandi, the seven-step process becomes merely an unstated way of life. But what really differentiates the very best from merely the good is the fact that this process is consciously thought about and implemented as one of the critical overt management processes.

Your Personal Game Plan

Best practices are, at best, moving targets. Yesterday's outstanding performance is tomorrow's business as usual. This reality is as true for I/T as for any other part of professional life. In fact, some might argue that there is more change in I/T than in many other parts of the business. My own research indicates this is not quite the case, but it is important to understand what is changing and how fast so you know how to invest your personal time keeping up. There are four "buckets" in which we can put various forms of change. Some we pour change into constantly, others only periodically. Figure 9.2 represents the bandwidth of change that we have to deal with. Change occurs at different speeds. The faster change occurs in an area of great importance to your organization's success, the more you have to do to keep up to take advantage of it. Everything is relative. Thus, for example, I suggest that the business realities generally change slower than the need for new technologies and skills. If you were in agriculture or teaching, you would probably agree with Figure 9.2. If you were working

FIGURE 9.2

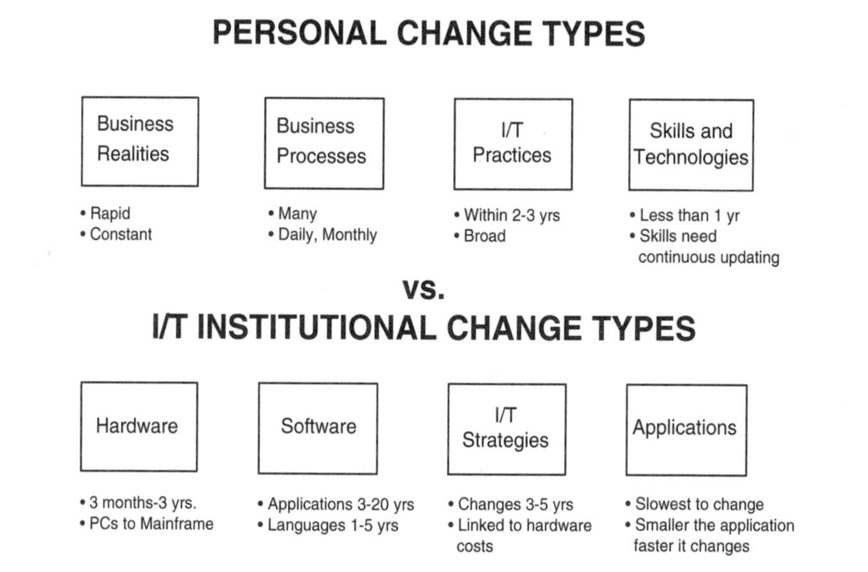

PERSONAL CHANGE TYPES

Business Realities	Business Processes	I/T Practices	Skills and Technologies
• Rapid • Constant	• Many • Daily, Monthly	• Within 2-3 yrs • Broad	• Less than 1 yr • Skills need continuous updating

vs.

I/T INSTITUTIONAL CHANGE TYPES

Hardware	Software	I/T Strategies	Applications
• 3 months-3 yrs. • PCs to Mainframe	• Applications 3-20 yrs • Languages 1-5 yrs	• Changes 3-5 yrs • Linked to hardware costs	• Slowest to change • Smaller the application faster it changes

at Microsoft, you would probably move the business realities bucket over next to skills and technology. It does not matter what the absolute relative positioning is of the buckets. What is critical is the realization that there are at least four buckets holding change that any I/T professional must be aware of and deal with. Effective leaders and change agents instinctively understand this concept. My own research, however, has yet to turn up an I/T executive who clearly articulates the range of skills and knowledge required for him or her to keep their organizations the best they can be. What you do find in best practices I/T organizations, however, is a climate of learning, exploring, questioning and a desire to understand how others deal with common problems and issues. That climate of curiosity and learning, however, begins with the senior I/T executive and is encouraged all the way down the organization. So how do you keep up, keeping your various buckets full of relevant, timely information and insights?

Business Realities

There are some common elements that conveniently fall into this bucket. Some of the obvious issues are

- Corporate business plans
- Business environment in which your company operates

- Economic performance of the firm
- Customer responses to your company's products and services
- National and international economic and governmental trends

These are broad based and are learned with the question in the back of your mind: How do I exploit technology to take advantage of broad business opportunities in a timely fashion? Do I look for printouts of data, hang out with the marketing people and stare at trends, or attend pricey seminars in my industry? The answers may all be the same: yes or maybe. However, the key element is the constant acceptance of information gained both through formal exercises (e.g., planning efforts and attendance at seminars) and from a wide variety of information data-gathering efforts (e.g., telephone calls to peers, meetings with employees).

In a fascinating study of how managers get the information they really need, two business professors—Sharon M. McKinnon and William J. Bruns, Jr., attempted to find out how effective managers did collect this kind of information (McKinnon and Bruns, 1992). They learned all kinds of things. For example, successful managers develop the ability to collect and use a broad range of information and do a good job of assessing it. They are also very, very good at asking crucial questions. One observation they made was that "information that is often of most use to them is timely, accurate physical measures of quantities or counts" (p. 15). This approach is evident in the gathering of information for our first two buckets—business realities and business processes—and even more so for our third bucket. Other researchers have found that about two-thirds of the information one needs comes from talking with other humans and of these about three-quarters from face-to-face discussions. Most sources are external to the company. In other words, executives and middle managers generally rely on a wide variety of contacts and access to people outside their companies for information of the type you would put into the first bucket. Increasingly, the same is becoming true for members of process teams

Business Processes

Since I/T is increasingly playing a very important role across the enterprise, and particularly in reengineered processes, we must have a detailed understanding of how these work. To a large extent, I/T professionals ask the same kinds of questions of processes across the enterprise as they would ask of their own. Unit counts by day, week, month or quarter are very much in evidence. Physical counts of how many things were done, moved, sold, changed, or conducted and why is important. If you are managing your I/T organization as a collection of processes, most of your information will come from the process teams that execute the processes. Much of that information is a combination of statistical hard data and conversations. The lower in the organization one goes, the more frequently computer-based data become important since I/T teams tend to capture data on transactions. The rationale and analysis of the meaning of such data, however, remain largely verbal, coming from face-to-face meetings. For that reason, the way you keep up with how your processes are doing and those versions implemented in other companies calls for organized and scheduled meetings and reviews. Reviews are particularly useful within one's own organization. Benchmark meetings with other companies to compare your process to theirs are considered some of the most productive uses of time by I/T professionals.

Research on the role of I/T-based data versus face-to-face data gathering is a growing field. What the experts are saying today is, in general, that managers select the medium in which they want information based on its ability to reduce uncertainty or equivocality. An unequivocal message can be received in written form very easily, for example, number of telephone calls received in the data center (McKinnon and Bruns, 1992). Where lack of clarity and uncertainty exist, face-to-face meetings are preferred by most managers. Human conversations provide a far richer exchange of information than a printed report or even a fine book!

Well-organized I/T managers spend a great deal of time discussing business processes outside their own departments. While a vast literature has emerged about what information you need to be effective in such areas as sales, accounting, and manufacturing, what is important to realize is that managers in those functions can and will drive your attention to the issues of greatest relevance to them. Since best practices I/T organizations invariably operate in well-managed companies, one can reasonably expect that your peers in other departments are focusing on crucial issues. Your participation in their discussions on a daily, weekly, monthly, and quarterly basis remains the single most effective way to gather information on the quality of business processes. If you are a member of a process team, then normal process management techniques still provide the most feedback because you need statistics and trend and problem analysis.

I/T Management Practices and Processes

Now let's get very parochial! Four very common practices are evident in well-run I/T organizations both among the management team and employees at large.

First, good process management practices are in clear evidence. Teams gather data on the physical performance of all key processes, set goals for improvement, and go after them. They frequently do root-cause analysis. Reviews of the performance of key processes are routinized, that is to say, they occur at prescheduled times (e.g., daily or weekly) and whenever a significant aberration in performance becomes evident. This disciplined approach is hard to implement and stick to, but the best do it.

Hunting for Best Practices Begins with Learning: The Case of the Rover Group

Famed for its MG sportscar and the Land Rover, this is a company that knows how to learn and to apply insight and experience. After hard times in the 1970s, it turned to a strategy that included becoming a learning organization. Extensive use of quality management practices across nine major processes reinforced tactical processes to improve. Revenue per employee climbed from £31 in 1989 to £122 in 1993, clearly world-class performance! Some of the tactical steps in this success involved sharing best practices, fostering learning through learning processes with tools and techniques, and by encouraging employees to learn outside the company, for example, by going to universities, teaching and encouraging learning among its stakeholders, and by promoting its image as outstanding.

One of the unique features of Rover is its life-long learning strategy to encourage employees to continue acquiring skills. It does this by a series of programs: stipends for courses that relate to work activities, higher education programs with the University of Warwick, career development program tools for employees to use to manage their own development strategies, self-administered diagnostic tools, personal learning and planning diaries, and learning facilities at each factory. Linked to these initiatives is empowerment driven by basic corporate values: Learning is a natural instinct; creativity, contributions, and participation are driven by learning and growth; everyone is expected to do their job, improve their job, and help others to grow; you own what you make; creativity is not exploited enough; and management is not all wise, employees have answers too.

For further information, see Economist Intelligence Unit, *The Learning Organization* (New York: Economist Intelligence Unit, 1996): 37–38, 51–57.

Second, benchmarking is a major activity. Everything important is benchmarked: key processes, overall departmental performance, how end users view I/T, and what they want from it. I/T managers establish monthly or quarterly benchmark meetings with neighboring I/T departments and with members of their own industry if they are not in direct competition. Industry benchmarking consortiums are used a great deal. For example, in higher education in the United States, a number of universities participate in the NACUBO benchmarking project which in part collects data on I/T. Vendors like IBM also regularly sponsor I/T-specific benchmarking studies. Results typically are unit counts, such as productivity indicators (e.g., cost of transactions, cost of I/T per dollar of sales) because they are the easiest to gather and the least expensive. However, benchmarking projects are becoming more sophisticated as they move to more qualitative issues. If anything, benchmarking studies are on the rise and are becoming broader in scope.

One quick example of formal work suggests excellent rules of the road. In 1996, the Gartner Group conducted a study for IBM on the total costs to companies in owning and operating PCs and local area networks (LANs). Using a life-cycle cost model that looked at industry data and stalking horse scenarios, a variety of useful observations that an I/T executive can use were obtained. For example,

- End-user operations account for about 55 percent of a Windows system's total cost.
- Count on technical support eating up 17 percent of your costs.
- Administration will absorb another 14 percent.
- Capital costs—often a great point of interest—only accounts for 14 percent.

The study led to the observation that one could bank on operating costs coming in at about five times the capital investment in the technology. Looking at things from the end-user's perspective, this and other studies have observed that an end user's time spent on nonjob related activities connected to the use of PCs can generate half the total cost of a company using PCs. Most studies of I/T expenditures, including this one, confirmed what had been occurring for over a decade: About 60 percent of all expenditures on this technology are now made *outside* the formal I/T organization. That fact alone would justify why best practices in I/T should be of interest to all managers! The point of this discussion is to suggest the kind of information that is coming out of comparative studies of I/T can feed the constant hunt for best practices.

Third, I/T practices are increasingly discussed at conferences. In the United States alone, well over a thousand conferences held annually on business topics contain discussion of I/T practices. These range from process reengineering conferences (e.g., like those held by Clemson University) to technical seminars provided by the American Society for Quality Control (ASQC), the Conference Board, and the American Management Association (AMA). Even functionally narrow organizations, like the American Society for Training and Development (ASTD), run meetings in which I/T processes are discussed. Well-run I/T organizations participate in these, either attending or presenting at such conferences. These should not be confused with seminars and conferences that teach skills or present products—the content of our fourth bucket.

Fourth, I/T personnel are buying more books and magazines devoted to their subject areas than ever before. We do not know if they are reading them, but the body of literature they are buying is substantial. Major publishers routinely bring out books on I/T management—McGraw-Hill, Van Nostrand Reinhold, Prentice Hall, John Wiley & Sons, Free Press, just to mention a few—and sell them at a profit. My own research on the bibliography of this industry, covering patterns of the past 50 years, indicates that more is being published today on the management and use of I/T than ever before. By the early 1990s, it had become routine to see a whole section in bookstores selling new books on I/T in Asia, Europe, Latin America, and the United States. Most are "how-to" books of a technical nature, usually product specific. This was not the case as recently as the late1980s. There are also now hundreds of newspapers, magazines and journals dedicated to I/T. Those which routinely discuss I/T management practices include

- *Computerworld*
- *CIO*
- *Datamation*
- *PC Magazine*
- *Beyond Computing*
- *Information Week*

Even Bankers Use Computer Games to Learn: Knowledge Growth at Bankers Trust

This New York-based wholesale banker defies its industry's stoginess by recognizing that its operations and customers live in a fast-paced world. Finding that traditional classroom teaching techniques just didn't enable employees to keep up, the company turned to faster, better ways to teach employees. One way I/T helped was through the use of computer games as part of a broader strategy of distributing training on demand and simultaneously to many, relying frequently on interactive software tools. Exploiting the addictive qualities of video games, Bankers Trust put gamelike training tools that they call "Corporate Gameware" into PCs across the enterprise. Employees use a combination of simulations and self-assessments to learn through extensive interaction. Some of the games include Battle of the Brains, "day in the life of" scenarios, conversations, and flashcards. What do employees get? Three things: interactive fun learning, learning when they want to do it, and just-in-time advantages. This bank is more than a best practice, or even world class; its training is a window into the future of I/T-based learning for all industries, including schools and universities!

For further information, see Economist Intelligence Unit, *The Learning Organization* (New York: Economist Intelligence Unit, 1996): 69–71.

Articles on similar topics now appear routinely in all major business journals. Figure 9.3 is a more extensive list of I/T publications that enjoy a wide circulation. Thus, you can go into an on-line database and pull down bibliography on some I/T best practices and find considerable amounts of material. When I do it, it is not uncommon to find dozens, even hundreds of articles, that have appeared just within the past 18 months on a topic. The subject of commercially available databases is a vast one. Most well-run I/T shops subscribe to several which they make available to the rest of the company as part of their duty to make information readily accessible. But assuming that is not the case for you, where can you go quickly to learn about these? Here are my favorite sources:

- Local university library—call the reference desk for details.
- Public libraries—they have discovered that subscribing to databases is cheaper than buying magazines and journals.
- Marketing departments—the bread and butter for many marketing organizations is machine-readable data, much of it obtained without going through your I/T organization.

- Chambers of commerce—they do the same thing as marketing departments.
- Local newspapers—they all have a business library function constantly doing on-line searches.

Let me tell you generally what are not good quick sources:

- Government agencies—either because you do not know which one to call or they don't return phone calls as promptly as you want.
- Industry associations—they are overwhelmingly still paper-bound.
- Business schools within local universities—for the same reasons as government agencies.

The point is, the amount of information readily available is skyrocketing. You could read a book a month on I/T management and still feel left behind. You could read several I/T journals a week and have the same reaction. However, subscribing to a clipping service that regularly sends you summaries or copies of articles on subjects of importance to you is an effective way of keeping up. Your corporate librarian or marketing department can make the necessary arrangements. Best practices I/T organizations have already made such services available to the end users, so become an end user yourself!

FIGURE 9.3

Key I/T Publications

Beyond Computing	*IBM Systems Journal*
BYTE	*IEEE Computer*
CIO	*IEEE Software*
Communications of the ACM	*Information Week*
Computer Weekly	*InfoWorld*
Computerworld	*Journal of Data Management*
Data Communications	*LAN Times*
Datamation	*Network World*
Electronic Business	*PC Computing*
IBM Journal of Research	*PC World*
and Development	*Software Magazine*

Skills and Technology

These are the two areas that always receive the greatest amount of attention. All the training seems to be in these categories: programming, new software tools, and products. These are the subjects of all the major industry conferences, GUIDE, SHARE, AIM, COMDEX, and those run by IDG, for example. All the vendors focus on these—IBM, DEC, Microsoft, Hewlett-Packard, Lotus to suggest a few. When people talk about keeping up with I/T, it is typically a discussion about skills and products. It turns out that these are the two most volatile subjects facing an I/T professional. Business realities and business processes change, but slowly in comparison to products and skill requirements. Your I/T processes, for example, how you support end users or even develop large systems, do not change as frequently as releases of software or new models of PCs. And some areas, such as local area networks and telecommunications in general, are even harder to keep up with. So it is understandable that most of the effort any I/T professional goes through to keep up focuses on skills and products.

Best practices organizations do invest extensively in training their people. It is not uncommon to see anywhere from 4 to 15 percent of an I/T organization's budget spent on training. It is also not uncommon to see well-run shops provide an extensive curriculum of training for end users, staffed either with their own people or vendors of software, hardware, and training. Well-run shops almost appear like in-house votech junior colleges when you see the laundry list of classes they offer on PC basics, others on using Windows, OS/2, Lotus products, and a myriad of word processing packages. They are also responsible for training and running feasibility labs for new software applications

Already discussed in earlier chapters is the practice of well-run organizations to inventory their skills, figure out what is missing, and fill the gap with training, hiring, or subcontracting for these. This applies as much to hardware as to software skills. It is not uncommon to see even general management of I/T participate in product briefings and technical education on a monthly basis. This is a very intense part of the business. If you are to develop strategies about what architectures to adopt, what software tools to standardize on, what products to install, keeping up is critical. Some of the most commonly used techniques found in best practices shops for doing this include the following:

• Vendor product presentations, demonstrations, and tours of product plants and labs

---

Sharing the Knowledge Wealth Using I/T—The Kao Group

Japan's leading manufacturer of household packaged goods is committed to learning, adding knowledge through its activities. This highly successful company is organized as a flat institution linked by a management philosophy encompassing search for truth and wisdom, quality management practices, focus on customers, all lashed together with computer systems. The I/T systems, called Value-Added Networks (VANs) can be accessed by all employees. This menu-driven collection of databases provides critically valuable information real time on a variety of topics from sales, production, and customer feedback to a series of marketing topics. Even budget data are updated daily and made available to all employees. I/Ts systems are intended to help customers by ensuring prompt delivery, minimum inventory for the company and customers, and for Kao specifically, efficient production. These marketing-oriented systems make it possible for employees in all departments to have a comprehensive perspective on the business as they go about making decisions.

Kao has complemented these VAN databases with a nationwide customer response application called "Echo of Consumers." Telephone operators respond to customer inquiries about products, for example, accessing a database with descriptions of these items, thereby providing instant answers. Thus if someone calls up to find out what to do because a child has swallowed a soap product, the operator can provide immediate advice on how to handle the crisis! Customer comments are logged, analyzed, and influence product development and marketing. Kao has data on 44 million customers.

For further information, see Economist Intelligence Unit, *The Learning Organization* (New York: Economist Intelligence Unit, 1996): 72–75.

- Attendance at key industry conferences and events (e.g., COMDEX)
- Attendance at seminars on products, skills, and technologies

- Reading industry and technology trend analyses (e.g., books and journals, and newsletters)

- Visiting users of other products and techniques

- Telephoning references provided by vendors

- Deploying consultants to advise on trends in the use of technologies and skills

In reality, effective I/T professionals use a combination of these.

Conclusions

Well-run I/T organizations have institutionalized learning. They learn about the business environment of their companies and customers; they learn about how to run the best collection of processes; and they learn about emerging technologies, acquire skills, and stay current. They have a formal process in place for understanding how to improve and report results. What is particularly obvious is the fact that a management philosophy exists of continuous improvement linked to satisfying the needs and wants of both end users and the customers of their companies. It is a mindset and collection of actions that ensure alignment of I/T activities and skills development to what the company wants to get done. Learning is not done because it is interesting; I/T professionals do it to ensure that they are continuously delivering compelling value to the companies and customers who depend on them.

This chapter ends the "formal" presentation of the subject of best practices strategies as applied to I/T. However, you might want to continue reading through the last chapter and the appendices because they are intended to buttress the material presented in this book. Chapter 10 summarizes "rules of the road," making this topic of best practices a way of life. Appendix A shows you how to conduct an assessment of the effectiveness of an I/T organization, with effectiveness meaning alignment of I/T with what the corporation as a whole needs to get done to be economically successful. Appendix B discusses in more detail quality management practices since these are now so common in corporations around the world but are only just now making their way into I/T organizations. Appendix C is a tool intended to provide a quick and ready reference of where to go to for more information on the topics discussed in this book. It is not enough to use only the bibliographies at the end of each chapter because they speak to what was and is, not necessarily to what is evolving or will in the future—considerations we must all keep in mind. Otherwise, this book, like those listed in the various bibliographies, will become dated, something I do not want to happen!

References

1. Cortada, James W. *Second Bibliographic Guide to the History of Computing, Computers, and the Information Processing Industry.* Wesport, CT: Greenwood Press, 1996 (the first was published in 1990, same publisher.)

Implementing Best Practices Now	
Action	**Why**
Drive all discussions about I/T in one direction: Toward how to deliver value to end users in measurable ways.	So that I/T investments chase business opportunities and help the company control operating costs.
Apply the four-step process now.	It is a proven way of working on the things that count.
Invest in business education of all I/T managers and in I/T "trends and directions" training for endusers.	This is a way to continuously stay current and to apply one's understanding of the business to effective use of I/T.
Apply some existing criteria for judging the performance of I/T, such as the Baldrige criteria.	Saves you from inventing one; use a set of criteria already proven to work in driving your focus toward delivery of value.

2. Davidow, W.H., and M. Malone. *The Virtual Corporation.* New York: Harper Business, 1992.
3. Economist Intelligence Unit and IBM Consulting Group. *The Learning Organization: Managing Knowledge for Business Success.* New York: Economist Intelligence Unit. 1996.
4. Goldman, Steven L., Roger N. Nagel, and Kenneth Preiss. *Agile Competitors and Virtual Organizations: Strategies for Enriching the Customer.* New York: Van Nostrand Reinhold, 1995.
5. Grantham, C.E. *The Digital Workplace.* New York: Van Nostrand Reinhold, 1993.
6. Luftman, Jerry N. (Ed.). *Computing in the Information Age: Strategic Alignment in Practice.* New York: Oxford University Press, 1996.
7. McKinnon, Sharon M., and William J. Bruns, Jr. *The Information Mosaic.* Boston: Harvard Business School Press, 1992.

8. Watson, G.H. *The Benchmarking Workbook.* Cambridge, MA.: Productivity Press, 1992.
9. Woods, John A., and James W. Cortada. *Qualitrends: 7 Quality Secrets That Will Change Your Life.* New York: McGraw-Hill, 1996.

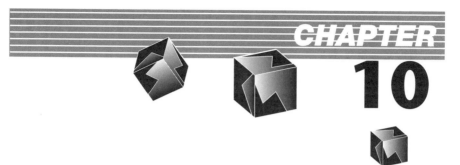

CHAPTER 10

BEYOND BEST PRACTICES

Excellence is not an act, but a habit.

—Aristotle

*T*his chapter provides an overview of six lessons best practices teach. It then presents actions management can routinely take to ensure the best application of these strategies.

The hunt for value, productivity, and profits is unrelenting in successful companies. At no time in the half-century history of the computer has this application of information technology been so true as it is today. Recent productivity data from the early to mid-1990s suggest that at last computers are delivering value in ways management had always wanted and rarely received since the 1960s. Thus with computing now having come into its own and expected to become even more ubiquitous, using this technology effectively becomes even more of a critical success factor than in the past for most companies and for all industries. To a large extent, this realization by managers, consultants, and business professors explains the resurgence in recent years in improving the application and management of this technology. While that had always been the case, the recent urgency to find better ways to use computers that we have seen beginning in the late 1980s can be explained by this enormous increase in dependency on these machines.

Best practices holds out the promise of being a strategy that makes it possible for organizations to find better ways to apply information technology, constantly improving all aspects of their operations. But best practices is a double-edged sword. On the one hand, it can inspire through example specific improvements over existing uses of information technology. On the other hand, best practices can default into "me too" strategies, a potential problem for those companies that must rely on innovation either to gain market share or to fight competitors. For a company that is not the most effective in using computers, a best practices strategy is wonderful because it is a path to better ways already proven to be effective. For other organizations already sophisticated in the use of computers, the strategy runs the risk of serving only to confirm that they already are good without encouraging the hunt for even better new methods and applications. That is why it is important for management, both in I/T and in functional areas, to understand how effective their organizations are in using computing. In fact, we can begin to catalog some of the most obvious methods and "rules of the road" concerning the use of a best practices strategy.

The Lessons of Best Practices

Managers have long found case studies and examples of productive uses of computing to be learning points. Benchmarking, roundtable discussions among CIOs, articles and books, influx of new personnel, and finally conversations among technologists have long been ways that successful uses of computing have moved from one company to another, across industries, and around the world. But by putting a name and some structure to much of this activity, by calling it best practices, many organizations have raised these efforts to the status of strategy. The key lessons about how to apply best practices strategies have become clearer over the past decade, thanks in large part to the adoption of quality management techniques and greater amounts of academic and consulting research on how best to run organizations. The lessons can be boiled down to six fundamental principles.

1. *Align all I/T decisions, actions, and measurements of performance with the business strategy of the organization as a whole.* Focusing I/T this way reduces wasted effort, concentrates attention on activities of value to the business, and gives purpose to this area of the company. Almost all the recent research on I/T strategies reach this same conclusion.

2. *Most effective applications of technology emerge from industry-specific applications that make it possible to do new things of value in the market place.* Other applications, not industry specific, tend to be most effective when they are driving down operating costs. This is a lesson that has emerged out of the research done by historians of computing in the past ten years. This kind of research, while still tentative, promises to fill in specific details by industry. To date, we know this rule of the road is true in the information processing industry, retail, airlines, banking, and some manufacturing applications, particularly in product design and fabrication.

3. *Technologies evolve fast enough that new economies of scale, and new functions, become cost-effective or practical, providing new opportunities to use information technology in innovative, productive ways.* Costs per calculation continue to drop at about 20 percent a year, while major new capacities in memory and processing are allowing for greater video, audio, and imbedded functions to emerge in many areas, ranging from laptop-based tools to office applications and simulations.

4. *Best practices in I/T require a coordinated and effective use of many resources simultaneously: best organization, best skills, best people, best processes, and best computing.* Nothing works well in isolation. For example, those businesses that have successfully transformed themselves in the past decade have learned that they must simultaneously change skills and people, organizations and policies, practices, work steps, applications, and processes. Leaving out even one spells failure because a successful transformation is a holistic exercise.

5. *Reorganizing organizations and redesigning workflows to make them technology friendly is rapidly turning out to be some of the most important ways to improve the value of I/T. It is the ultimate best practice in computing.* Experts on computing productivity are pointing to these two actions—both designed to exploit I/T as opposed to bolting computing onto existing structures—as the primary reasons why computing is beginning to pay off well, especially when careful attention is paid to such

human elements as rewards, training, and making systems easier to use. Computing in this way is leading to smaller, leaner organizations, and to new applications that exploit market conditions faster and which contribute productivity rapidly while reducing overall cycle times. Technology-friendly approaches to management have finally come into their own. Support of users is key to Bob Evans, editor-in-chief of *InformationWeek* (May 12, 1997, p. 6): "Never before have the demands been so relentless, both in number and intensity . . . are forcing managers of technology in business to confront a seemingly impossible support situation."

6. *Since technology and business circumstances keep changing, the best believe and practice habits of continuous improvement, being curious to learn how others do things and adopting the most relevant to their operations.* We have been moving slowly from talking about learning organizations to building intellectual capital systems, from teaching people about quality practices to vigorous process reengineering and management. IBM's intellectual capital systems, for example, are at the heart of many of the company's activities in product development, sales, support, and consulting. Quality management practices have long been recognized as the body of success factors at such companies as Motorola, Xerox, Kodak Chemical, IBM, and Hewlett-Packard, to mention just a few. ISO 9000 registrations are almost doubling each year in the United States while in Europe and Asia, ISO 9000 is a basic way of life. In short, many well understood sound management practices, combined with a little science and a great deal of technology, are coming together with I/T organizations increasingly finding themselves leading the way. In fact, just in 1996 alone, we began to see reengineering and quality management practices in some companies being put under the control of the I/T organization.

Beyond Best Practices

What if you already do the things cited in this and other books, and are clearly already delivering value, have I/T aligned with the business strategy, and enjoy the most efficient computing operations in the land? What's next for you? The answer has been scattered all through this book, implied and sometimes explicitly stated. But the question deserves a crisper answer because most companies will forecast using far larger amounts of information technology in the next few years than they ever have before. Networking alone is already causing business people to topple industries and change others, while compelling companies to change in fundamental ways not seen since the creation of the corporation a century ago. Already organizational borders are becoming fuzzy as people outsource processes and extend networks into departments of their customers, suppliers, and partners. If the forecasts are even remotely correct—and they have historically always underestimated demand for I/T—then we are entering a period of profound expansion of applications in highly integrated formats.

Regardless of all the change currently underway and anticipated, the truly best of the past and the future share some common patterns of behavior. These patterns help get us to the answer to our question about what happens beyond today's best practices. The outstanding performers have long known that the best practice identified today may already be yesterday's news because by the time you find out that company X is doing such-and-such, chances are that X is already moving on to a higher level of value and productivity which, at the moment, it is not sharing with its competitors. So just coming up to par may not be doing more than treading water. To gain true competitive advantage requires more.

If the history of best practices is any guide, then what we learn is that there are two actions any management team can take to get ahead in the effective use of I/T. First, challenge the organization to come up with new and better ways of using computing to provide services not readily or quickly replicated by the competition. The issue here is offering it first, even if this is only a temporary advantage until your competitors can catch up, because it provides revenue and profit streams denied to other firms. Citicorp's introduction of ATMs is the classic example of applying technology in a new way and enjoying a temporary competitive advantage until all banks installed ATMs. The fact is, during that short period of time when it was unique, Citicorp attracted customers. Other cases demonstrate that the competitive advantage provided by I/T can be sustained for many years through continuous improvements of key applications. The American Airlines reservations system remains the ultimate example of this strategy at work.

Second, one can execute a leapfrogging strategy, bypassing currently accepted uses of applications or technologies. If you guess right, you can come to hold great competitive advantages, guess wrong, and you just spent a great deal of money. History would suggest that guessing wrong about emerging technologies or their use is less of a problem than one of economic timing. In other words, worst case, you may attempt to apply a technology three or four years before anyone else, finding it still not fully operational or very expensive. But eventually such firms catch up and possibly continue to be ahead of the curve because in those years of development management they will have learned how to exploit the leapfrogged I/T. A recent example was the attempt by some insurance companies in the late 1980s to use imaging systems to have a paperless office. Today, we can hardly imagine an insurance company not doing that. Some of the massive customer service systems being implemented by U.S. utility companies represent a whole class of examples in the mid-1990s.

Those who go beyond best practices first build effective I/T operations that, by today's standards, work well. They provide value, are cost-effective, and contribute to the overall well-being of the organization. They also make sure everyone in the organization understands how I/T is contributing. These actions are simply doing the basics well. But then those that go beyond best practices constantly look for innovative ways of applying I/T. Those individuals and organizations, whether I/T or functional executives, managers, technologists, centralized data centers, corporate I/T headquarters, or small end-user departments, perform differently than their peers. Their actions can serve as suggestions for what you can do.

1. *Keep looking at what is going on with I/T in other industries.* Most managers tend to be like schools of fish within an industry. Someone makes a turn to the right and everyone else in the industry quickly follows. While there are good reasons to do so, particularly if the first fish has just spotted a nearby source of food (read, marketing opportunity), not all the fish in the school will get to eat. There is much to be said about also operating as the lone shark exploring larger bodies of water in search for food.

2. *Pay attention to how technology is evolving and emerging.* I am not suggesting that everyone become a computer scientist. I am urging you, however, to be sensitive to three things: What new devices, software tools, and base technologies are beginning to appear; patterns concerning changing costs of these technologies since cost per transaction always drops at predictable and in continuous ways; and perking up your ears when the thinkers about these technologies share what is on their minds. All three sets of awareness are just that; paying attention to changes around you either through some formal process within the I/T organization, or by observing and reading about computing.

Rate of Change in Technology

Historians of computer technology have discovered that various types of machines and technology change at different rates. The implications for I/T management are enormous since they base part of their migration from one generation of machines to another on the rate of change. This process also affects strategies in marketing, capital acquisitions, cost justification of applications, and the way productivity is measured. The key finding is that there are five types of changes in I/T:

- Hardware
- Software
- Strategies
- Applications
- Management Practices

With hardware, for example, PCs are replaced every year or two, while mainframes tend to stay in place closer to a period of 3 to 5 years. Software on a PC often has a life span of less than a year, while a large mainframe application may be used for two decades. I/T strategies—when they really exist— have a life span of between 1 and 5 years. Tactics change so much that we do not have hard data on their patterns of change. Applications tend to last a very long time—between 3 and 20 years is normal. Management practices—such as how people are appraised or billing policies—often last decades.

These diverse rates of change are caused by different patterns of change—a subject still under study by historians—but the lessons for management are already clear.

1. Change hardware when it makes economic and functional sense to do so.
2. Develop a strategy for what technology to rely on and why.
3. Plan on keeping core applications longer than originally intended.
4. Ensure I/T management uses the same management practices as the rest of the organization.
5. Finance and cost-justify each type of I/T change differently.

The basic insight is that one cannot generalize about the rate and types of changes that go on in I/T. The best understand that there is a bandwidth of changes underway and that each must be treated distinctly yet at the same time as part of the overall whole. They are specific about the kinds of change affecting their organizations but also deal with the general theme of change as it affects the entire enterprise.

For further information, see James W. Cortada, *Before the Computer* (Princeton, NJ: Princeton University Press, 1993)

3. *Put two or more existing ideas together in new ways.* We know that effective uses of technology have always surfaced by evolving existing devices and methods into new uses. The wisdom of that several thousand-year-old strategy remains very relevant today, particularly with all the restructuring going on within industries. The strategy does not even require great imagination. Invariably new uses come about precisely because someone has asked, "Is there a way we can use a particular technology to solve an existing problem, or reach a newly identified opportunity?" All through the history of technology, people have asked and answered that question by putting tools and techniques together in new ways. In business, doing that earlier than a competitor brings a company first-entrant competitive benefits. We do not know so much that the question can be ignored. The best continue to ask it as well as the following:

- With our workers going mobile, how might we use wireless computing?
- With networks finally becoming ubiquitous, where is the opportunity to partner with others to go after new markets?
- How can I get more information into a product or service to differentiate my supermarket chain from competition?
- How can I use computing to exploit my size?
- To what use can I put networking technologies, more powerful PCs, and all this new telephonic/GUI hardware and software that dominate so many COMDEX shows today?
- How can I use technology and my information with those of the local utility company to sell in a new territory?

4. *Set your own business goals and then ask the I/T community (your experts and computer and software suppliers) how to help achieve those targets.* To a certain extent, people will set targets that they think are reasonably achievable, even if a stretch. The best do something different: They take a page out of reengineering and set outrageous targets and ask their staffs to find new ways of achieving them since the old ways are what make the targets appear impossible to achieve in the first place. Left to their own devices, most people will set targets that are limited by the capabilities of existing systems, rewards, risks, and applications of technology. The best say things like, "let's see what it would take to do this same work in 90 percent less time," or "how can I get to all my potential customers on the West Coast using a firm already there and not having to open up offices in the region?" Taking another example, this time from GE, also insist that each project or organization turn a profit on these dramatic new ways of doing business.

5. Explore with your suppliers of I/T how to work jointly on projects that lead to new forms of computing or different technologies. For example, in the electrical utility industry in the United States, there are several projects underway in which homes are being made "smart," that is to say, a computer chip is being installed that helps keep track of electrical usage by type. This application required the "invention" of a PC on a chip just for that purpose. Motorola has experimented for years with various portable wireless communications devices in partnership with various companies. One project that has not proven terribly successful was the airphone that GTE installed on the backs of some seats in commercial airplanes; moderate successes or outright failures are also part of the process. The best always experiment to learn and to push the edges of the technical envelope. Bill Gates, in his book *The Road Ahead*, repeatedly emphasized the role of experimenting with new ideas. Like Thomas Watson, Sr. and Jr. at IBM decades ago, Gates continues the tradition of experimentation. While focusing his comments on the problem of how the Internet will finally become practical for businesses to use, his advice to experiment has long been a hallmark of successful companies.

Before we leave this chapter of "rules of the road," there is one other set of corroborating findings that can help you, drawn from a study done by the U.S. General Accounting Office in the mid-1990s in an attempt to find practices that could be used across the entire government to improve I/T operations. It went to 12 well-run I/Ts in organizations outside the government and then to those that did a good job within, to find out their best practices. The companies visited were American Airlines, Kodak, Royal Bank of Canada, United Services Automobile Association (USAA), and Xerox. They also looked at operations in state governments: California, Florida, Minnesota, Oregon, and Texas and then those perceived to be outstanding within the U.S. government: Army Corps of Engineers, Coast Guard, Environmental Protection Agency, Housing and Urban Development, Soil Conservation Service, Veterans Affairs, Department of Commerce, Federal Trade Commission, and the Social Security Administration. Because the GAO worked on the assumption that government I/T operations were not the best and thus needed to be improved, their findings focused on how to get things improved, the theme we deal with in both Chapters 9 and 10. In short, this was an important "best practices" study. They boiled their findings down to 11 best practices listed below using the exact wording from the report to ensure clear communications of their discoveries (U.S. GAO, 1994).

Since they are relatively straightforward, here they are.

1. *Recognize and Communicate the Urgency to Change Information Management Practices*

- Assess mission performance and contribution made by information and technology assets.
- Clearly understand how information management is critical to solving performance problems and exploiting opportunities.
- Communicate specific mission-related performance problems and make the business case for changing the current information management approach.

2. *Get Line Management Involved and Create Ownership*

- Hold line management accountable for the mission impact of information management.
- Get line management meaningfully involved in critical information management decisions.

3. *Take Action and Maintain Momentum*

- Act short term: Exploit or create windows of opportunity to signal or reinforce an improvement initiative.
- Think long term: Clearly set directions, goals, and milestones for information management.
- Pick and place internal champions to shepherd day-to-day improvement actions.
- Establish incentives tied to successful resolution of performance problems identified by top management.

4. *Anchor Strategic Planning in Customer Needs and Mission Goals*

- Match external and internal customer group needs with specific products and services.
- Link customer group needs to specific mission problems and assess corresponding opportunities.
- Focus strategic planning on highest priority customer needs and mission goals.
- Set explicit mission goals tailoring products and services to the needs of key customer groups.

5. Measure the Performance of Key Mission Delivery Processes

- Focus performance measures on gauging service to key external customers within individual customer groups.
- Embed performance measures in key management processes—including planning, budgeting, investment selection, and performance evaluation—to influence decision making and support continuous improvement.
- Use internal and external benchmarks to help assess relative performance.
- Tailor performance measures to gauge the mission value of information management (e.g., clearly show whether information systems projects make a difference).

6. Focus on Process Improvement in the Context of an Architecture

- Establish and manage a comprehensive architecture that (1) ensures the appropriate integration of mission-critical information systems through common standards and (2) emphasizes local control and flexibility in adapting to new processes and technologies.
- Distinguish large-scale improvement efforts from others by concentrating on order-of-magnitude improvements in cost, quality, or timeliness.
- Focus strategic resources, at the right time, on a limited number of large-scale process improvement efforts.
- Target efforts at core mission delivery processes—defined as those that, because of their cost and/or importance to customers, have a unique potential for return on investment.
- Use a combination of controlled development and rapid prototyping to minimize risk and maximize benefits.

7. Manage Information Systems Projects as Investments

- Link information systems decisions tightly to program budget decisions and focus them on mission improvement.
- Establish a high-level investment review board that fully involves senior program and information managers to help in key decisions through a project's life cycle.
- Use a disciplined process—based on explicit decision criteria and quantifiable measures assessing mission benefits, risk, and cost—to

select, control, and evaluate information systems projects using postimplementation reviews.
- Make information systems projects as narrow in scope and brief in duration as possible to reduce risk and increase probability of success.
- Balance the proportion of maintenance expenditure versus strategic investment.

8. *Integrate the Planning, Budgeting, and Evaluation processes.*

- Put all five elements of the strategic planning cycle in place: long-term strategic and information planning, systems life cycle and project level planning, budget review, performance assessment, and architecture management.
- Require executives and senior management to fully participate in and take responsibility for all major information management project decisions throughout their life cycle.
- Integrate key elements of the strategic planning process by ensuring that outputs of one are used as inputs for the next.
- Use the strategic planning process to manage operations and make key decisions and assessments by top management—especially those involving program budgets and information systems investments.

9. *Establish Customer/Supplier Relationships between Line and Information Management Professionals*

- Make line managers responsible for identifying critical information and performance needs, work requirements, and economic benefits of mission improvement projects.
- Make information management professionals responsible for supporting line managers as investment counselors and product/service providers.
- Clarify roles and responsibilities at the corporate, mission, and project levels—focusing corporate management on reinforcing accountability and facilitating mission success.
- Manage the organizational architecture with a bias towards local control and ownership, but also a strong central counterbalance to maximize cross-cutting systems integration needs.
- Rigorously understand the economics of information management functions as well as product/service needs of line management customers.

10. *Position a Chief Information Officer as a Senior Management Partner*

- Understand the mission and work closely as a peer with top management to help increase awareness, understanding, and skill in identifying and resolving information management issues.
- Catalyze, design, and facilitate implementation of new organizational capabilities by clearly articulating the role of information systems in mission improvement.
- Bridge gaps between top management, line users, and the information management unit by acting as an adviser and architect.

11. *Upgrade Skills and Knowledge of Line and Information Management Professionals*

- Teach line executives and management how to identify important information management issues, opportunities, and decisions.
- Ensure that information management professionals acquire line management and leadership skills.
- Identify existing skills, explicitly target future skills, and move systematically to new levels of capability.
- Find the right mix of technology dependent and independent skills.

Conclusions

After all is said and done, the best experiment, to keep up with what others are doing and learn at every turn. They do the basics well, are prepared to challenge their own assumptions and the way they do business, and always align I/T activities with the critically strategic imperatives of the business. They find ways to build a culture willing to change, where people grow in skills, are rewarded simultaneously for innovation and change, yet move quickly to sound practices and new applications. These I/T organizations, however, do not operate in isolation. They invariably function in companies and government agencies where the application of best practices strategies are evident in many functions. In these organizations senior management encourages the best performance. They measure quality and results, first, in terms of how the very best do it today and second, by how innovative the company is in going beyond simply copying others. They worship organizational agility, speed to market, cycle time reduction, innovation, a willingness to take risks and to experiment, and a curiosity to find out what happens when things are changed. Their organizations constantly collect talent and information, hire and retain smart employees, while everyone seems to be acquiring new skills. In I/T that means learning more than just about technical topics, it includes management, strategy, industry knowledge, and interpersonal skills.

You see the results all around in such organizations. People work long and hard hours; empty pizza boxes lie next to full trash cans in the morning. Drive by their offices on a Saturday afternoon and you see a few folks at work on *their* projects. The fact that these are also the company's projects is almost irrelevant. They talk about *their* initiatives, *their* objectives, which invariably *they* came up with in the first place. The bottom line can be simply stated: Best practices exist when whole departments are delivering compelling value. Most exciting, however, is that today there are many I/T organizations doing exactly that!

Implementing Best Practices Now	
Action	**Why**
Align I/T investments with the business strategy of your company.	So you use I/T most effectively in support of the company.
Constantly look for new uses and new technologies.	New uses and new technologies always present new opportunities to generate revenue and clip competition.
Use yours and anybody else's organization necessary to apply I/T.	Because some other firms do specific I/T functions cheaper, faster, and better than you.
Look inside and outside your industry for new uses of I/T.	Because industries vary widely in their effective and creative uses of I/T.

References

1. Chawla, Sarita, and John Renesch (Eds.) *Learning Organizations: Developing Cultures for Tomorrow's Workplace.* Portland, OR: Productivity Press, 1995.

2. Davidow, William H., and Michael S. Malone. *The Virtual Corporation: Lessons from the World's Most Advanced Companies.* New York: Harper Business, 1992.

3. Editors, *Forbes.* "Silicon Wealth Explosion," *Forbes* (July 7, 1997): Entire issue.

4. Evans, Bob. "The Next Dilemma," *Information Week* (May 12, 1997): 6.

5. Gates, Bill. *The Road Ahead.* New York: Viking, 1995.

6. Handy, Charles. *Beyond Certainty: The Changing Worlds of Organization.* Boston: Harvard Business School Press, 1996.

7. U.S. General Accounting Office. *Executive Guide: Improving Mission Performance through Strategic Information Management and Technology, Learning from Leading Organizations.* GAO/AIMD-94-115. Washington, DC: U.S. Government Printing Office, 1994.

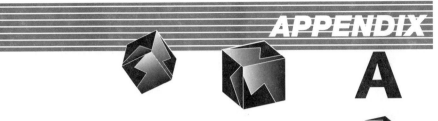

HOW TO TAKE A SNAPSHOT OF YOUR I/T EFFECTIVENESS

You get what you measure. Measure the wrong thing and you get the wrong behaviors.

—John H. Lingle

*T*he purpose of this appendix is to describe how an I/T organization can do an annual appraisal of its own performance. Since best practices departments already have process and departmental measurements in place, we will assume for this appendix that you do too. If not, a one-time assessment exercise is useful to identify where your gaps are in how the I/T function is run. Address those—the alignment theme we have discussed throughout this book—and then run annual inspections to determine how well you are providing services and how effectively the entire operation works together. The key here is to check alignment of I/T activities with business strategies on a regular basis because business priorities change. Annual inspections seem to be about right for many firms with more frequent assessments of specific issues. This assessment should not be a replacement for ongoing inspections and dialogues with end users.

209

Rather, it is in addition to these. To a large extent the discussion below is linked to the Baldrige criteria since these are widely used.

What Gets Inspected

There are essentially three purposes for any inspection:

- To help improve performance practices and capabilities
- To facilitate communication on objectives and results
- To serve as a working tool for managing performance, planning, training, and other assessments

It is critical to realize that over the years organizational assessments have increasingly focused on both results against objectives and how effectively activities are performed in order to achieve results. In other words, just looking at a set of month-end numbers does not represent an effective inspection process; the news is too late. Since problem prevention-based strategies are becoming more widely used, the need for early warning assessments becomes more critical to the successful functioning of an organization. This strategy is particularly important for base processes that facilitate change and speed of agile performance. The challenge is to understand how the organization can deliver ever-improving value to customers and end users, resulting in marketplace success and improving the service capabilities of the company at large.

Any inspection criteria, like the Baldrige, should have a set of core values and topics of concern—something you must define if they are not already in place. In the case of the Baldrige, they are

- Customer-driven quality
- Leadership
- Continuous improvement and learning
- Employee participation and development
- Fast response
- Design quality and prevention
- Long-range view of the future
- Management by fact
- Partnership development
- Corporate responsibility and citizenship
- Results orientation

These are embodied in seven categories (Baldrige chapters) which in turn are the groups of questions that a well-run organization asks of itself. They are

1. Leadership
2. Information and Analysis
3. Strategic Planning
4. Human Resource Development and Management
5. Process Management
6. Business Results
7. Customer Focus and Satisfaction

What you initially look for through these seven categories is the role of management, particularly senior management, in setting directions, creating values, goals, expectations and systems, while pursuing customer and business performance excellence. This set of management actions are frequently called drivers. You should inspect the systems that facilitate execution. These systems are the defined and designed processes for meeting the company's customer and end-user performance criteria. The goals remain clear: Perform well in the market place in meeting customer requirements and expectations and well in the eyes of the end users by facilitating their achieving their goals.

These seven categories can serve as the main parts of your inspection. They link together well in providing a framework for judging the overall performance of the organization. The leadership section deals with the role of senior management and the strategic direction and values of the I/T organization. Information and analysis focuses on what information you gather on your operations and how you use it. Strategic planning is both about your quality management practices and how you align I/T operations with the strategies of the corporation as a whole. Human resources are the only real assets that you have to make a difference; thus how they are hired, cultivated, motivated, trained, and deployed is crucial. Process management concentrates on what processes you have and how effectively they are managed. Business results emphasizes performance against internal business goals, both I/T's and the corporation's. Customer focus can be read as both customer and end user. Throughout this book I have pointed out that value is in the eye of the beholder—the receiver of your services. Here we ask the tough questions about how your end users, exec-utives, and your company's customers judge your performance.

From these seven categories can come suggestions for improvement and a judgment of how well you did, much as an accountant's audit defines the quality of the accounting performance of the previous year and makes suggestions about where to improve. Companies that perform such perfor-mance audits document these, communicate findings to employees, and use the assessment as a tool for guiding next year's improvement initiatives.

How You Inspect

Essentially what you do is ask a lot of questions by categories about your operations. There are many books out on how to do Baldrige-like assess-ments running into hundreds of pages so I do not need to list them here. However, it is helpful to understand the structure of such an assessment. Let's take Leadership as an example.

The various Baldrige guides will make a statement which you then react to by assessing the quality of your approach, extent of deployment of that approach, and then the results achieved. You give yourself points and, after all seven categories are studied, you add them up and give yourself an overall score. The value lies in the discussion about the extent to which the organization does perform well. Let's try one example.

Our senior executives have a process for being actively and visibly involved in establishing customer focus and personally leading our organi-zation's efforts (vision, values, goals, etc.), reviewing and recognizing out-standing performance.

Under Approach you might have any of the following be true:

- World Class
- Proven innovation with benchmarked processes
- Process improvement through cycles of learning
- Systematic, documented, well-integrated, and controlled process
- Beginnings of a sound, systematic, prevention-based process
- Reactive beginning of awareness of need
- No process

Each has a number of points associated with them with "World Class" being the best and "No process" the worst. A similar set of phrases are developed for deployment and for results. Let's take a look at results from top to bottom.

- Part of the culture
- Environment is one of customer and end-user focus
- Recognition given, collaboration encouraged
- Regular reviews conducted of all key processes
- Vision, goals, and strategy established
- Training received by most executives

The same process is applied to other Leadership issues. For example,

Our senior executives have a process to demonstrate their commitment to best practices by regularly communicating the organization's vision, values and goals internally and through sharing with external groups.

We have a process to translate our customer and end-user focus and quality values and goals to requirements for all levels of management and employees.

We have a process to analyze, benchmark, and improve the organization structure to most effectively accomplish the organization's goals, implement innovation, and cycle time reduction.

We have a process of regular reviews which include quality, performance, assessment (ISO 9000), audit, and how well our values are integrated into the organization.

Our management team has a process to evaluate, benchmark, and improve the effectiveness of their leadership and involvement, and the integration of our corporate values throughout the I/T organization.

I drew the examples from Leadership because it all begins with management, but the process is then extended through the other six categories. This process causes you to ask tough questions of yourself in a methodical manner. The Baldrige approach, now a decade old, is a proven approach and covers all the major issues reviewed in this book.

Benchmarking I/T operations with those of other organizations is an example of Information and Analysis within the Baldrige framework. Questions that should be asked in a benchmarking exercise include

- What are the best practices associated with each I/T critical success factor?
- What makes a best practice "best" in I/T?
- Which best practices apply in different circumstances?
- What cultural, organizational, and other factors should be understood well to implement a best practice?

- How does your organization compare to others? What are the gaps? Why is a gap important to fill?

Switching the questions over to a format similar to the organization of this book, answer the following questions on a regular basis.

1. How do other companies (and ours) manage human resources to achieve business objectives?
2. How does rapid change affect the ability of companies (and ours) to change?
3. How should I/T be designed and assimilated?
4. How do companies manage their application portfolio to maximize return on investment?
5. How can business and I/T plans, funding, and communication be best coordinated?
6. What techniques are most effective for selecting, justifying, and monitoring activities to ensure value?

These critical success factor questions are asked, for example, by IBM consultants when they perform assessments of the performance of I/T organizations. It turns out these are the same questions well-run I/T organizations have been asking themselves for years. It does not matter what industry you are in. I have seen them applied in banking, high-tech manufacturing, railroads, health care, insurance, package delivery, petroleum, utilities, financial services, retail, telephone companies, and automobile manufacturing. These kinds of questions are being asked from Asia to Eastern Europe by small and large companies.

Often the topics of each chapter in this book are considered a family of Critical Success Factors (CSF) to be assessed from time to time. When you translate into CSF language, you can inspect your organization by answering basic questions:

Architecture: What architecture do we need for application development and maintenance?

Legacy systems: How can we use such systems—the workhorses of the I/T organization—most effectively?

Governance: What partnerships and processes can we develop or use more effectively?

Culture: How can culture and commitment be used to work for us?

Human resources: What competencies and skills do we need?

Alignment: How does business need to engage I/T?

Value delivery: What value do we deliver? What value do we have to deliver?

If you were to establish a process for inspection, it might work as it does for many other companies.

The first time, you would probably take a shortened Baldrige questionnaire and gather your managers or peers together and spend several hours taking it collectively, and discussing key issues. The effort invariably leads you to the conclusion that everything is broken! Don't panic; you are just reacting to new questions. Second, you might then make up a detailed list of processes and other departmental activities that need to be inspected. Third, criteria would then be written up as a basis for comparing performance from one year to the next or with some other company's I/T organization. Fourth, you would collect data to answer the critical questions using questionnaires, existing process and departmental documentation, and round tables, and, of course, involving your customers (e.g., end users).

Companies sometimes hire a consulting firm to lead the assessments. While assessments last on average from one week to four months, the efforts are very similar. The distance in time is a function of the level of detail you want. The best consulting firms also have a best practices database to compare your performance against those of other companies. For example, when IBM consultants perform such assessments, they use that kind of information to guide their work. The steps they take are predictable:

- Define goals and objectives of the enterprise.
- Understand existing business realities.
- Conduct workshops, document reviews and interviews concerning key departmental activities.
- Interview executives and end users.
- Document results, make recommendations to close gaps between what the I/T department must do versus what it is doing.

The output of an inspection or a benchmarking study should define the strengths and areas of improvement opportunity. The best of these studies also include specific recommendations on next steps and provide detailed business cases for change. They also define the value that must be obtained.

These kinds of assessments lead to a number of actions by management. They find ways to streamline existing processes. They clarify roles and responsibilities as a way of improving productivity and increasing the effectiveness of decision making. They have a list of things that can be done right now to capitalize on current strengths and that deal with needed improvements. They learn what the gaps are between the perceptions of I/T and end users, making it possible for I/T to concentrate on improving communications while appreciating more accurately what their end users need and want.

Role of Critical Success Factors

In addition to using a Baldrige-like approach, some of the best run I/T organizations like to analyze their critical success factors. While these vary from company to company and change over time, a common set is emerging that generally applies to most organizations. You have seen them presented throughout this book. IBM's own work in this area has led to as good a list of general critical success factors as you can find. For that reason they are listed below as an additional tool to help you identify your CSFs.

Alignment
- I/T and business planning processes
- Coordination and communication
- I/T funding

Company Culture
- Values
- Vision
- Leadership
- Capacity for change

Governance
- I/T roles and responsibilities
- Decision making
- I/T structuring

- External option assessment
- Working relationships

Human Resources
- Resource planning
- Training and coaching
- Resource deployment
- Career path planning
- Goal setting and rewards

Legacy Systems
- Identification
- Migration
- Resource allocation

Architecture
- Architecture design
- Assimilation of new technology
- Infrastructure development
- Compliance process

Value Delivery
- Value measurement
- Customer/end-user communication
- Change selection
- Monitoring I/T investment performance

The silver bullet answers on best practices for each of these areas do not exist. They do for a few areas—the one's discussed in this book—and are constantly emerging and changing. The value of the list is not to depress you with all the work that has to be done to be effective for your customers and end users. Rather, it is to comfort you with the knowledge and confidence that there are ways of determining how to improve!

References

1. Bogan, Christopher E., and Michael J. English. *Benchmarking for Best Practices: Winning through Innovative Adaptation.* New York: McGraw-Hill, 1994.
2. Cortada, James W. *TQM for Information Systems Management.* New York: McGraw-Hill, 1995.

3. Criner, James C. "Benchmarking Data Processing Installations," *Capacity Management Review* 22, no. 3 (March 1994): 1–6.

4. Davenport, Thomas H. *Process Innovation: Reengineering Work through Information Technology.* Boston: Harvard Business School Press, 1993.

5. Grady, Robert B. *Practical Software Metrics for Project Management and Process Improvement.* Englewood Cliffs, NJ: Prentice Hall, 1992.

6. Jordan, Daniel W. "Using the Baldrige Criteria for Self-Assessment," *Engineering Management Journal* 6, no. 2 (June 1994): 16–19.

7. Myers, Dale H., and Jeffrey Heller. "The Dual Role of AT&T's Self Assessment Process," *Quality Progress* 28, no. 1 (January 1995): 79–83.

8. Wilson, Paul F., and Richard D. Pearson. *Performance-Based Assessments.* Milwaukee: Quality Press, 1995.

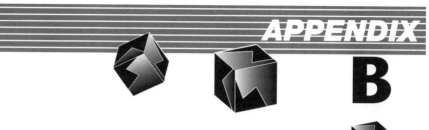

B

Applying Quality Management Practices to I/T: The Short Course

Never tell people how to do things. Tell them what to do and they will surprise you with their ingenuity.

—George S. Patton, 1944

Every "best practices" organization that I have seen executes many of the same elements evident in companies and government agencies that overtly practice quality management principles. This is not an appendix devoted to the pros and cons of quality management practices; the fact is, these are evident in well-run organizations. This is no different than the experienced highly successful salesperson who denies that he or she has a planned sales call technique. You go out on a sales call with that person and you walk away absolutely convinced that you just saw the finest demonstration of the classic sales call, yet the salesperson didn't think he or she was doing that because it came natural, an integral part of how they work. The same applies to quality management practices. They come naturally to a well-run organization. In fact, some of these organizations will deny that they are applying the principles espoused by such quality gurus as the late Dr. Edwards Deming, Joseph Juran, and others. They might not even know who these people are, but their spirit is alive and well in the best I/T organizations. So what do they do?

To begin with, they subscribe to three basic principles.

- One: The most effective way to gain and sustain competitive advantage is to shorten the amount of time it takes to do something.
- Two: They add value to whatever products and services they provide.
- Three: The great difference makers are your employees, treat them like the golden geese who lay golden eggs.

Managers in this environment delegate more frequently than in the past and make their organizations customer and end-user focused in all that they do. Employees don't just worry about improving efficiencies, they also pay equal attention to better effectiveness. Increasingly they have been moving away from a strict project approach to one characterized as process focused. Teams are more the norm and these groups of people are increasingly being measured as a team, not just as individuals. Management is moving from a centralized approach to highly decentralized deployment.

The quality experts have taught us many key lessons, some of which are learned in best practices organizations through dint of experience and hard work. Summarized in a nutshell they are

- Approach quality performance specifically and systematically.
- Quick fixes don't work on big problems, major changes take time.
- Involve all employees and give them freedom to make informed decisions.
- Best practices come through hard work, focus, and comparison to others.
- Continuous and radical improvement is a constant way of life.
- Customers and end users are the central focus of all improvement initiatives.
- Good managers are coaches; bad managers are why organizations fail.

Quality Is a Strategic Tool

Quality management is a set of practices that make it possible for leaders to introduce continuous improvement initiatives across all functions. The integration of various practices and tools include such techniques as benchmarking, Quality Function Deployment (QFD), Statistical Process Control (STP), Just-In-Time (JIT) practices, root-cause analysis, and vision-based strategic planning. Once implemented, you cannot turn back; life is changed forever because they lead to positive results. So one must systematically apply order and common sense to all of these wonderful tools. Successes are predictable, while failures become opportunities for learning and improving, not punishing. I/T executives have found that as a result of applying such tools, their department's contribution and hence, stature, in the corporation as a whole rose. Published accounts from Monsanto's Fiber Division, Black & Decker, IBM, and Appleton Papers simply confirm the benefits of this approach to the management of I/T.

All good quality management practices incorporate four basic ideas:

- Continuous improvements
- Zero defects
- Doing it right the first time
- Reliance on employees closest to the situation to improve it

Customers and end users become the benchmark against which to judge the effectiveness of these four strategic imperatives.

Looking at all the tasks that I/T has to perform as collections of processes is also at the heart of a quality strategy. There is now a vast body of best practices associated with the management and improvement of processes that is fundamentally changing how businesses are being run. It would be difficult to underestimate the sea change currently underway in the industrialized world. Major surveys of quality management practices indicated that by the early 1990s some two-thirds of all medium to large corporations had quality management practices underway and that the heart of these related to process management (*Quality Progress*, 1988–1996).

When you look at tasks as processes you find that they can be improved. This concept is called entitlement; that is, all existing processes have built into them room for improvement that you are "entitled" to, since the process exists today in some imperfect form. You measure the time it takes to do it today and the number of mistakes made. You then speed it up, cut out wasted valueless steps, and reduce errors and waste. You keep doing this until it works squeaky tight. Then you have what the experts call a stable process. If you want even more performance out of the process, you have to replace it with something very different—enter process reengineering. Benchmarking often leads to the conclusion that a process can be improved and if yours can't be, you have the makings of a business case for a total replacement.

When you treat tasks as processes, you gain profound knowledge of a function (Deming's idea), design out defects (Crosby's suggestion), and create an atmosphere of constant improvement and customer focus (Joiner's notion). What best practices organizations find is that these various techniques apply across the board from applications to hardware, from data management to business, and ultimately, to all work.

What commonly appears in quality management strategies are actions in five areas:

- Processes
- Measurements
- Organization
- Rewards and incentives
- Education

The challenge is to get employees to behave in ways that quality-driven enterprises value. The effort begins with a clear list of attributes that must be reflected in the work of the organization, woven into the five areas.

So what are the attributes evident in quality-focused I/T organizations?

- Service to customers, both internal and external
- Leadership involvement in directing, rewarding, inspecting, and coaching
- Continuous improvement through process work
- Employee involvement as reflected in empowerment and commitments
- Quality assurance which is the application of assessments
- Measurements, including self-assessments
- Supplier relationships which involve shared management disciplines
- Strategic quality planning involving everyone

Experience shows that the application of these eight attributes does cause changes in corporate culture, improves operational effectiveness, and ensures that I/T's link to the company's overall objectives remains solidly in place.

A common and chronic worry is what measurements of progress to implement. A quality-focused organization typically has four types: customer/end-user satisfaction feedback, employee success or morale indicators, company profit, revenue, or market share, and budget attainment or taxpayer satisfaction (if government). I/T goals are measurable. Those are normally achieved by a four-step process:

1. Everything worthwhile is measured numerically.
2. Measurements should indicate progress toward goals, not hurt the individuals gathering the data.
3. Define the process, then formulate measures of its performance.
4. Expect to change measurements as circumstances and experience dictate.

You Do Not Live in Isolation: The World Influences You

This book, and certainly any others that you read about quality management practices, will argue the case that megatrends outside of your company in your industry and in the economy of the world will influence how you perform. While the list of major influencers is subject to much debate, my own research suggests there are at least seven that appear in the minds of quality-focused managers and which economists and social commentators watch closely. They affect your employees and organizations directly. They are a combination of values, insights, and warnings of things to come. However you look at them, they cannot be ignored as they influence the workings and thinking of quality-focused organizations.

Emphasis is on teams and empowerment which means your ability to understand how to work with others, and taking pride in team and organization achievement over individual gain maximizes your contribution.

Viewing work as process, not individual performances, implies that the analysis and documentation of processes, along with the establishment of standards, make individual and organizational performance more efficient and effective.

The widespread use of measurements and statistical analysis to determine how well a system is functioning and how to improve it is on the rise. That means you base decisions and actions on real data gathered over time, not on the latest event, seat-of-the-pants idea, or whim are the basis for all decisions and changes.

People are focusing increasingly on services and the complete bundle of benefits an organization can offer its customers and end users. Defining, delivering, and continuously improving the value of the services you offer customers make for a sustainable competitive advantage and a profitable, growing company.

Continuous upgrading of knowledge and skills is a must for personal survival. That means fast-changing technological and economic environments are causing successful employees—and their managers—to constantly renew themselves to remain competitive.

Globalization of competition is a reality: Customers and suppliers can be found in any country on the planet. Someone is competing against you around the clock seven days a week which means to compete and survive you are required to deal with diverse suppliers and customers from many countries, cultures, and industries.

Blurring of organizational boundaries and increasing worker mobility are obvious results of corporate downsizing, rightsizing, and hunt for productivity. It is not slowing down; in fact, it is increasing. That means the new competitive and technological environment requires more flexibility in business alliances, use of consultants and contract workers to meet customer and end-user needs and to take rapid advantage of opportunities.

Since this appendix is the short lesson on quality, here are the seven bumper sticker versions of these major trends:

- A world of teams and empowerment.
- Your job is your process.
- Statistics and data are our friends.
- Your business is unrelenting service to customers.
- Training and continuously upgrading your skills are a way of life.
- Our competition is now global.
- The virtual corporation has arrived; do you have a place in it?

This short tour through quality management practices is too brief to even suggest the large and growing body of management practices and tools sweeping across the industrialized world. This phenomenon is as much a set of attitudes as it is a rapidly expanding collection of tools and methods. The references below can get you started learning more. Each has bibliography on the theory and philosophy of quality management.

References

1. Berry, Thomas H. *Managing the Total Quality Transformation*. New York: McGraw-Hill, 1991.

2. Cortada, James W., and John A. Woods. *McGraw-Hill Encyclopedia of Quality Terms and Concepts.* New York: McGraw-Hill, 1995.
3. Cortada, James W., and John A. Woods. *Quality Yearbook.* New York: McGraw-Hill, annual.
4. Harrington, H. James. *Total Quality Management.* New York: McGraw-Hill, 1995.
5. Manganelli, Raymond L., and Mark M. Klein. *The Reengineering Handbook.* New York: AMACOM, 1994.
6. Nanus, Burt. *Visionary Leadership: Creating a Compelling Sense of Direction for Your Organization.* San Francisco: Jossey-Bass, 1992.
7. Sashkin, Marshall, and Kenneth J. Kiser. *Putting Total Quality Management to Work.* San Francisco: Barrett-Koehler, 1993.
8. Woods, John A., and James W. Cortada. *Qualitrends: 7 Quality Secrets That Will Change Your Life.* New York: McGraw-Hill, 1996.

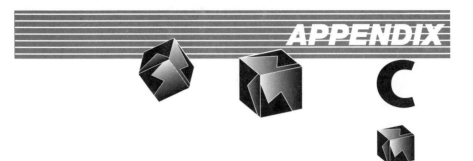

ORGANIZATIONS THAT CAN HELP YOU IDENTIFY BEST PRACTICES

The new source of power is not money in the hands of a few but information in the hands of many.

—John Naisbitt

Everything in this book will eventually become dated because organizations improve; so also do the best examples, and new lessons are learned. Simply reading *Computerworld* or *CIO* will not keep you completely current for the truth is that the most current information is usually not published. But there is one place you can always go to for current information: organizations that collect data about changing circumstances. We have mentioned several obvious types already—consulting firms and major providers of equipment and software—which can be supplemented with specific industry-focused organizations. A good example of this latter type is the Southern Gas Association which provides services to some 150 firms in the utility industry because it pays particular attention to I/T issues in the belief that computing is a central change agent in any company.

But in addition to industry associations, there are others that represent major sources of information, pointing to organizations that are innovating and managing well. This list below is not definitive, nor international in scope, but it is a start!

American Management Association
135 West 50th Street
New York, NY 10020 USA
Tel: (212) 586-8100
Fax: (212) 903-8168

The AMA pays a great deal of attention to innovative management practices, incorporating these into its large number of management seminars and publications. Its key journals are *Management Review, Organizational Dynamics*, and *HR Focus.*

American Production and Inventory Control Society (APICS).
500 West Annandale Road
Falls Church, VA 22046 USA
Tel: (703) 237-8344, (800) 444-2742
Fax: (703) 237-1071

This is one of the premier organizations for manufacturing professionals, providing education. Its seminars and annual conferences always contain a great deal about best practices in I/T. APICS has local chapters scattered across the United States.

American Productivity and Quality Center (APQC)
123 North Post Oak Lane
Houston, TX 77024 USA
Tel: (713) 681-4020
Fax: (713) 681-8578

APQC has a quality research center that specializes in finding benchmark data and best practices. If you could go to only one organization for help, this might be the one to pick! It does research, supplies articles on processes, conducts seminars, and sells publications. It publishes *Continuous Journey.*

American Society for Quality Control (ASQC)
P.O. Box 3005
611 East Wisconsin Avenue
Milwaukee, WI 53201-3005 USA
Tel: (414) 272-8575, (800) 248-1946
Fax: (414) 272-1734

After APQC, the ASQC is a major source of information on all aspects of quality management, best practices, and process improvement techniques. This is the most important quality association in the world. It has committees studying major areas of management, publishes *Quality Progress, Journal of Quality Technology, Technometrics,* and *Quality Engineering,* among other journals, dozens of books, and videos, and conducts seminars on a wide range of topics. I/T issues are constantly the subject of its attention. It has chapters all over the United States.

American Society for Training and Development (ASTD)
P.O. Box 1443
1630 Duke Street
Alexandria, VA 22313 USA
Tel: (703) 683-8100
Fax: (703) 683-8103

This is the premier American association dedicated to those developing corporate training programs. It also focuses attention on performance improvement strategies, sells publications, and conducts seminars. Its key publications are *Training & Development, Technical & Skills Training,* and *InfoLine*—all of which discuss I/T issues.

Association for Manufacturing Excellence, Inc.
380 West Palatine Road
Wheeling, IL 60090-5863 USA
Tel: (708) 520-3282
Fax: (708) 520-0163

Its member companies focus on how to excel in manufacturing through education, documentation, research, and sharing of experiences.

Association for Quality and Participation (AQP)
801-B West 8th Street, Suite 501
Cincinnati, OH 45203 USA
Tel: (513) 381-1959
Fax: (513) 381-0070

AQP focuses on quality improvement strategies through employee involvement, labor-management cooperation, redesign of processes, and education. It runs seminars, does research, and publishes *Journal for Quality and Participation.* It has chapters all over the United States and Canada.

Computer Channel
6801 Jericho Turnpike
Syosset, NY 11791 USA
Tel: (516) 921-5170

The Computer Channel has published hundreds of videos dealing with a broad range of I/T management issues, many of them best practices topics. These range from technical management issues, to organizing and managing I/T organizations, and improving operations of all types and technologies. Its services are provided on a subscription basis.

Conference Board, Inc.
P.O. Box 4026, Church Street Station
New York, NY 10261-4026 USA
Tel: (212) 759-0900
Fax: (212)-980-7014

This is one of the most widely respected national organizations in the U.S. business community. It is best known for its research on all manner of business issues, runs dozens of conferences on major management issues each year, and publishes the results of its research.

Madison Area Quality Improvement Network (MAQIN)
2909 Landmark Place, Suite 201
Madison, WI 53713 USA
Tel: (608) 277-7800
Fax: (608) 277-7810

This is an active organization best known for its annual Hunter Conference on Quality, usually held in June. It covers all aspects of quality management, best practices, and includes I/T subjects. Its annual conference is one of the most important of the "new" management conferences.

National ISO 9000 Support Group
9964 Cherry Valley, Building No. 2
Caledonia, MI 49316 USA
Tel: (616) 891-9114

This organization helps its member companies to comply with ISO 9000 standards which, of course, invariably involve I/T's participation. It does research, connects companies, hosts seminars, and publishes *Contin-*

uous Improvement, a very tactical "how-to" journal on ISO 9000 subjects; a "must talk to" organization.

Quality & Productivity Management Association (QPMA)
300 North Martingale Road, No. 230
Schaumburg, IL 60173 USA
Tel: (708) 619-2909
Fax: (708) 619-3383
   This is a network of business professionals focused on implementing continuous improvement strategies. It hosts seminars, workshops, and distributes publications.

Beyond Computing's Partnership Award Winners

Results are gained by exploiting opportunities, not by solving problems.

—Peter Drucker

Outstanding performance within I/T organizations has long been recognized primarily by technical societies honoring achievements in the development of new components and other engineering and scientific innovations. Recently, however, the management of I/T has started to get recognition. An example of "best practices" recognition was recently launched by the magazine *Beyond Computing*, which concentrated its selection on I/T organizations that were doing an outstanding job of aligning information technology with business objectives—a key best practice and the subject of the first several chapters of this book. The first set of awards—called the Partnership Awards—went to ten companies in the fall of 1996. The criteria used by the judges provide even more evidence of the growing use of best practices strategies: effectiveness of alignment between I/T and business strategies, business benefits achieved, business management's involvement in I/T, strategic value placed on I/T by senior management, and I/T management's involvement in business. Like many of the sidebars in this book, they are outstanding case studies of how to do it right. The article below is *Beyond Computing's* report on the ten best practices firms.

Partners in Excellence

by Walter A. Heinschrod

Partnerships. They can be powerful or perishable. The best are priceless. Beyond Computing is honoring 10 extraordinary business/technology alliances with our first annual Partnership Awards. The winners are organizations in which I/T and business executives not only recognize the benefits of aligning their strategies, but demonstrate a bond that has brought unprecedented value to the enterprise.

Getting there "takes a lot of work at the business level and the personal level," observers Amy Wohl, president of Narbeth, PA-based consultancy Wohl Associates and one of the five independent judges who chose the winners. "In some entries, the level of cooperation between I/T and the business is as high as you'd ever expect."

Another judge, Frank Dzubeck, president of Washington, DC-based consulting firm Communications Network Architects, adds that "top management involvement is significant in these partnerships." However, to pass muster with him, an organization also had to have strategic goals, not just tactical or technological objectives.

Each award entrant had to provide specific examples of how I/T is aligned with the broader goals and strategies of the business. Key benefits had to be cited, and entrants had to detail the size and nature of their enterprise and its I/T operation. Only when all these criteria were met to the judges' satisfaction was an entrant called to the winner's circle.

And the Partnership Awards go to . . .

Inland Steel Industries

It's amazing how much they sound alike. Robert Darnall, chairman and CEO of our Chicago-based Platinum Award winner, and H. William Howard, vice president and CIO, mirror each other almost to the word as they speak about a partnership that has markedly increased revenues, lowered costs and improved customer service.

"We have a real partnership between the technology experts in our organization and the management people running our various operating companies," Darnall declares. "And Bill Howard is key to making that happen."

"The secret to our success is the relationship I/T has with the business," Howard adds. "There's a lot of teamwork, and that helps tremendously."

What does it take to maintain a partnership like this, which has been formally in place at Inland for about three years? "Strong and regular communication at all levels of the organization," Darnall replies.

Of course, the most visible measure of success is on the bottom line. At Inland's main operating units—for bar steel, flat steel and international operations—three separate I/T projects aimed at improving order fulfillment, inventory tracking and productivity will result in a total one-time saving of $50 million, plus ongoing annual savings targets set at the project's inception are likely to be exceeded.

Howard, who is part of the executive planning committee, and Inland's other senior managers understand the importance of involving users in projects such as these. As the systems were being designed, representatives from the business areas were placed on the development teams. Once the systems were in place, Inland invested heavily in worker training.

These systems bring more disciplined, timely and accurate customer interactions. MANIX, a client/server-based package used in the bar steel unit, allows all price quotes, delivery times and orders to be handled during a single phone conversation. Status data is available on every pending order, and all shipments are invoiced within one business day, with 99 percent of those invoices accurate upon receipt.

Inland invested more than $40 million in MANIX and a system for flat products called OFS (Order Fulfillment System). Along with re-engineered business practices, OFS reduced obsolete inventory and resulted in better use of plant and machinery.

"The greatest benefits are going to come from our increased responsiveness to customers," Darnall points out. "From order entry through the whole manufacturing process, we're taking lead time out of the cycle with these systems."

Inland's expansion into international markets has been similarly predicated on strong business-technology teamwork. At a Mexican subsidiary, Howard's group set up a client/server system that supports logistics and metals distribution and they did it in only 100 days.

International sales volumes mirror that pace, growing from zero in 1994 to $150 million in 1995 to a projected $300 million this year. "We've become more productive, and the technology has helped us do that," Darnall says.

"In all, our I/T team has played an integral role in helping the company make the leap from a product-focused model to a customer-focused business model," Howard says. "In the process, I/T management transformed our company's view of technology. Today, we are a real business partner in support of Inland's growth and profitability."

One Vision, One Language: Citizens Utilities

The vision: To transform Citizens Utilities from a good utility to a world-class growth company. The challenge: To build such an aggressive company out of an extremely diverse enterprise.

Citizens offers electric, natural gas, water, waste water treatment and telecommunications services to customers in 20 states from New England to Hawaii, with administrative offices in Stamford, Conn., and Dallas. The many different processes and technologies supporting these businesses were becoming a hodgepodge—unfocused and redundant.

Senior management realized that if Citizens was going to maintain leadership in its markets, it had to develop an enterprise wide business model adaptable enough to meet the rapidly changing conditions that were being created by deregulation and increased competition. For that model to pay off, a strong bond between business and technology was essential.

To strengthen that bond, senior management created the Operating Technology Team (OTT) to govern information technology and elevated the senior I/T position to officer level. The OTT consists of six officer-level executives who represent operating, financial, technology and support services throughout Citizens. These executives plan strategically and ensure that the company's I/T investment is protected.

Against this background, president and chief operating officer Daryl Ferguson teamed with Michael Love, vice president for corporate planning, and Nicholas Ioli, vice president and CIO, to create Vision 2002, a long-term vision for Citizens. Central to Vision 2002 are common practices and a common language that all employees understand. "This broader understanding of what we are doing and where we are going has dramatically improved employee morale," Ioli says.

The governance model at Citizens includes four levels of hierarchical structure that guide I/T. At the top is the senior team: president, CFO, CIO, the vice president of strategic planning and vice presidents from all the business sectors. Next is the OTT. "Management commissioned the OTT as a subset of the senior team," Ioli explains. "The mission and charter of the OTT is to focus on the business implications of I/T."

The nuts and bolts of I/T are handled by the third and fourth levels: Ioli's own Office of the CIO, within what's called the Office of Information Technology; as well as the CITT (Citizens Information Technology Team), which involves the business sector technology managers.

The results of this structure, as well as I/T's involvement with Citizens' new strategic vision, have been impressive: Economies of scale are being realized through a leveraging of processes, people and technology infrastruc-

ture. Millions of dollars are being saved through cost-reduction initiatives, and revenues will be increased significantly through a better prioritization of business initiatives. And, key to all, there's now an enterprise wide business model.

"We've already done a lot of the theory, strategy and planning," Ioli says. "Now we're into tactics and implementation."

Trying to describe this year-and-a-half effort in 500 words or less, as our entry rules required, was "a monumental task," according to Ioli. But so was the visionary partnership that he and his business colleagues launched. It has transformed Citizens into a stronger, leaner and unified— yet still diversified—organization.

Where Smiles Are Serious Business: Oticon

"We began turning this company around when we realized that we had to be in the smile business," says Dr. Peter Hahn, president of Somerset, N.J.-based hearing-instrument maker Oticon. "That meant we had to absolutely delight our customers with products and service. To make that happen, we had to rely on information technology."

Five years ago Oticon was, by Hahn's admission, a marginally profitable firm. Quality was inconsistent, and employees mostly had to sort through records manually when customers called for service.

One of the first things Hahn did after coming on board was to learn about customers. "A lot of the frustrations with hearing care hinged on our not having access to information that could make those hearing aids provide the most benefit," he says. Today, much of that information is available via PC. If needed, the history of past interactions with a customer can be accessed. Other vital information on hearing-aid fitting techniques can be captured in real time.

"Our industry," Hahn explains, "is moving from instruments that were adjusted with screws to what we call programmable hearing products. Modern instruments change programs automatically and thus change how the instrument sounds in different environments." It's this exciting use of technology, which was driven by a complete change in company thinking and by personal commitments from employees, that has propelled Oticon into the ranks of the top five firms in its industry.

The key players on the employee team include Oticon's I/T staff, under director of information systems Peter Miska. "I/T is the key to competitive differentiation," Hahn says, "and it's been essential to achieving our market position."

Miska's unit continues to roll out technologies that hone the company's competitive edge. For example, bar coding is now widely used for rapid capture of data among audiologists and dealers. In the near future, telephone and computer applications will be linked for customer service and telemarketing. And they've set up a home page for customers and healthcare professionals on the Internet.

This partnership makes employees, as well as customers, smile. Executives like CFO Gene Cancellieri, who with Hahn has final I/T budget approval, relish the fact that technology greatly enhances production planning and workflow.

And employees feel more empowered. "Everyone is encouraged to use query tools to improve quality, service and success with the company's products," Hahn says. "The result is a better understanding of our business and better-informed decision making."

Small Company, Big Results: Aetna Industries

Being a medium-sized company in the auto-supplier business doesn't stop Centerline, Michigan-based Aetna Industries, from pursuing ambitious policies: It seeks to minimize waste and maximize quality, as illustrated by its certification under the International Organization for Standardization's ISO 9002 and the auto industry's QS 9000 quality standards.

These goals are also recognized by the partnership between I/T, under information systems manager Mark Shuttleworth, and senior management, particularly vice president and CFO Harold Brown. To operate more efficiently, Shuttleworth's group uses leading-edge software and outsources when appropriate.

The I/T department also seeks to raise the quality of information. To minimize the possibility of corrupting mission-critical data, the testing program changes take place in experimental environments that are separate from the main system. The results can be seen in Aetna's inventory data: Accuracy has risen from 40 percent to more than 98 percent since mid-1995.

I/T also supports product quality, on-time delivery and communications. Process-control software improves products, while bar coding speeds the gathering of data from Aetna's nine plants. Electronic data interchange, a mainstay with Aetna's customers for several years, is now being extended to suppliers.

Quality and accuracy are so prevalent that one vendor who paints parts made by Aetna ships them directly to the customer, saving time and money for everyone. Another supplier will be increasing its efficiency by pulling data directly from Aetna's computers.

As this forward-thinking organization illustrates, partnerships between I/T and business operations need not be limited by corporate boundaries.

Building an Electronic Marketplace: Boston College

The lecture halls, libraries and dorms fit the image of any university campus. It's only when you delve beneath the brick and mortar of Chestnut Hill, Massachusetts-based Boston College that you can appreciate the extraordinary technological resources that support this renowned institution.

However, it's not simply the vast array of networks and access capabilities, the E-mail, voice mail and Internet feeds, or the cable TV and Ethernet jacks at each student's bedside that make this massive infrastructure so noteworthy. What commands attention here is the high level of commitment from all sectors of the university in launching, financing and fulfilling Project Agora (marketplace in Greek). This project is more than a network—it's a goal. "We want to become an electronic community where people can gather to exchange information and ideas," explains Bernard Gleason, associate vice president for information technology.

Agora delivers a variety of electronic resources to students, faculty, researchers and administrators. Launched in 1995, it is one phase of an overall network strategy begun in 1986. And while Gleason, who reports to executive vice president Frank Campanella, was heavily involved in the strategy sessions, he also had some purely technological issues to resolve. For one, the plan had to balance Boston College's sizable investments in legacy systems with an innovative approach that uses cable TV technology for high-speed data access. Also, the always-pressing issue of operating cost had to be addressed.

Gleason partnered with vendors to bring in superior service at the lowest possible cost. The portions of the system aimed at operations reduced staff and lowered overhead. Further, by timing the laying of wire with renovations and new construction on campus, the university also saved. As a result of these moves, Gleason got it all done without adding to his I/T staff or cutting services. The benefits, brought to fruition by a sound alignment of management strategy and technology, fulfill a mission expressed by the university's motto, "Ever to excel."

Medical Cost Recovery Program: Department of Veterans Affairs

Recovery, as in "cured," is the highest aim of the many hospital and outpatient services provided by the US. Department of Veterans Affairs (VA) to its millions of beneficiaries. But there is another important recovery mission going on: collecting payment for healthcare services.

Run by the VA's Medical Care Cost Recovery (MCCR) Program, this effort has grown in five years from a minimal system to one rich in technology. In 1991, the program returned $267 million to the US. Treasury. Last year, recoveries soared to $573 million.

What drives the effort, says director of systems development Samuel Georgeson, is the program's vision of efficiency enhanced through partnership. This effort aligns I/T not only with directions set at the executive level under MCCR director Walter Besecker, but also with other VA areas, such as financial, administrative and clinical.

In a key example, Georgeson's unit upgraded the billing software in the VA's accounts receivable sector so it could interface with existing medical-data software. Now, comprehensive patient information is always available, even when a patient's paper records aren't. This enables MCCR's National Data Base to effectively prepare bills for recovery.

In addition, MCCR's National Data Base provides coordinators with summary information to gauge the performance of MCCR's 2,000 employees. This automated rollup of financial and program status displays data such as recovery totals, cost-to-recovery ratios and recoveries per employee.

MCCR's achievements do more than fulfill its strategic mission: They also carry forward a broader mission to recover funds that can be used to reduce the federal deficit.

Where Partnering Rings Up Benefits: Fred Meyer

In the roster of who gets involved in planning and implementing I/T programs, Portland, Oregon-based retailer Fred Meyer brings together all the right players—corporate management, outside consultants, I/T management, end users, business unit managers, vendors and customers.

"Our goal is to please all our customers every day and thereby increase shareholder value," remarks CIO Ron McEvoy, who reports to CEO Bob Miller. McEvoy participates in the planning work of such core committees as logistics, human resources and real estate. This involvement is full-time, and McEvoy practices what he preaches. He recently spent a day in a Fred Meyer store selling merchandise, loading groceries and helping customers locate items—all in an effort to learn more about the needs and expectations of shoppers and store associates.

Internally, McEvoy's team confers with the various departments to keep abreast of their issues and special I/T needs. Sometimes these needs can be easily met by exploiting existing information in new ways.

Recently, for example, store management wanted to know how many in-store customers shopped at each location at given times. The I/T staff was able to provide this information quickly, enabling the store managers to serve their customers better during peak traffic periods.

PACE, the company acronym for "Please All Customers Every Day," means just as much to Fred Meyer's information technology team as it does to the employees who work in the stores. It's a theme that's constantly reinforced at meetings and training sessions. And, as this award-winning enterprise, a strong partnering effort is what truly sets the PACE.

A Mony-Making Partnership: The Mutual Life Insurance Company of New York

The corporate vision of The Mutual Life Insurance Company of New York (MONY), a New York-based insurer, is to become the company of choice for policy-holders, field associates and employees. This goal has been crafted with keen awareness of the many competitive challenges that MONY faces.

To reach its goal, MONY developed the Information Systems Strategic Plan (ISSP), which vice president and CIO E.P. Rogers calls "a blueprint for the company's technology infrastructure for the year 2000 and beyond."

"The plan was developed after interviews with senior management, department heads and departmental officers," explains Rogers, who reports to Keith Baker, vice president for management resources. Samuel Foti, president and COO, has the final I/T budget authority.

ISSP is just one part of a sturdy I/T-business partnership. The company also reviews I/T allocations six times a year so it can quickly address new challenges. This year, I/T resources were reallocated in support of a sales campaign that was initiated because of changing business priorities.

In addition, MONY correlates its business and I/T strategies on an annual basis. This helps ensure that the technology supports all aspects of the business plan.

These efforts have reaped significant benefits for MONY: There are fewer cost overruns and more projects meet expectations. MONY has crafted a policy that insures smooth operations through the partnering of business and I/T.

Beefing Up Sales: Sedgwich James

"Our job is to help our clients get a handle on their property and casualty claim losses so they can create real-world business plans," explains Alan Josefsek, managing director of Sedgwich Information Systems (SIS), part of Sedgwick James, a Memphis, Tennessee-based insurance broker and risk advisor. To help achieve that business objective, Josefsek's group implemented the Information System for Risk Management (INFORM).

"INFORM contributes to this goal in important ways," he reports. "Previous systems were too difficult and time-consuming to use, so this kind of information was denied to large populations of risk managers and claims analysts. With this system, we democratized information, making it available to everyone who needs it."

As a key member of the firm's national resource groups, Josefsek was charged by the senior management of Sedgwick James with helping to create new opportunities to generate revenue in a climate of flat sales. SIS responded with an enhanced version of INFORM. Within a year of its implementation in early 1995, unit revenues increased by 60 percent. In 1996, SIS revenues continued to be on track. The system's biggest benefit, states Josefsek, "is that decision makers can get immediate feedback on risk- and claims-management trends." This enables companies to identify potential problems, and then plan to minimize risks and maximize profits.

The partnering of information technology with Sedgwick's insurance and risk services has enabled the firm to provide more value to clients by giving them the tools to help lower the cost of potential risk.

Making Partners of the Disadvantaged:
The Private Industry Council of Southwest Indiana

"Our customers used to cause a large volume of paperwork," says Sue Hardwick, I/T systems manager for the Private Industry Council of Southwest Indiana (PICSWI). "Now we see them as partners in information processing."

The Evansville, Indiana-based agency's mission is to provide economically disadvantaged or dislocated workers, youth, adults and older workers with quality training and job placement services. What turned things around for PICSWI was a bold gamble to computerize the information system on which its work depends. This benefits not only PICSWI and those it serves, but also the taxpayers of Evansville.

Partnering closely with Hardwick on the project was Jerry Yezbick, PICSWI's executive director. Ultimately giving their okay were PICSWI's board and Evansville's mayor, Frank McDonald II.

If this were simply a case of computers helping to speed up procedures, PICSWI's effort would be commendable but hardly unusual. What this small agency actually set in motion was an ongoing partnership that reviews and revises goals frequently, updates data daily, corrects errors quickly and better serves the customer.

"The staff spends more time with our clients now that everyone has a networked PC," Hardwick concludes. "I/T provides everyone on the staff with

immediate access to the information they need. They no longer have to say, 'I don't know.'"

"In addition, we are spending less time on the mundane tasks that are a daily part of any nonprofit agency. So we have more time to plan and prepare, and can eventually become a total quality enterprise."

INDEX

of making applications computer-
friendly, 195-196
Telecommunications, at Xerox, 87; how
changes entertainment applications,
76; trends survey in, 107-110
Texas Instruments (TI), skills process at,
133
3M, 2; I/T as a corporate strategy, 20; role
of learning at, 169
Toyota, 2, 3; productivity at, 66
TQM, role in I/T, 158-159
Training, I/T-based, 186; role of, 128-133
Transformation strategies, how implemented, 93-97
Trends, influencing organizations, 223-
224
Tucker, John L., 48

—U—

Universal Product Code (UPC), 76
USAA, 74-75; use I/T in customer service,
47
US Army, inventory control and, 3
US workers, automation and, 62-69
Users, role in justifying I/T projects, 45-46
Utility, effective uses of I/T, 72

—V—

Value, defined, 43-44, 47-48; history of in
I/T, 26-27; how perceived, 55-58; linking cost of I/T to, 149; of I/T architectures, 97-101; strategy for delivering,
44-49, 176-179; survey on how to
gain, 21
Value-Added Networks (VANs), case of,
189
Values, of I/T profession vs. corporation's,
13-136
Venkatraman, N., model of, 31-33, 36

—W—

Warehouse management, savings in, 68
World Class, versus Best in Class, 9-11
Work, how changed by I/T, 170; mobility
and savings, 68

—X—

Xerox Corporation, 2; role of legacy systems in, 87